RETURN from SIBERIA

The LTCB International Library Trust

The LTCB (Long-Term Credit Bank of Japan) International Library Trust, established in July 2000, is the successor to the LTCB International Library Foundation. It carries on the mission that the foundation's founders articulated as follows:

The world is moving steadily toward a borderless economy and deepening international interdependence. Amid economic globalization, Japan is developing ever-closer ties with nations worldwide through trade, through investment, and through manufacturing and other localized business operations.

Japan's global activity is drawing attention to its political, economic, and social systems and to the concepts and values that underlie those systems. But the supply of translations of Japanese books about those and other Japan-related subjects has not kept pace with demand.

The shortage of foreign-language translations of Japanese books about Japanese subjects is attributable largely to the high cost of translating and publishing. To address that issue, the LTCB International Library Foundation funds the translation and the distribution of selected Japanese works about Japan's politics, economy, society, and culture.

International House of Japan, Inc., manages the publishing activities of the LTCB International Library Trust, and Sumitomo Mitsui Trust Bank, Ltd., manages the trust's financial assets.

LTCB International Library Selection No. 40

RETURN from
SIBERIA

A Japanese Life in War and Peace, 1925–2015

Oguma Eiji

translated by David Noble

 LTCB International Library Trust / International House of Japan

Transliteration of Foreign Words

The Hepburn system of romanization is used for Japanese terms, including the names of persons and places. Except in familiar place names, long vowels are indicated by macrons. An apostrophe is used to distinguish syllable-final *n* from *n* at the beginning of a syllable. The spelling of non-Japanese words that have been incorporated into Japanese reflects the way these words are pronounced by Japanese speakers.

The local custom of placing the family name first has been followed for the names of Japanese, Chinese, and Korean persons.

All uncredited photographs courtesy of the author.

This book originally appeared in Japanese as *Ikite kaette kita otoko: Aru Nihon-hei no sensō to sengo* (Tokyo: Iwanami Shoten, 2015). International House of Japan retains the English-language translation rights under contract with Ogima Eiji and through the courtesy of the Iwanami Shoten.

First English edition published March 2018 by International House of Japan
11-16, Roppongi 5-chome, Minato-ku, Tokyo 106-0032, Japan
Tel: +81-3-3470-3211   Fax: +81-3-3470-3170

URL: http://www.i-house.or.jp/

Printed in Japan
ISBN 978-4-924971-45-5

Contents

Oguma Kenji (right) and his son, Eiji, the author of this book. (photo by Lee Soon-Koo).

Oguma Family Tree

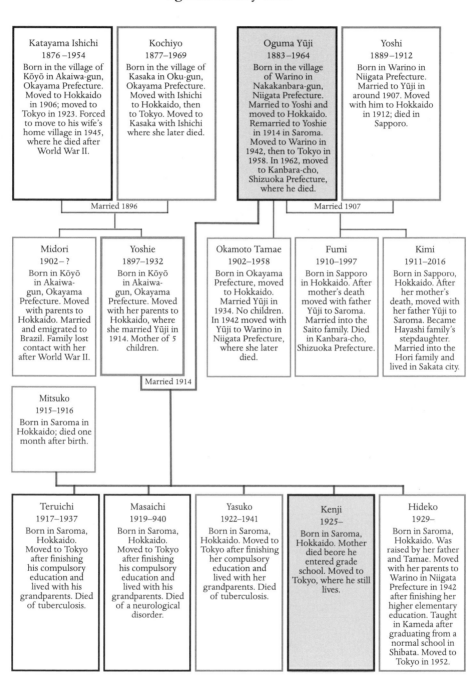

Katayama Ishichi
1876–1954
Born in the village of Kōyō in Akaiwa-gun, Okayama Prefecture. Moved to Hokkaido in 1906; moved to Tokyo in 1923. Forced to move to his wife's home village in 1945, where he died after World War II.

Kochiyo
1877–1969
Born in the village of Kasaka in Oku-gun, Okayama Prefecture. Moved with Ishichi to Hokkaido, then to Tokyo. Moved to Kasaka with Ishichi where she later died.

Oguma Yūji
1883–1964
Born in the village of Warino in Nakakanbara-gun, Niigata Prefecture. Married to Yoshi and moved to Hokkaido. Remarried to Yoshie in 1914 in Saroma. Moved to Warino in 1942, then to Tokyo in 1958. In 1962, moved to Kanbara-cho, Shizuoka Prefecture, where he died.

Yoshi
1889–1912
Born in Warino in Niigata Prefecture. Married to Yūji in around 1907. Moved with him to Hokkaido in 1912; died in Sapporo.

Married 1896

Married 1907

Midori
1902–?
Born in Kōyō in Akaiwa-gun, Okayama Prefecture. Moved with parents to Hokkaido. Married and emigrated to Brazil. Family lost contact with her after World War II.

Yoshie
1897–1932
Born in Kōyō in Akaiwa-gun, Okayama Prefecture. Moved with her parents to Hokkaido, where she married Yūji in 1914. Mother of 5 children.

Okamoto Tamae
1902–1958
Born in Okayama Prefecture, moved to Hokkaido. Married Yūji in 1934. No children. In 1942 moved with Yūji to Warino in Niigata Prefecture, where she later died.

Fumi
1910–1997
Born in Sapporo in Hokkaido. After mother's death moved with father Yūji to Saroma. Married into the Saito family. Died in Kanbara-cho, Shizuoka Prefecture.

Kimi
1911–2016
Born in Sapporo, Hokkaido. After her mother's death, moved with her father Yūji to Saroma. Became Hayashi family's stepdaughter. Married into the Hori family and lived in Sakata city.

Married 1914

Mitsuko
1915–1916
Born in Saroma in Hokkaido; died one month after birth.

Teruichi
1917–1937
Born in Saroma, Hokkaido. Moved to Tokyo after finishing his compulsory education and lived with his grandparents. Died of tuberculosis.

Masaichi
1919–940
Born in Saroma, Hokkaido. Moved to Tokyo after finishing his compulsory education and lived with his grandparents. Died of a neurological disorder.

Yasuko
1922–1941
Born in Saroma, Hokkaido. Moved to Tokyo after finishing her compulsory education and lived with her grandparents. Died of tuberculosis.

Kenji
1925–
Born in Saroma, Hokkaido. Mother died beore he entered grade school. Moved to Tokyo, where he still lives.

Hideko
1929–
Born in Saroma, Hokkaido. Was raised by her father and Tamae. Moved with her parents to Warino in Niigata Prefecture in 1942 after finishing her higher elementary education. Taught in Kameda after graduating from a normal school in Shibata. Moved to Tokyo in 1952.

Japan and East Asia

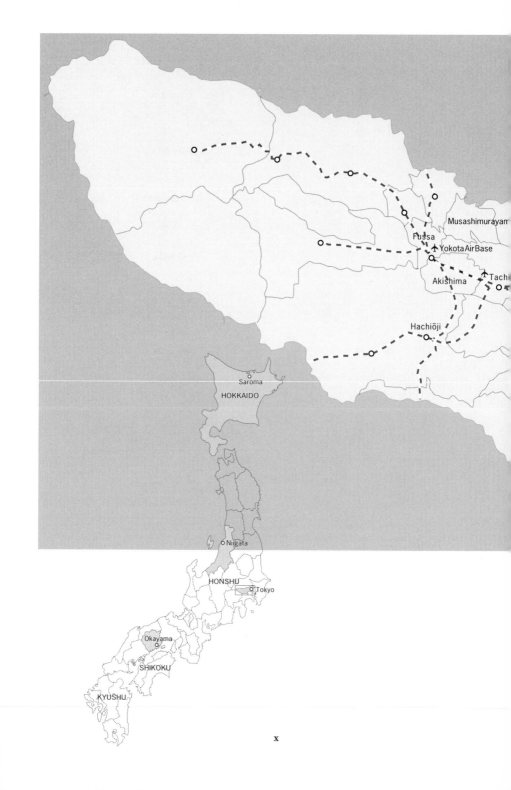

Musashimurayama

Fussa

Yokota Air Base

Akishima

Tachi

Hachiōji

Saroma

HOKKAIDO

Niigata

HONSHU

Tokyo

Okayama

SHIKOKU

KYUSHU

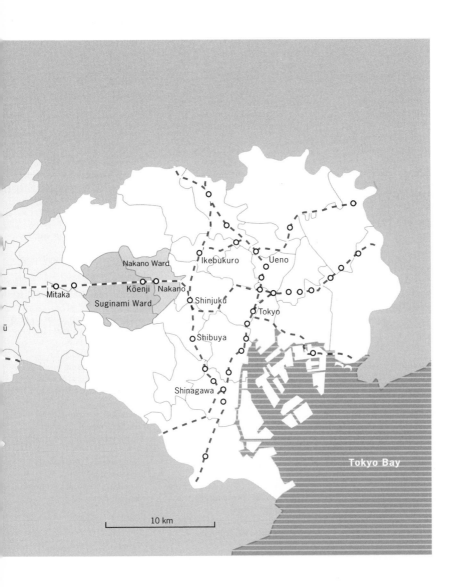

Tokyo Metropolitan Area

This map shows the different areas where Kenji lived and worked.

Chronology

WORLD	JAPAN	OGUMA KENJI
1868	Meiji Restoration	
1876		Ishichi born
1877	Satsuma Rebellion	Kochiyo born
1883		Yūji born
1914	World War I begins	Yūji and Yoshie marry
1917	Russian Revolution	
1918	World War I ends	Siberian Intervention (to 1922)
1923	Munich Putsch	Great Kantō Earthquake
1925		Universal Manhood Suffrage Law	Kenji born
1929	Great Depression begins	
1930	Salt March in India	
1931		Manchurian Incident	Teruichi comes to Tokyo
1932	Military seizes power in Siam	May 15 Incident (failed coup)	Kenji comes to Tokyo; Ishichi opens shop in army commissary
1933	Hitler takes power in Germany		Masaichi comes to Tokyo
1935			Yasuko comes to Tokyo
1936	Spanish Civil War begins	February 26 Incident (failed coup)	
1937		Second Sino-Japanese War begins	Teruichi dies; family moves to Nakano
1938			Kenji enters Waseda Jitsugyō
1939	World War II begins		
1940	Paris falls to Nazi Germany		Masaichi dies
1941	War between Germany and Soviet Union begins	Pacific War begins	Yasuko dies; Ishichi suffers strok
1942		Battle of Midway	Waseda Jitsugyō hit in air raid
1943		Japan withdraws from Guadalcanal	Kenji graduates Waseda Jitsugyō employed by Fuji Telecommunications
1944	Normandy landings	Battle of the Philippines	Kenji conscripted
1945	World War II ends	Japan surrenders	Kenji interned in Siberia
1946	Nuremberg trials	Constitution of Japan promulgated	Fellow internee Kyōsaka Kichiji dies
1947	Indian independence		"Democracy movement" in the camps intensifies
1948	Berlin Blockade	Verdicts in the Tokyo Trials	Kenji repatriated from Siberia
1950	Korean War (to 1953)		
1951		Treaty of San Francisco	Kenji enters tuberculosis sanatorium
1953	Stalin dies	Television broadcasting begins	Kenji has word of his aunt in Bra
1954	Algerian War	Anti-nuclear protests against Bikini Atoll test	Ishichi dies
1955	Afro-Asian Conference	Long-term dominance of Liberal Democratic Party begins	
1956	Suez Crisis		Kenji released from sanatorium
1957	Sputnik launched		Kenji moves to Tokyo
1958			Kenji employed by Tachikawa St
1959			Family moves into Municipal Housing No. 6
1960	Year of Africa	Protests against US-Japan Security Treaty	
1961	Berlin Wall built		Kenji and Hiroko marry
1962	Cuban Missile Crisis		Eiji born
1964	Nelson Mandela sentenced to life imprisonment	Tokyo Olympics	Yūji dies
1965	American bombings of North Vietnam begin		Tachikawa Store bankruptcy
1966	Cultural Revolution in China begins		Tachikawa Sports opens for business

Chronology

	WORLD	JAPAN	OGUMA KENJI
1968	Prague Spring	Radical students occupy universities	Kochiyo dies
1969	Apollo moon landing	Agreement on return of Okinawa to Japan (implemented 1972)	Family moves to Musashi Murayama
1972	Munich Olympics terrorist incident	United Red Army terrorist incident	Gōichi dies; family moves to Tachikawa
1978			Family moves to Nan'yōdai
1979	Soviet Union invades Afghanistan		Kenji reads The Gulag Archipelago
1980	Solidarity movement in Poland		Kenji sympathetic with Solidarity
1981	Reagan becomes US president		Kenji travels in connection with Chita-kai activities
1982	Falklands War	International controversy over Japanese history textbooks	Movement opposing motor vehicle station at Nan'yōdai
1983			Kenji meets Kyōsaka's brother
1987	June 29 Declaration in South Korea		
1988		Government initiates solatia to Siberian internees	Kenji joins Veterans Against War
1989	Democratization in Eastern Europe	Death of Emperor Shōwa (Hirohito)	Kenji participates in environmental protection movement in Nan'yōdai
1990			Kenji receives government solatium, shares it with Oh Unggeun
1991	Collapse of Soviet Union		Kenji revisits Chita
1995	Cease-fire in Bosnia	Controversy over Diet resolution commemorating 50th anniversary of war's end	
1996			Kenji joins Oh's lawsuit for compensation from Japanese government
1997	Asian financial crisis		First hearing of case; Tachikawa Sports closes
2001	September 11 terrorist attacks		
2002	Summit conference between Japan and North Korea	Suit by Oh Unggeun et al. rejected by Supreme Court	Kenji has stroke
2008	2008 financial crisis		
2009		Transfer of power to Democratic Party of Japan	
2010	Economic crisis in Greece	Siberian Special Measures Law enacted	
2011	Egyptian Revolution	Tōhoku earthquake and Fukushima Daiichi nuclear disaster	Kenji receives solatium under Siberian Special Measures Law
2012	Eurozone debt crisis	Liberal Democratic Party returns to power	Kenji installs solar panels in home in Nan'yōdai
2014	Protest movements in Taiwan and Hong Kong		
2015	Intensification of Syrian civil war	Protests against new national security bills	Hiroko dies; Japanese edition of this book published;South Korean and Taiwanese editions published
2016	Candlelight protests in South Korea		
2017	Trump inaugurated as US president		Chinese edition of this book published

Oguma Kenji in February 1945 in Mudanjiang, Manchuria, before his Siberian internment.

Preface to the English Edition

To the people all over the world whom I will come to know through this book:

What image comes to mind when you hear the words "Japanese soldier"? Is it one of arrogance and cruelty, the impression that remains in so many Asian and Western countries?

I do not intend to argue otherwise. Each of us has aspects of our personality that can be domineering, cruel, or lustful. The Japanese soldier was only human, and possessed these traits as well. And these aspects of human personality come to the forefront most forcibly in situations such as war or colonial domination. I do not think this has anything to do with what we refer to as "race" or "ethnicity."

Yet at the same time, it is not fair to judge people solely by these aspects of their personality. Nor is it an accurate understanding of them. The soldier who is brutal on the battlefield can be a loving father when he returns home. To see only one side means failing to comprehend the whole.

Because of this, if we wish to achieve an accurate understanding, we cannot turn our attention only to wartime. This is true of Japan and the Japanese as well. What sort of life did the men who became Japanese soldiers lead before they arrived at battlefronts across Asia and the Pacific? What was on their minds? Under what circumstances did they leave their homes and set out for war? What were their lives like after they returned home to Japan? Without looking at all these questions it is impossible to adequately understand them.

This book is a life history of my father, who was born in 1925. He worked in a small shop before the war. Drafted late in the war and sent to Manchuria, he was interned by the Soviets in Siberia, where he spent three years doing forced labor. After his return to Japan he went through a series of different jobs and was ill with tuberculosis. But after this bleak and difficult period in his life he started a small business and raised a family. This is the story of the life of this rather ordinary human being. And writ large, this story depicts the contemporary history of Japan. The Japanese people—my father among them—experienced the Great Depression, the war with China that began in 1937, and the war with the United States and its allies that lasted from December 1941 to August 1945. In the course of those events, 3,100,000 Japanese died—about 4 percent of the population. Almost all of Japan's cities were reduced to ashes and rubble by US bombing raids, and a quarter of the nation's wealth was destroyed. The Japanese economy recovered from these dire circumstances by the late 1950s, entering an era of high growth that by 1968 made its GDP second only to that of the US among the Western nations. However, from the 1990s onward the economy stagnated, while at the same time Japan was called to account by its Asian neighbors on issues of war responsibility and postwar compensation. The life of my father, born in 1925, thus reflects this period in Japanese history. And through this book, readers are provided a chance to review the contemporary history of Japan through the life of a single individual.

My father did not lead an affluent life before the war, and after it was over he continued to experience hardships for quite some time. In the decade after he returned from internment in Siberia, he changed jobs more than ten times. The image of the Japanese man that seems common to people in other countries is that of the salaryman with lifetime employment, but this has always been limited to university graduates who have found jobs with major corporations. And in any country, it is people who have completed higher education who tend to leave literary or documentary evidence of their lives, and whose lifestyles typify their nation to people from other countries. On the other hand, anthropologists and ethnologists have done much to record the ways of life of people in settled farming communities, but there are few records of the life of the urban lower classes who, like my father, led unsettled lives and changed jobs frequently. This book may help readers come to know something of this "silent majority" of ordinary people who lived through the changing times of wartime and postwar Japan.

There are two things I hope the reader will take away from this book.

The first is that there is nothing particularly special about my father. Late in life, my father joined with another former Japanese soldier, who was of Manchurian Korean ancestry, in bringing suit against the Japanese government to seek redress for those from Japan's former colonies who had been interned by the Soviet Union. Some people, when they hear of this, think he must be a very special individual, a man of conscience. But I am his son, and I can vouch for the fact that he is no saint.

Human society is not made up of a minority of "good people" and a majority of bad ones. Every one of us has good and bad sides. To see only the good and regard someone as a saint is—like seeing only the bad and regarding him as a sinner—not an accurate perception.

What my father has done is no more than what any human being has the potential to do. Rather than praising his deed as an individual act, it is more important to activate that potential among a broader range of people. To see my father as exceptional, and different from the common run of humanity, risks obstructing that goal.

The second thing I hope the reader will take from this book is the analysis of the societal background. My book differs from a standard biography in the attention given to the impact of the contemporary economic and social situation, government policies and law, foreign relations, and other factors on the trajectory of my father's life. I am a historian and a sociologist, and in writing the biography of my own father, I have worked hard to keep my analysis as objective as possible.

Why is such analysis necessary? As I have said, there are good and bad aspects to all human beings. Generally speaking, adverse circumstances such as war and colonialism tend to bring out the worst in people. In such situations, individual effort to maintain and uphold the better aspects of our nature is crucial. But even more important is the creation of circumstances in which a greater number of people will find it easier to display their better aspects. To this end, we need to analyze what we should do to eliminate circumstances such as war and colonialism, poverty and inequality.

In this book, "war" and "everyday life" as my father experienced them will be treated as constellations of the factors comprising them—government policy, foreign relations, political institutions, commodity prices, income, social conditions, and so on. In order to depict this, for each period of my father's life I have woven in analyses of policies and institutions and how they affected daily life and the economy—frequently resulting in suffering, poverty, and mutual distrust. But I have also written of the policies and institutions that proved helpful to my father in his efforts to make a better life for himself. In this sense, this book does not merely deal with past history, but will hopefully offer hints for the present as well.

Finally, I would like to say a few words regarding what I respect about my father. This book is based on a lengthy series of interviews with him between 2013 and 2015, and what impressed me the most amid the many stories I heard from him was the empathy he has for other people.

For example, during the hardest period of his life, his internment in Siberia, his friends were dying of hunger and cold, and he was one step away from the grave himself. Yet even when he spoke of this experience, my father did not demonize the Russians. Instead, he spoke of how desperately poor Soviet society was at that time, how undemocratized and full of injustice. And he spoke of how this had influenced his own situation and treatment. For him, the Russian people were, like himself, the victims of a dysfunctional system and bad policies.

My father is not an educated man. Nor is it the case that education and knowledge will automatically produce an outlook like my father's. There are people who use their knowledge only to aggrandize themselves and to denigrate others as fools or devils. I believe that my father's perspective on the Russian people is a result of the empathy he has for others. And this empathy is the quality I most respect in my father.

It is this type of empathy that is most needed in today's world. Our world is divided by nationality, culture, religion; differences in birthplace, educational experience, economic situation. To overcome these divisions and build a better world, one of the things that is required is empathy for other people. And it is critical that we put our knowledge and analytical abilities to work in expanding the potential for such empathy. One of the things I hope to convey through this book, and through my father's life, is the potential that such empathy gives to us.

We are all human—despite differences in country, language, and social class, we are all human. I will be happy if this book is useful in helping to remind everyone of this obvious fact.

Oguma Eiji
August 2017

September 1934.
Ishichi (58), Teruichi (17), Masaichi (16),
and Kenji (8).

Summer 1941 in Okayama.
Kenji (15) and Kochiyo (64).

Chapter 1

Before the Army

At 7:30 am on 25 November 1944 the skies were overcast. The war with the United States and its allies that had begun in December 1941 was entering its final phase; Japan would surrender nine months later in August 1945.

A small group of relatives and acquaintances had assembled in front of the family home in Nakano Ward, Tokyo, to see nineteen-year-old Oguma Kenji off. He was being inducted that day into the Imperial Japanese Army as a private second-class. The day before, 24 November, Tokyo had been subjected to its first full-scale air raid, with a flight of American B-29 bombers passing high in the skies over their neighborhood.

The induction notice had arrived five days earlier, on 20 November. A telegram had been sent to Kenji's father in Niigata telling him to come to Tokyo, but there had been little time for other preparations.

A few years before, the neighborhood association or the local branch of the Women's National Defense Association would have organized a flag-waving sendoff. But nowadays young men were being called up with such frequency that people had grown indifferent. The city was still tense after the air raid the day before, and the atmosphere among the small group of family and friends of his grandfather who gathered to wish Kenji farewell was far from festive.

Dressed in his khaki national uniform, Kenji gave the expected farewell message, "I will do my best to serve my country!" and then turned to his grandfather and grandmother and said quietly, "Well, goodbye for now." His grandfather, overcome with emotion, wept loudly. This was quite unusual in those days—virtually taboo. His grandmother said, "Ken, get going!" and almost pushed him in the direction of Nakano Station before turning to lead his grandfather back into the house.

It would be four long years before Kenji would return to Japan from his postwar internment by the Russians in Siberia.

1

Kenji was born on 30 October 1925 in the village of Saroma in Hokkaido. Northernmost of the main Japanese islands, Hokkaido is a bit larger than Ireland. Its cold climate is not well suited to traditional Japanese agricultural techniques, and until the middle of the nineteenth century it was largely undeveloped. As in Siberia and Australia, the first settlers were soldiers, convicts, and poor pioneers seeking a new life. Braving winter conditions that frequently went below −20°C and occasionally below −40°C, they began to cultivate the forests and plains where the indigenous inhabitants—the hunters and gatherers known as the Ainu—had lived. The place name Saroma derived from an Ainu phrase, *sar oma pet*, that meant "river of the reed plains." The village was partly settled in 1911 by a group of refugees from Tochigi Prefecture who had relocated there after their own community was devastated by pollution from the Ashio copper mine.

The Ogumas had been a well-to-do rural family in Niigata Prefecture. But Kenji's grandfather got involved in rice futures trading and other ill-fated ventures, and ended up losing the family land and sinking into poverty. At the time the Ogumas had five children: three sons and two daughters. The second son, Yūji, born in 1883, was Oguma Kenji's father.

Oguma Yūji graduated from elementary school and at the age of eighteen apprenticed in a dry goods store in Sapporo, the capital of Hokkaido. Not long afterward, he was conscripted into the army and served as a medical corpsman in the Russo-Japanese War. After the war ended in 1905, he married in Niigata and returned to Sapporo, where he opened a bookstore. But he was unsuccessful in this business and lost the store itself in a fire that spread from a neighboring building. Then, in 1912, his wife died. So the next year Yūji moved on to Abashiri, a town on Hokkaido's western coast known for the fishermen who plied its cold offshore waters, as well as for its maximum-security prison holding those convicted of serious crimes. With his one- and two-year-old daughters in tow, Yūji found work as an assistant in a scrivener's office located across from the town hall.

In the newly settled towns and villages of Hokkaido, there was a considerable amount of legal paperwork to be submitted to the government concerning the sale and purchase of land and other matters. The Japanese government had expropriated the forest and plains of Hokkaido from their Ainu inhabitants, and was selling them off to poor pioneers resettling there from other parts of Japan. Few people had the skills to fill out all the required forms by themselves, and scriveners set up shop in the vicinity of local government offices to meet this need. Brought up in an affluent family, Yūji had the skills to engage in this kind of clerical work despite having only completed his primary education.

In those days local inns provided long-term accommodations to a fair number of people, and Yūji stayed at one such establishment while working in Abashiri. Through the good offices of the innkeeper he was able to find an adoptive home for his younger daughter, relieving his responsibilities somewhat, but further prospects did not seem to be in the offing. Eventually he learned that a new government office was to be built in the recently settled village of Saroma, not far from Abashiri. Thinking that a new office would create demand for scriveners, he packed up and moved to Saroma in October 1914.

Settlers with skills and talents tended to find jobs as carpenters, merchants, or other professionals, and formed small urban enclaves in the vicinity of the local government offices. Yūji established himself at the Katayama Inn in Saroma, and ran his scrivener's business out of a small office building across from the government office.

The innkeeper was a man named Katayama Ishichi. Born in 1876 in Okayama Prefecture, he had moved to Hokkaido in 1906. As a newly developing area, Saroma was in the midst of a construction boom, and the Katayama Inn bustled with customers. Ishichi himself had started out as a homesteading farmer, gotten

Katayama Inn (4 March 1913).

3

involved in the construction business, and used the proceeds to build the inn, which was managed by his wife, Kochiyo, who was a year younger.

In December 1914, Yūji remarried. His bride was the Katayamas' elder daughter, Yoshie. At the time of their marriage, Yūji was thirty-two; Yoshie was eighteen.

Initially, Yoshie's parents had been opposed to the marriage. The Katayamas had two daughters and no sons; they had been hoping that Yoshie would marry someone the family could groom to take over the inn business. An apparent ne'er-do-well in his thirties with a child of his own probably did not seem the best match for their daughter. But in the end it was agreed that if there were any children from the marriage, the eldest son would be heir to the Oguma family name, while the second son would be adopted into the Katayama family as its heir.

In any event, Yūji began to prosper. Raising funds and making contacts through his scrivener's work, he rose to be managing director of the Saroma buyers' cooperative and eventually became a major figure in the producers' cooperatives for the eastern region of Hokkaido.

The producers' cooperatives were originally created to protect small farmers from poverty. With the enactment of the Producers' Cooperative Law (Sangyō Kumiai Hō; also known as the Industrial Association Law) in 1900, producers' and buyers' cooperatives were created among farmers in rural villages and consumers in the cities and towns—the precursors of today's agricultural and consumer cooperatives. Many people at the time, including the renowned folklorist and Ministry of Agriculture official Yanagita Kunio, hoped that the cooperatives would help free villages from the stifling grip of rural poverty.

Oguma Yūji and Yoshie had six children: three boys and three girls. The boys were named Teruichi, Masaichi, and Kenji; the girls were Mitsuko, Yasuko, and Hideko.

Kenji, now ninety years old, explains the children's names as follows:

"My father was originally from Niigata, and my mother from Okayama, so the boys' names were based on the names of feudal lords in those regions from several hundred years ago [Uesugi Kenshin, in the case of Kenji]. This was the way people without much education named their children at the time—and neither my father nor my mother had more than an elementary education."

Their eldest daughter died about a month after her birth. Of the remaining five children, as will be related later, three would die of illness around the age of twenty.

In 1923, Yoshie's father, Katayama Ishichi, and his wife, Kochiyo, let go of the Katayama Inn and moved to Tokyo. The reason they gave up the inn is unclear but, according to Kenji, it was probably a result of Ishichi either failing in the construction business or being swindled in some fashion.

In 1930, Kenji's mother, Yoshie, was diagnosed with tuberculosis, dying of the disease in July 1932 at the age of thirty-five. At the time, tuberculosis was untreatable and often fatal. Underlying her death were overwork and poor nutrition. In an era before electric appliances, giving birth to six children and caring for them was a tremendous burden. As her mother, Kochiyo, later recalled, "Yoshie said to me, 'Mama, these days I am just worn out.' She'd borne six children, and then she was worked to death." Regarding this, Kenji comments,

"I suppose my grandmother thought my dad killed her daughter with overwork. But everyone in Japan was overworked in those days; it's a pity to blame my father. My father had lived in poverty for a long time. Even when things eased up a little, I doubt he ever thought of hiring a maid."

Even after Yoshie fell ill, Yūji was busy at work, and had little time to spare to care for the children. After Yoshie's death he married for the third time, but sent the children one after another to live with the Katayamas in Tokyo. Saroma did not have much by way of industry, and office jobs like those with the producers' cooperatives were limited. He seems to have judged that it was better to send the children to Tokyo rather than having them grow up in the country where they would probably wind up farming or tending livestock.

First to be sent to Tokyo was the eldest son, Teruichi, upon his graduation from higher elementary school in 1931.* In July 1932 he was joined by Kenji, who had just entered elementary school. The last

---

* In prewar Japan, elementary school was six years, secondary school five years, higher school three years, and university three years, with only elementary school being compulsory. After completing elementary school, many students went on to a two-year higher elementary school instead of secondary school. In postwar Japan, elementary school became six years, middle school three years, high school three years, and university four years, with both elementary and middle school education being compulsory.

5

child, Hideko, would remain in Saroma, but as we will see, Masaichi and Yasuko were also sent to Tokyo. The agreement seemed to be that Yūji would send money for child support to Tokyo, but the Katayamas would raise their grandchildren.

After World War I, Japan passed through a period of boom and bust from the 1920s into the 1930s, as the market economy permeated and reshaped society, and finance and trade became increasingly internationalized. On the one hand, this encouraged the rise of an urban middle class and established the foundations of Japan's later consumer culture. But from another perspective, there was a sudden rush of population from the countryside into cities, and a concomitant swelling of the urban population. The advent of producers' and buyers' cooperatives was a sign of the poverty, instability, and inequality that underlay both rural and urban life. And these were harbingers of the war and unrest of the 1930s.

2

Kenji has almost no memory of his mother. By the time he was old enough to remember anything she had already developed tuberculosis and was confined to an outbuilding of the family home. All he can recall is a vague image of a woman who must have been his mother sitting on the veranda. His father was always busy with work and had little time for him.

In July 1932, Kenji's grandmother Kochiyo took him back to Tokyo with her. She had come to Saroma to care for her daughter Yoshie in her final illness, attend the funeral, and collect Kenji, who was six years old at the time and had no idea of why he was going to Tokyo. He says, "I didn't think much about it—it was like going on a school trip." Much later Kochiyo told him that he'd given her trouble when they were in the bus on the way to the train station, saying, "Maybe I won't go after all." His first impression of Tokyo was simply that there were certainly an awful lot of people.

His grandfather Ishichi was operating a sweet shop near the Sericulture Experimental Station in Kōenji, which had formerly been a farming village on the outskirts of the city but was rapidly being populated by people moving to Tokyo from the countryside.

Many, without education or specialized skills, ended up running small businesses of this sort, and a sweet shop was among those that required the least experience. There was no food service licensing system and anyone could open a shop. As a result, there was an oversupply of such microbusinesses. At the beginning of the 1930s in metropolitan Tokyo there was one sweet shop for every sixteen households and one rice shop for every twenty-three households. It was an uncertain livelihood: the average life expectancy of a small retail shop in the Tokyo suburb of Urawa was one year and eleven months during this period.*

Kenji recalls Katayama Ishichi as "a man of many talents." Before arriving in Tokyo he'd been a homesteading farmer, a construction contractor, and manager of an inn. The frontier region of Hokkaido had offered many opportunities for someone who was good with his hands and who also had some managerial skills. Ishichi had never had any training or experience in the confectionery business. Nevertheless, when he arrived in Tokyo he opened a sweet shop in the family's rental house in Kōenji, making sweet bean-paste buns and stocking other inexpensive sweets and candies from a wholesaler. Though still quite young at the time, Kenji remembers going with Ishichi to the wholesaler on several occasions. Some treats came with little lottery markings and if you won you got a small prize—this was quite popular with the neighborhood children.

The rental property that the family lived in was a typical two-story merchant's duplex, divided in half down the middle to accommodate two storefronts on the ground floor. Immediately inside the ground-floor entrance was a three-mat shop area where the sweets and candies were displayed for sale. (The tatami mat determined the basic unit of area for traditional Japanese floor plans, measuring about one by two meters, or three by six feet). This was divided by sliding papered doors (shōji) from the interior, which consisted of a six-mat room, a three-mat room, and the kitchen, behind which was a work area that Ishichi had built onto the back of the house with a large cauldron and bamboo steamers for making the sweets. On the second floor was a small veranda for drying laundry, fronted by the shop sign, and, inside, another set of three- and six-mat rooms.

---

* Arata Masafumi, Shōtengai wa naze horobiru no ka (Kōbunsha, 2012), p. 70.

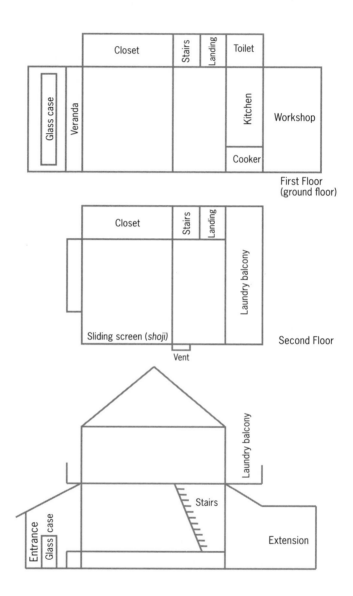

First Floor
(ground floor)

Second Floor

The Katayamas' House in Kōenji

In this rented house, Teruichi, the eldest boy, slept on the second floor, while the grandparents and young Kenji slept on the first floor. A large traditional dresser was virtually the only furniture, but Ishichi was fond of novelty, and by around 1934 the household had acquired a radio, still a relatively rare item in a Japanese home.

Running water came from an outdoor spigot shared by about ten households, with responsibility for the key to the faucet rotating regularly among them. Laundry was done by Kochiyo in a large tub; underwear was changed only once every four or five days. In fact, ordinary people in Japan began daily changes of clothing only after washing machines came into widespread use following the postwar economic boom of the 1960s. Once every four or five days was also the frequency with which the family bathed, and this was done at the local public bath, for the house was not equipped with bathing facilities. Neither running water nor gas for cooking or heating were common in Japanese households at the time; to have a bath in one's home was still an upper-class amenity.

Meals centered on rice and pickled vegetables. Kenji says, "We would eat fish maybe once in three days or so, but I don't recall eating meat much at all." The distribution system was underdeveloped, so the majority of fish the family consumed was dried. Fresh fish was limited to sardines—and they were often none too fresh.

On the rare occasions when they did eat meat, it was mostly pork. Vegetables were bought at a neighborhood greengrocer; fish and meat from a market near the Sericulture Experimental Station. Kochiyo was so busy with household chores she rarely had time to prepare anything fancy for dinner.

Kenji figures the proportion of income spent on food to have been about 60 percent, but also says, "We had running water nearby, and I think we ate better than we did in Saroma. In Saroma we had to draw water from the river or a well and carry it home, and the food wasn't very good." In Saroma, the Oguma family was regarded as well-to-do, so if the meager rations he ate in Tokyo seemed like better fare to Kenji, it is suggestive of the immense economic inequalities that existed between urban and rural areas in those days.

Kenji does not remember ever eating fresh fish while living in Saroma. There was no established transport route to bring fish inland and there were not even any bicycles in Saroma in those days. Aside from carrying things by hand, horses and horse-drawn sleds were about the only conveyances, and horses and their handlers were costly—prohibitively costly for the transport of fish, which would have to have been sold at a price that consumers in the village could not afford.

The tenant in the other half of the duplex was a Western-style tailor. Among the ordinary folk of their neighborhood it was common for the women to wear kimono and for the men to wear either work clothing or a kimono as their everyday dress, but men also usually possessed at least one Western-style suit for formal occasions such as weddings and funerals. These were usually not bought off the rack at a store, but made to order at a tailor's shop. Men also commonly wore Western-style underpants rather than the traditional loincloth, which Kenji said he was only made to wear for his military conscription exam and after he was inducted into the army, since it was part of the official military uniform.

Their neighbor the tailor had six children to care for, and life appeared hard. The family had been living in the old Tokyo working-class neighborhood of Fukagawa east of the Sumida River, but had moved to Kōenji after the Great Kantō Earthquake of 1923. Ordinary residents of Tokyo in those days were almost all renters, and after much of the old *shitamachi* (the "downtown" working-class enclaves) was destroyed in the terrible fires accompanying the earthquake, a fair number of them moved to the western parts of the city, which until that time had still been largely rural.

Kenji recalls that the Katayama house was part of a small shopping street, largely made up of providers of daily necessities—a greengrocer, a tofu shop, a charcoal seller, a drugstore, a public bath, and so on. For the more affluent, there was also a laundry, a sushi shop, a nightclub, and a bookstore. In this period, Kōenji began to be populated not just by small shopkeepers like the Katayamas, but by middle-class office commuters into central Tokyo.

The Katayamas were definitely not middle class. They never took their clothes to the laundry nor ever ate at the sushi shop. As Kenji puts it, "Back then, ordinary people had no pensions or health insurance, so they scrimped and saved to provide against illness and old age. Grandpa kept close track of the family expenditures in addition to the store accounts, and in the evening he would ask Grandma how much she had spent that day and on what. In those days there were a lot more small local banks than there are now. And among longtime residents of the area I think there were still some traditional mutual-loan associations."

In Japan, local or regional mutual-loan associations had begun to spread during the course of the eighteenth century. Many local banks developed out of such associations as the capitalist economy matured. But as we shall see later, they disappeared in the 1940s as the war escalated and the government tightened its control over the economy.

Kenji recalls that by this time farmland was disappearing from the neighborhood, and there was a great deal of new housing construction. Kōenji Station was opened by the national railway in 1922, and the area was also served by a private tram line running westward out of central Tokyo from Shinjuku to Ogikubo. The result was the development of the area into a commuter suburb of central Tokyo.

In the early 1930s the population of the Kōenji area was growing rapidly, fed by a mixture of three different groups: first, families like the tailor's, who had lost their homes in eastern Tokyo in the great earthquake and moved to the western part of the city; second, families like the Katayamas, who moved to Tokyo from the provinces; and third, a new commuter middle class. In 1932, the year Kenji moved to Tokyo, the neighborhood was formally incorporated into the city of Tokyo as part of the newly created Suginami Ward.

The neighborhood nightclub served Japanized "Western food" such as curry over rice and pork cutlets at lunchtime, and Kochiyo called it the "Western food shop." In the evenings, two or three waitresses would be there pouring drinks. One night young Kenji, still in elementary school, peered in beneath the shopfront curtain to see what was going on. He remembers seeing one of the waitresses and a customer in an interior dimly lit with colored lightbulbs and decorated with artificial sprays of cherry blossoms.

Nearby was Ōme Kaidō, one of the principal highways running westward out of the city, but the other roads and streets of the neighborhood were narrow lanes that a hand-drawn cart could barely negotiate. On the highway one would see bicycles, "rear-cars" (large two-wheeled carts on bicycle tires pulled by hand or towed by bicycle), buses, and trams, as well as the occasional truck or taxi. But personal automobiles were almost nonexistent, and the taxis were almost all American-made. The drivers were usually accompanied by a barker or tout in the front seat who called out to passersby to drum up business.

Kenji does not remember his grandfather Ishichi having anything to do with any sort of local residents' council or neighborhood association—organizations basic to any village or established urban neighborhood. He says he doesn't think there were any organizations of this kind because the area had been so recently developed.

In Japanese elections, neighborhood and block associations played an important role in gathering votes for local politicians. In 1925, enactment of the General Election Law expanded suffrage to all males twenty-five years of age or older, giving Ishichi the right to vote for the first time, but Kenji does not recall ever seeing him vote in an election or have his vote solicited for a particular candidate or party. About all he can remember with regard to such matters are some of the slogans from a major campaign around 1935 to reform the election process and combat pervasive vote-buying and bribery.

The eldest boy, Teruichi, helped his grandfather with the family business. When Kenji arrived in Tokyo, Teruichi was still only fifteen, but in Kenji's eyes he had become quite grown up. About two years after Kenji got to Tokyo, Teruichi opened a take-out tempura shop in a public market in Nakano. The customers were mainly the wives of office workers, shopkeepers, and day laborers in the area, according to Kenji. The tempura Teruichi sold was not high-class restaurant fare, but an economical ready-made meal for working families without a proper kitchen at home. For such families it was common to cook only their rice at home, and buy accompanying dishes as takeout.

Ishichi had worked to train and assist Teruichi in establishing himself as an independent tradesman. Kenji recalls, "In those days ordinary folks like my father and grandfather had no concept of providing their kids with formal education. They only thought in terms of how to make it possible for them to survive on their own."

The market where Teruichi had his shop fronted on the Ōme Kaidō highway at one of the stops on the tram line going into central Tokyo.

"There was a rice-cake shop and a drugstore at the entrance and then a lot of little shops—tempura, saké, fruits and vegetables, sewing materials and sundries—you could get just about anything you needed there. At the entrance there was a sort of mezzanine balcony set up as a stage, where musicians hired by the market would perform on the first and fifteenth of each month to advertise the regular bargain days."

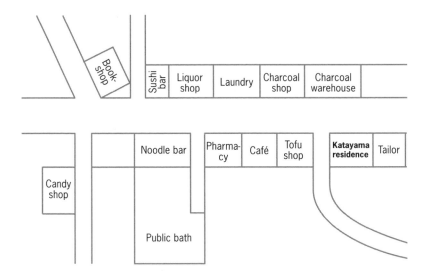

The neighborhood of the house in Kōenji

Across the highway to the south was Nakano Shinbashi, a government-licensed entertainment district where restaurants, drinking establishments, and lodgings catering to geisha, prostitutes, and their clients were concentrated. In prewar Japan, prostitution was legal if it was overseen by government-licensed businesses in specifically designated areas. During the war, many of these entrepreneurs would procure women to staff "comfort stations" that they managed in occupied territories of Asia to serve the Imperial Japanese Army. Kenji remarks that "this was an area where rich old guys came to sport with geisha. It was a completely different world from ours."

Public markets like the one in Nakano were established by local government. In a pattern common in the developing world today, a public entity would provide the buildings and other infrastructure to enable small retailers to open and run their shops. Individual micro-businesses catering to individual consumers could not compete with big capital and were inherently unstable, vulnerable to unfair sales practices and unpredictable price fluctuations. The famous Rice Riots that occurred throughout Japan in 1918 had been triggered by a sudden radical jump in the price of rice, and stabilizing commercial transactions became an urgent task for the government. As a result, local governments took the lead in encouraging cooperatives, and the year after the Rice Riots, public markets were created in six locations in Tokyo. The Nakano market was part of this government policy of restoring order and stability through urban cooperatives similar to the producers' cooperatives that were already being implemented in rural areas. The cooperatives were one attempt at countering the instability exhibited by the capitalist economy of this era.

Another attempt to develop cooperative businesses proceeded simultaneously: the creation of shopping streets. From about the time the Great Depression began in 1929, small shopkeepers had begun to organize, pooling their capital to create shopping streets as a way to compete with the big department stores and other large retailers. The Katayamas lived near a stop on the tram line where there was a shopping street with a covered arcade, called the Mutual Prosperity Association Market. Both sides of a narrow pedestrian street (more like a passageway) were lined with two-story buildings with residences above and shops on the ground floor—a fish shop, a greengrocer's, a sundries shop, and so on.

Kenji remembers Teruichi in his tempura-shop days as a typical working-class kid with a bright, outgoing personality. He played on the baseball team formed by the young men of the public market, and a photograph has survived showing him in the team uniform. And Kenji recalls him climbing the drum tower to play the big drum providing rhythmic accompaniment to the song "Tōkyō ondo" (Tokyo Dance) for the midsummer Bon festival dances in Kōenji.

"Tōkyō ondo" was the hit song of 1933 and a major contribution to the growth of the Japanese recording industry, selling an astonishing 1.2 million records. The secret of its success was an arrangement that recalled Japanese folk tunes and captured the hearts of people who had moved to Tokyo in great numbers from rural areas and were still unfamiliar with Western music, encouraging them to organize in Tokyo the kind of Bon dances they had once enjoyed in their home villages in the summertime. According to Kenji, "Tokyo natives like the tailor and his family were scornful of both 'Tōkyō ondo' and the Bon dances as entertainment for hicks from the countryside. Their popularity probably reflects just how many people in Tokyo had recently moved there from the provinces."

After arriving in Tokyo from Saroma in July 1932, Kenji was enrolled as a first-year pupil at an elementary school in Kōenji. Boys and girls were schooled separately; the first-year pupils were divided into four classes, two of boys with male teachers and two of girls with female teachers. (After the war, the reforms implemented by the Allied Occupation would replace this separation of the sexes with a coeducational system.) His grandparents bought Kenji the traditional *randoseru* (a sturdy rucksack—the best of which were made of leather—carried as a book bag by Japanese elemntary school students), but it was a flimsy thing of cheap leather over a cardboard core.

Teruichi (center) in his baseball uniform.

The classes were a mix of children of small shopkeepers, tradesmen, and day laborers and those from the middle-class families known as "monthly wage-earners" (*gekkyū-tori*). In the early twentieth century, hardly anyone other than white-collar workers in government offices or large corporations received monthly wages or salaries, and those who did formed a privileged urban elite. Their ranks swelled during the 1930s, but they remained a middle class that was distinctly better off than the self-employed shopkeepers and day laborers who still made up a significant percentage of the urban population. Kenji does not remember any farmers' children: "I don't know for sure, but the middle-class kids made up maybe 40 percent. If you looked at the class graduation picture you could spot them by their clothing and appearance.

"In those days the schools were not egalitarian, like they are today. I never participated in any of the school plays. That was for the middle-class kids. Nowadays everybody in the class would be given a chance to play a part, but back then nobody thought about it. School plays and such were put on to impress the local notables, not for the sake of the parents. And in any case, my grandpa and grandma were so busy working they didn't have time for events like that.

"I think it was when I was in fifth grade, but after playing in the schoolyard the kids were washing up and one of the middle-class kids

15

pulled out a handkerchief to dry his hands. One of the female teachers who was passing by praised him for his good manners. But the rest of us weren't particularly embarrassed—we just thought, "Oh, so that is what you're supposed to do."

The families of day laborers and street vendors were even poorer than small shopkeepers like the Katayamas. Kenji remembers seeing one child of a street vendor helping his father pull their cart. The street vendors, who did not have their own shops, did most of their business on Saturday and Sunday nights off of carts set up along the main highway. The rest of the week they mostly worked as day laborers. There were also itinerant peddlers with spiels like this to sell anything from fountain pens to bananas: "Hey, hey! Look at this fountain pen! It was rescued from a fire in a fountain pen factory . . . It's a little dirty, but that's because of the muddy water that saved it from burning. This is normally a top-priced item—if you don't buy it here, it's your loss!"

Incidentally, in Fukagawa, where the tailor's family had lived prior to the 1923 earthquake, there was a sizable Korean population, and the area elected the only Korean-born member of the House of Representatives in the prewar period.* But in Kōenji, Kenji does not recall ever seeing any Koreans or Chinese.

Kenji says, "We were just kids, so we didn't pay too much attention to the inequalities among our parents," but the children of merchants and tradesmen played in different groups from the middle-class kids. Kenji and the children of other shopkeepers played with *menko* (heavy square or circular decorated cards thrown down to flip an opponent's card and win it) and fighting tops called *beigoma*, and also played war games like "torpedo-boat commander." Their play areas were vacant lots that had been abandoned as farmland but had still not been built up, or the alleyways behind the shopping street, where bicycles did not pass.

Ishichi and Kochiyo loved little Kenji, whom they affectionately called "Ken," but they were always busy with work or the household chores and had little time for him. If he tried to cling to them, they would shoo him outdoors, so he never stayed inside to study but spent most of his time playing with the neighborhood kids.

---

* At the time, Koreans possessed Japanese nationality and could vote if they lived in Japan. See chapter 11 of Eiji Oguma, *The Boundaries of 'the Japanese,'* vol. 2, *Korea, Taiwan, and the Ainu, 1868–1945* (Melbourne: Trans Pacific Press, 2017).

The children formed groups led by the older kids, fifth graders or so, and defined a "turf" of about a hundred meters in every direction that they would play within. If you wandered off your turf, the kids in the neighboring turf would chase you back to where you belonged. So even without parental supervision, the older kids would keep an eye on the younger ones, and prevent them from straying off on their own or getting lost. Then, about halfway through fifth grade, the older kids would leave the groups as they began to prepare themselves for the responsibilities of adult work.

Kenji (left) at a field day at Suginami Elementary School No. 3.

They did have some contact with the middle-class kids, but even their houses were built differently. In the shopkeepers' houses the storefront let immediately into the living area. "The middle-class houses usually had a fence, a front gate, and a formal entryway. They were also equipped with baths. And the children themselves were somehow just more refined."

The middle-class kids were provided by their families with children's books and magazines like *Shōnen kurabu* (Boys' Club), which the shopkeepers' and tradesmen's kids would then borrow and pass around. Kenji and one of the tailor's sons became friends with a stockbroker's son who lived in a house with a big gate, and cajoled him into getting his parents to buy books and magazines so they could read them. Kenji himself never received any kind of regular allowance.

Kamishibai (lit., "paper plays")—a type of street theater in which a storyteller would set up a small stage with a set of illustrated placards to accompany his narrative—also came to the neighborhood from time to time. Kenji remembers, "The *kamishibai* usually consisted of three shows. The first was nonsense cartoons, the second a weeper for girls, and the third would be an adventure story like *Ōgon Batto* [Golden Bat] or *Shōnen Taigaa* [Tiger Boy]."

Ishichi and Kochiyo also were fond of theater, and took Kenji to see kabuki, which in those days was still a popular entertainment. Near the Mutual Prosperity Association Market and the tram stop there was a little local playhouse that offered the Japanese-style vaudeville known as *yose*, a mixed evening of entertainment featuring storytellers, comics, musicians, singers, sleight of hand, and so on. Kenji was taken there by his grandparents: he remembers seeing a popular outlaw drama. He also remembers being taken on the tram line to visit the big Isetan department store in Shinjuku.

The other major form of entertainment was the movies. In nearby Nabeya Yokochō ("Potsellers' Alley"), a bustling shopping and entertainment area of Nakano, there were two cinemas. Kenji's grandparents loved movies, and frequently took him along. There weren't any children's films at the time, but Kenji remembers going with his grandparents to see *Hitozuma Tsubaki* (Tsubaki, A Married Woman; 1936), adapted from a popular novel of the period by Kojima Masajirō. Cinemas were gradually driving out the little local playhouses, and around 1937 the local playhouse succumbed to this trend, becoming a movie theater.

Another pleasure of Kenji's elementary school days was the local shrine festival: "There was a kagura shrine dance with performers wearing comic masks, and a night market with treats and toys. We hardly ever went to the shrine otherwise, but the night market was fun. Unlike today, there really wasn't anyplace else kids could go at night to enjoy themselves."

But this lower-class urban lifestyle was already changing with the drumbeats of war.

3

In September 1931, the year before Kenji entered elementary school, Japan invaded northeast China and set about establishing the puppet state of Manchukuo. By the time he was enrolled in elementary school, the children were all talking about the "Three Human Bullets"—three members of the Imperial Japanese Army's corps of engineers who had perished in a suicidal bombing attack on enemy lines in Shanghai. Among the books kids were passing around to read were titles such as

Ajia no akebono (Asian Dawn) and *Shōwa yūgekitai* (Shōwa Commandos). Yet Kenji says, "The war stories at that time were not as absurd as they became later on. They began to get really crazy after the Second Sino-Japanese War began" in 1937.

For example, the May 1932 issue of the weekly magazine *Shōnen kurabu* featured an article by military affairs expert Hirata Shinsaku positing war between Japan and the United States entitled "Nichi Bei moshi tatakawaba" (If Japan and America Go to War). This later appeared as a book, which Kenji borrowed from a classmate and read. Based on a realistic consideration of the economic and military power of both nations and their strategic planning at the time, this book envisaged a pitched battle somewhere in the western Pacific. In contrast, Kenji recalls reading another such hypothetical account of a Japan-US war in the summer of 1941 that had Japanese forces landing on the West Coast and eventually conquering Washington, D.C.

When the Japanese government had begun its policies of modernization after the Meiji Restoration of 1868, it placed a high priority on unifying the nation around the figure of the Japanese emperor. The Imperial Rescript on Education, promulgated in 1890, was an articulation of this ideology grounded in patriotism and Confucian virtues. From around 1930, patriotic education in the schools intensified, though it was still not as oppressive as it became in later years. In addition to being forced to listen to the Imperial Rescript on Education "so many times we developed calluses in our ears," the children were set to memorizing the names of all 124 Japanese emperors from mythological times to the present. But Kenji says he never learned more than the first four or five generations, and does not recall being made to salute the Rising Sun flag or to bow in the direction of the Imperial Palace.

"In my fifth or sixth year of elementary school, they built a special shrine in the school to house a photograph of the emperor, but at the time I didn't think of it as anything more than an odd new building. I don't think we were made to bow to it when arriving at or leaving school until after the Second Sino-Japanese War began. In February 1938, when I was a sixth-grader, I went on a school trip to the Ise Grand Shrine,* though I don't remember much about it aside from thinking that riding the train was fun.

---

* The Ise Grand Shrine was dedicated to Amaterasu Ōmikami, the ancestral deity

"However, on the four great holidays related to the imperial house we always had ceremonies, and the principal would read the Imperial Rescript on Education. While he was reading the students all had to stand at attention with bowed heads. In those days kids all seemed to have runny noses, but it was not yet common for them to carry handkerchiefs or tissues, so there was usually a lot of sniffling going on as the principal read."

Kenji's fourth year of elementary school in 1936 was punctuated by the February 26 incident, an attempted coup d'état by young Imperial Army officers influenced by right-wing thought who led their troops in attacks on the prime minister's residence, Tokyo Police Headquarters, the Ministry of the Army, and the offices of major newspapers. Several government ministers and high-ranking military officials were assassinated before the coup could be suppressed. For the general public, though, a lurid murder case of the same year, the Abe Sada incident, left a deeper impression. Sensationally covered in the mass media, it was much discussed in the neighborhood among grown-ups and children alike.

The tramp of marching feet was drawing nearer, but the lives of ordinary people were still fairly relaxed. If anything, military demand after the outbreak of the Manchurian Incident in September 1931 spurred a recovery from the deepening economic depression. The Katayama family directly benefited from this upturn. In 1932, Ishichi opened a shop in the commissary of the army's First Signal Regiment, which was stationed in Nakano. Somehow he had secured the concession to sell items such as sweets and noodles in this shop on the base catering to off-duty soldiers. This became a secure outlet for the sweet buns that the Katayamas were making at home. Sales to a state organization such as the military represented a stable livelihood to a small business owner like Ishichi. He hired three assistants and expanded his operations.

Then, in 1933, Kenji's older brother Masaichi, Yūji's second son, graduated from higher elementary school in Saroma and came to Tokyo to live with the Katayamas. Masaichi found work as an assistant in the Imperial Army General Staff's Land Survey Department.

---

of the imperial family. The "four great holidays" were New Year's Day, Kigen-setsu (Imperial Foundation Day; 11 February), Tenchō-setsu (the reigning emperor's birthday; 29 April), and Meiji-setsu (Emperor Meiji's birthday; 3 November).

Such assistants were recruited from elementary and higher elementary school graduates and entered a type of apprenticeship program to train lower-ranking technical staff. They would never rise above the intermediate grades, but it was a stable career. Kenji has no idea how Masaichi managed to secure this position.

Although Teruichi and Masaichi were brothers, they had strikingly different personalities. Teruichi was an outgoing, salt-of-the-earth type: an older brother Kenji could talk to freely about anything. By contrast, Masaichi was a bit moody and seemed to Kenji to have more of an intellectual bent. Under the agreement at the time their parents married, the second son to be born—Masaichi—was promised to the Katayamas as their adoptive son, and he was thus known as Katayama Masaichi. Ironically, however, unlike his brother Teruichi, Masaichi had no desire to become a merchant. Both Teruichi and his grandfather Ishichi were indifferent to the idea of academic advancement, but Masaichi was attending secondary school at night while working at the Land Survey Department.

Meanwhile, Teruichi was learning to play go from Ishichi, who loved the game. When Masaichi was off at night school, Teruichi might be found poring over books on go and replaying famous games. Later, when Kenji had a look at Teruichi's diary, he found an entry in which Teruichi wrote that he and Masaichi were like "oil and water." The differences between the two were probably rooted in their personalities. But their circumstances were different as well: Teruichi was already running a small shop, while Masaichi was working in a bureaucratic institution in which one's academic record had a direct impact on wages and promotion.

In 1935, Kenji's sister Yasuko also arrived from Saroma upon finishing elementary school. After graduating from a higher elementary school in Kōenji, she used connections their father had made as an important figure in the producers' cooperatives to find a job as an office worker in the National Center for Agricultural Cooperatives in central Tokyo. Yasuko, a gentle soul, commuted to a women's clerical school in the evenings.

So it seemed as if life was stabilizing for everyone, but in 1935, when Kenji was in fourth grade, the storm clouds began to appear. Not long after Yasuko arrived in Tokyo, Teruichi began showing the first symptoms of tuberculosis. In those days there was no effective treatment for tuberculosis aside from rest and proper nutrition. As no national health insurance system yet existed, caring for a victim of the disease was a tremendous burden for an ordinary family. Thanks to Yūji's relative financial success back in Saroma, Teruichi was able to enter a sanatorium in Tokyo, but died in August 1937 at the age of twenty.

Teruichi's tuberculosis may have resulted in part from a physical susceptibility inherited from his mother that was also no doubt exacerbated by poor nutrition and the urban environment. But his grandfather Ishichi did not see it that way—he persuaded himself that Teruichi had ruined his health by staying up late at night studying go, and bitterly regretted having introduced him to the game. Ishichi gave away his go board and set of stones to friends, and never played the game again. He also got rid of all of Teruichi's clothing and other possessions.

Around the time of Teruichi's death, in the early summer of 1937, the Katayama family moved from Kōenji to a rental house in Nakano Ward. For some reason Ishichi had given up the concession at the army commissary and decided to take over Teruichi's tempura shop in the Nakano public market. The move put their home closer to the shop, but also meant closing the sweet shop they had operated in Kōenji. It had lasted for a little over five years, which was doing well for a small business in those days.

The Nakano house was one story, with a six-mat living and dining area, a kitchen, and additional six-mat and three-mat rooms. In terms of living space it was about the same size as the two-story house in Kōenji, but the kitchen was equipped with a gas range and running water, which was an improvement.

Ishichi, who had been a carpenter in Hokkaido, added a work area and a bath onto the house. Displaying his native versatility, at the age of fifty-eight he also learned the trade of cooking tempura. The eight-mat work area had an icebox in which the sardines, squid, and other perishables for making tempura were stored. The ice was delivered from a local ice merchant.

A day in the tempura business went something like this. Ishichi and his wife, Kochiyo, would get up at six or seven and spend the rest of the morning in the work area at home doing the prep work—slicing vegetables, filleting and deboning the sardines, and so forth—assisted by Kenji. Ishichi would then take the materials to the shop in

22

the public market, where he would begin the deep-frying in the afternoon, in advance of the rush of customers in the early evening picking up tempura for dinner. The cooking would be finished about four or five, and then family members would take turns manning the sales counter. Masaichi and Yasuko, who were both working in the daytime and going to night school, always got home late. Given this schedule, the entire family almost never sat down to dinner together.

Leftover tempura would be sold at a discount the next day. An inadequate distribution system meant that the sardines used for tempura were not the freshest. But customers knew they were getting day-old goods and had to judge the quality for themselves. Nor were the government authorities particularly strict about enforcing health regulations. Once an official from the Tokyo municipal health department visited the shop and advised that the tempura be displayed in a glass case to protect it from dust and dirt. But Ishichi protested that a glass case would fog up and prevent customers from seeing the product, and the official said nothing more.

Prices were one sen (a hundredth of a yen, the equivalent of about twenty cents today) for a piece of vegetable tempura and two or three sen for sardine. These prices were so low that quite a large volume had to be sold in order to make a profit. Time off simply meant loss of income, so the only days off were the first and fifteenth of each month, when the market itself would close, or for important family occasions such as weddings and funerals.

Soon after the move to Nakano, Kochiyo's sixteen-year-old nephew Tokioka Kiyoshi arrived in Tokyo. He moved in with the Katayamas and began working in the tempura shop. Kiyoshi was from a poor farm family and had only completed elementary school, but was studying on his own using published transcripts from classes at Waseda Secondary School (the school, affiliated with Waseda University, offered these as a kind of correspondence course for the general public). It appears that having lost Teruichi, Kochiyo had proposed that her nephew come to Tokyo to live with them and work in the shop, and Kiyoshi had agreed because he wanted the opportunity to study in Tokyo. He aspired to become a writer, and when he was not on duty at the shop he was working on a novel about rural life.

When the family moved to Nakano in 1937, Kenji was in sixth grade. Even after the move, he continued to attend elementary school

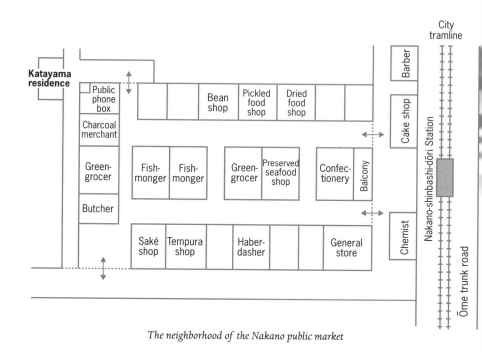

The neighborhood of the Nakano public market

in Kōenji, taking the tram to get there. He was not an outstanding student. His grades were average, and he was not good at sports. He had no special talents, nor any particular hopes for the future. He never did any homework and, in contrast to Kiyoshi the budding writer, his reading had not progressed beyond ninja thrillers for children like *Kaiketsu Kurozukin* (The Black Hood).

After Kenji finished elementary school his father Yūji and grandfather Ishichi intended to send him to higher elementary school for two years, and then put him to work. In prewar Japan, the children of farmers and workers generally were expected to go to work after completing higher elementary school; only middle-class children would advance to the five-year program of secondary education. This was what Kenji himself expected. Instead, Kenji became the first among his siblings to attend a regular daytime secondary school.

The opportunity to do so was created by his elder brother Masaichi. In the fall of 1937, Masaichi strongly urged Ishichi to have Kenji continue in school, telling him, "From now on it's going to be tough for anyone

24

who hasn't at least graduated from a day school." As mentioned previously, Masaichi himself was going to night school while working as an assistant in the Land Survey Department, where his chances of promotion were limited by his educational background. For him, attendance at a day school seemed like the key to personal advancement.

In the prewar educational system, secondary school was not part of compulsory education, and required the payment of tuition. In 1929 the monthly salary of an elementary school teacher was ¥46 (about $2,000 today); tuition and fees for a first-year student at a municipal secondary school in Tokyo were ¥146 (about $6,500). For the Katayamas, who were making a living selling tempura at the equivalent of 20 cents a piece, this was a very large sum of money. Many students who passed the entrance exams and were admitted to secondary school had to drop out before completing their studies for financial reasons. Moreover, aside from the very small number of people who could find jobs in the government bureaucracy or in large corporations, academic advancement and an academic record had little or no meaning. It is not surprising that Kenji's grandfather and father, who had made their way in the world on their own strengths with no more than an elementary school education, thought of further schooling as a waste of time and money.

But the times were changing. In 1937, only 13 percent of students advanced beyond elementary education—6 percent entering trade or commercial schools like the one Yasuko was attending, and 7 percent entering the secondary schools that opened the way to a university education. But in urban areas these percentages were rapidly increasing. Kenji recalls that at his elementary school other kids started studying for entrance exams in fifth grade, and about half his class ended up continuing their education.

One important factor behind the change was the wartime economic boom powered by corporate suppliers of the military, and the spur this gave to the rapid growth of Japanese heavy industry. In addition to an increase in white-collar employment, where promotion was directly connected to academic achievement, the stratum of people who could come up with tuition for their children also broadened. As Kenji says, "The percentage of children continuing their education was going up, to the point that in Tokyo even kids like me, with mediocre grades and no real sense of purpose, were continuing on in school."

So Ishichi accepted Masaichi's advice and negotiated with Yūji to pay the tuition fees. It may have been boom times, but Ishichi still did not have the economic wherewithal to make such academic advancement possible. Kenji recalls that the majority of the kids in his class who went on to secondary school were from middle-class salaried families. Although it was decided that Kenji would go on to secondary school, he didn't begin to study for the entrance exams until three months before they were given. At the beginning of sixth grade the children who were planning to advance to secondary school were all seated in the center of the class facing the blackboard, while those who were not were shunted off to either side. After regular classes were over, the advancing group would stay for another two or three hours of additional classwork in preparation for the exams. Kenji began to participate in these supplementary sessions, but he was not at the level of the other pupils. He got by in Japanese language, but floundered with arithmetic.

In the end, Kenji took the entrance exam for Waseda Jitsugyō, a trade school that, like the school that ran the correspondence course that Kiyoshi had been taking, was affiliated with Waseda University. His grades were such that he had no hope of getting into the more prestigious secondary schools his middle-class classmates were aiming for. Today, Waseda Jitsugyō is one of the best-known elite schools in the country, but at the time, as Kenji points out, it was just a trade school. "Grandpa seems to have thought that as a shopkeeper's kid it was appropriate for me to go there."

So Kenji succeeded in getting into Waseda Jitsugyō. But once he did, he found that despite its being a trade school, there weren't too many students who seemed interested in learning a trade. "Most of them were like me—they had no idea of what to do with themselves, and had simply found a school that suited their level." To commute there, Kenji began taking the tram line as far as Shinjuku.

For a while, life was peaceful. With his classmates he would go to Jingū Stadium to watch college baseball games or go hiking. Beginning in about his third year he became fond of Western movies and would go twice a week to cheap second-run cinemas in Shinjuku, where he saw films like *Pépé le Moko* (1937) and *Too Hot to Handle* (1938). He still wasn't much interested in reading, and when the budding writer Kiyoshi gave Kenji the manuscript of his novel to critique, "about all I could do was point out a few miswritten characters." Even so, Kenji began to develop an interest in the international page of the newspaper, beginning to pay attention to news of the Spanish Civil War, which began in 1936, and other events.

Meanwhile, the war with China, which everyone had thought would end in a swift Japanese victory, dragged on. At first people were only mildly irritated at reading news of the ongoing fighting, but eventually the war began to have a palpable effect on everyday life.

4

According to Kenji, the first harbinger of change in everyday life came around the end of 1937, when taxis started to disappear from the city streets. Up to that time, when Ishichi wanted to get some particularly fresh fish for his tempura, he would get together with the fishmonger at the public market and share a cab ride to the great fish market in Tsukiji on the Tokyo waterfront. One of the first effects of the war in China was a shortage of gasoline, and in May 1938, with the enforcement of the National General Mobilization Law, government-issued rationing coupons became required in order to purchase gas.

Such gasoline rationing had a direct impact on their tempura business. Since the stores in the public market were not provided with natural gas lines, the burners used to deep-fry the tempura had been fueled with gasoline. Ishichi was forced to switch to burning coke, which provided a weaker flame, and was harder to light and keep burning.

The boom driven by military procurement combined with shortages spurred inflation, and in October 1939, the government issued a price freeze. Official prices were set for approximately 100,000 items. As a result, sellers lost the ability to freely determine the prices of their goods, and distribution stagnated. Kenji recalls that by late 1939 it had already become difficult to obtain the cooking oil and fish to make tempura.

The controlled economy was sinking the public market. Meanwhile, across the way in the Nakano Shinbashi pleasure quarter, business was booming, at least temporarily, as war profiteers flocked to amuse themselves with geisha. Kenji recalls that in 1938, the name of the tram stop in front of the public market was changed from its previous name to Nakano Shinbashi-dōri. "Grandpa said that was because the folks on the other side of the street were making money off the wartime boom and had paid the tram company for naming rights."

Then, in June 1940, coupon rationing for sugar and matches began in Tokyo and five other major cities. The coupons were only proof of authorization to purchase; consumers still had to pay cash for these basic commodities. Around this time sweets disappeared from the shops in Kenji's neighborhood. In November this rationing was extended nationwide, and other daily necessities such as charcoal and clothing were included. As the war dragged on, even planned rationing began to malfunction as a result of both shortages of commodities and distribution bottlenecks resulting from the shortage of gasoline. More and more frequently, commodities might be unavailable at the rationing stations even if you had the proper coupons and rice-rationing booklet issued by the government.

In the autumn of 1939, "foreign rice" became a part of the household menu. Even before the war, Japan had been unable to supply all of its own rice, and it was common for lower-class urban households to eat rice imported from Taiwan, Korea, or China. But now, even rice from these sources was in short supply, and long-grain rice from Southeast Asia began to be imported. In the same year the government issued an ordinance prohibiting the sale of rice polished 70 percent or more in order to increase the bulk of the grains, even by a fraction. Use of sweet potatoes and other "substitutes" was encouraged, and after rice became subject to rationing in 1941, people began to also eat millet and barley. Kenji comments, "For ordinary people such things were more shocking than any news items about the seemingly endless war."

Meanwhile, formation of the organizations that would serve as the lowest-level units of the centrally controlled economy proceeded apace. It became impossible to procure cooking oil or fuel without being a registered member of the local take-out tempura association (tempura restaurateurs had a separate organization of their own). Shops that in ordinary times would have been rivals were forced to join together in such officially recognized organizations if they wanted to stay in business.

Households as well had to be enrolled in the neighborhood association (*chōnaikai*) and the smaller block groups (*tonarigumi*) if they wanted to be sure of getting their rationing. For Ishichi and his family, this was the first experience in Tokyo with such community organizations. The available rationed goods, however, were insufficient to supply the actual number of households in the neighborhood. There were also frequent imbalances of supply—scarcities of much-needed commodities and an abundance of unnecessary goods. Kochiyo attended a meeting at the house of the head of their block group and reported back that the neighbors were complaining about such problems.

Ishichi was originally from Okayama and still had family there, but the lack of transport and government controls on the major cereal crops meant that he could not have provisions sent from the countryside—except once, when they received a shipment of mixed grains.

Precious items such as sugar and gasoline were prioritized for military use. And even when there were shortages of foodstuffs in the cities, inadequate transport frequently meant that certain commodities would remain stuck in the countryside. When a controlled economy is introduced into a situation of prevailing maldistribution, the result is almost inevitably a proliferation of illegal channeling by those with special "connections." The term *yami-ne*—denoting a higher black market price for commodities outside the controlled economy—began to come into common use around 1939; regardless of the official price, the *yami-ne* was subject to severe inflation.

During the war, in contrast to the immediate postwar period, there was a general sense that buying things on the black market was somehow immoral, and it tended not to be done openly. But in fact it was quite common for neighborhood and trade association leaders and others in a position to do so to siphon off rationed items to sell at inflated prices on the black market, and for ordinary people to suck up to such "big shots" in order to secure the commodities they needed. This created considerable resentment, as expressed in a popular satiric poem of the time: "The world is ruled by / The stars [the army] and anchors [the navy] and connections and clout / Only fools stand in line."

Kenji remembers, "If you had your rice ration book you could buy rice, but for anything else, if you didn't know the person behind the counter you were out of luck. The slogan of the day was 'Luxury is the enemy,' but there were quite a few people who learned how to maneuver in the black market. 'Pull' and who you knew had become very important. The shortages of food and other items were one thing, but what everybody complained about was the sense of helplessness and unfairness."

In Kenji's recollection, the reaction of his neighborhood to the war was unenthusiastic. A neighborhood association and block groups were formed, but about all they did was pass around circulars with government directives and the like; hardly anyone was seriously active in them. When Nanjing fell to Japanese forces in December 1937, there was a nighttime lantern parade, but no one in Kenji's immediate circle participated. "Those above us had a lot to say, but the further down the hierarchy you went, the more indifference there was.

"In 1940 there was the New Order Movement, and bowing in the direction of the Imperial Palace began. If you were in a tram passing Hanzōmon, the conductor would announce, 'We are now in front of the Imperial Palace,' and all the passengers would bow. The straphangers on the opposite side of a crowded tram would not be able to turn around, but would bow anyway, with their backsides to the palace. No one took this sort of formalistic business seriously, and after a while they stopped doing it.

"The only news coming in about the war was that of victories. When Nanjing fell, or we attacked Wuhan, they would pin another little flag on the classroom map. But no matter how many flags they put up, the war went on and on."

The association of take-out tempura shopkeepers only functioned for about six months to a year. By mid-1940, it was impossible to get fuel and ingredients even through the association, and at the end of the year Ishichi was forced to close the business.

"A lot of shops were closed in all but name because they couldn't procure stock. About the only shop in the neighborhood that managed to keep going was one selling cleaning supplies like brooms and scrub brushes. You could no longer go out to eat anywhere. Every once in a while you'd hear that some shop had managed to find something to sell, and everyone would be excited."

In these circumstances, many shops simply closed for good. Workers outside of essential sectors such as food production and sale of daily necessities were redeployed into defense industries and supplying the military. Services that had catered to the new urban middle class, such as the nightclub and laundry in Kōenji, now vanished. The tailor who had lived next door to the Katayamas went out of business, and his children, now grown, worked to support the family.

In December 1941 the Business License Act required all private businesses to receive official authorization. This was followed in May 1942 by the Business Reorganization Act, which allowed for the merger and reorganization of business by administrative order. The result was a wave of business closings in the nonmilitary sector, and the merger and reorganization of such businesses into defense industries dominated by affiliates of the great conglomerates. In April 1942 the Financial Enterprise Reorganization Act forced a large number of smaller local banks and other regional financial institutions to be merged into the big banks, under the slogan "One bank per prefecture." The small banks in Kenji's neighborhood disappeared at this time.

These changes were paralleled by further misfortunes in the Katayama family. In the autumn of 1939, Masaichi, still working in the army's Land Survey Department, was stricken with a neurological disorder.

"Masaichi suddenly began having problems seeing, and then became unable to walk. A neighborhood doctor examined him, but was unable to make a diagnosis. I remember that when he came by on a house call he told my grandfather that a physician who was his mentor had said, 'That sounds a bit like Parkinson's disease.'

"At the end of that year, Masaichi entered a hospital attached to the medical school of a university, where they recorded footage of his symptoms. Since he had a rare disease, I guess they let him into the hospital as a guinea pig. Otherwise there was no way the grandson of a tempura shop owner could have afforded treatment at a university hospital."

After some six months of struggle and hospitalization, Masaichi died in June 1940 at the age of twenty-one. Kenji, in his third year of secondary school, wept along with his sister Yasuko, one year his elder.

To bury Masaichi, in July 1940 Ishichi erected a family grave for the Katayamas at Tama Reien cemetery on the outskirts of Tokyo. Extending between what are now the cities of Fuchū and Koganei, Tama Reien was opened in 1923 by the Tokyo Municipal Parks

Department to respond to the growth of Tokyo's urban population. Ishichi had already gone in with two friends who had moved from Hokkaido to Tokyo to buy rights to a plot. Nearby were grave sites dedicated to young officers killed in the ongoing Sino-Japanese War.

With both his older brothers gone, Kenji became closer to his sister Yasuko. But in March of the following year, 1941, Yasuko herself showed the first symptoms of tuberculosis. At about the same time, Kenji came home from school at Waseda Jitsugyō one day to be told that Ishichi, who had just closed down the tempura shop, had collapsed from a stroke. So Ishichi and Yasuko became bedridden invalids in the cramped confines of the Katayama rental house. Ishichi remained paralyzed on his right side, but survived. Yasuko's condition, however, progressively worsened, and in October 1941 she died at the age of nineteen.

Of the four children sent to Tokyo from Saroma, three had died of illness. A number of factors were probably involved: the strain of attending night school while working full-time, as well as poor nutrition and the anxieties of life under a wartime regime. Kenji says, "My older brothers and sister died one after the other. I wondered what was going to happen to me—and when. But I think all this was even tougher on Grandpa and Grandma."

Yet Ishichi was a stoic man of his generation (born in 1876), and even as the children left him by his deceased daughter also died in turn, and as he coped with his own stroke and paralysis, he never lost his composure or wept aloud. "He probably thought it wouldn't do to behave that way in front of me. He just sat there and took it. Grandma would complain a bit, but Grandpa would scold her, saying, 'What's the point of useless talk?'"

The aspiring writer Kiyoshi, who had lived with the family as an assistant at the shop, also came down with tuberculosis. Not long after arriving in Tokyo he'd not been feeling well, but the doctor diagnosed the problem as pleurisy and Kiyoshi continued working. Soon after the tempura shop closed, he had to return to his hometown in Okayama for his conscription health exam, and it was then that he found he had tuberculosis. The conscription officer called him disloyal and said that was why he had come down with the disease. Kiyoshi remained in his family home, where he died in the summer of 1944.

Left now were only sixty-five-year-old Ishichi, sixty-four-year-old Kochiyo, and sixteen-year-old Kenji. The family had lost its working members; the tempura shop was closed. They managed to get by somehow on Ishichi's savings from the business and money remitted to them by Kenji's father, Yūji.

Changes were also taking place at Kenji's secondary school. In 1937, the National Spiritual Mobilization campaign had been introduced, "and every year after that the slogans proliferated. By around 1939, the atmosphere started to change in earnest." Even so, in his second year there was still some freedom remaining from the old prewar secondary school days. His Japanese-language instructor indirectly criticized General Nogi Maresuke, hero of the Russo-Japanese War, saying, "Everyone in Japan thinks General Nogi is great, but overseas, especially in places like Britain, they say he was an incompetent general who sacrificed too many of his soldiers." One of the business instructors, Shio Kiyoshi, always dressed in an informal kimono and would chat critically with the students about current affairs.

In September 1939, World War II began in Europe, "but we didn't really feel like it had anything to do with us." However, when Germany defeated France in 1940, "there was a lot of talk about not missing a chance to bet on the winning horse." The National Spiritual Mobilization campaign began to make its influence felt on campus as well.

Kenji belonged to an extracurricular student club called the Commercial Management Club, with only four members. But beginning in 1940, all members of arts and science clubs were ordered to also enroll in sports clubs for physical training. Forced into it, he chose the basketball club because it sounded like it might be the easiest, but he never went. Eventually he was summoned by the club members and punished by being slapped around for his failure to attend.

As the war progressed, empty slogans and hollow ideology remote from the realities of life or the economy proliferated. In 1941, classes at Waseda Jitsugyō, which had been named with letters of the roman alphabet—ABCD—were suddenly changed to single Chinese-character slogans: Faith, Filial Piety, Honesty, Righteousness. The clubs were renamed "squads" (*han*), using military nomenclature.

The civics instructor, always wearing the khaki-colored civilian "national uniform" (*kokuminfuku*) introduced in 1940 by the government, delivered a series of endless, repetitive lectures on loyalty to the emperor, and it was rumored that if you simply wrote "Long live the emperor!" at the end of a quiz or paper he would give you a perfect score. The thirty-something army officer who taught the two-hour-per-week military training class was so delighted when one of Kenji's friends put a beautiful protective cover on the drill manual that he gave him a good grade simply for that.

Government controls gradually encroached on the foreign films that Kenji loved to go see. The last American film he saw was *Mr. Smith Goes to Washington* in November 1941. After that imports were cut off, and the only foreign movies screened were previously imported French and German films. The aging film stock was run so many times in different theaters that it became scratched and worn, and sometimes broke. Some films were so badly patched together that the storyline was lost.

Then, on 8 December 1941, about a month after his older sister Yasuko died, Kenji was getting ready to go to school when the radio announced the commencement of hostilities with the United States and Great Britain. Japan had attacked Pearl Harbor.

5

When Kenji arrived at Waseda Jitsugyō on the day Japan entered the war with the United States, the civics teacher came into the classroom, dressed as usual in his national uniform and grinning from ear to ear, and declared, "We've done it!" The students played along with his enthusiasm, and he remained in high spirits throughout the class. Later in the day, when it was reported that the emperor had made an official declaration of war, this instructor went into the school courtyard and shouted, "Banzai!"

But many of the other faculty members were more reserved. In class, one of the students asked Shio, the business instructor, a question about the news of Pearl Harbor: "Why is it that there are Nine Military Gods?" and he answered flatly, "Because one of them was taken prisoner."

During the attack on Pearl Harbor, five two-man short-range submarines were released from their mother ship as it neared Hawaii. None of them returned, and their crew members were lauded in the press as the "Nine Military Gods" for the fearless sacrifice of their lives. Yet even a secondary school student might harbor some doubts regarding why there were only nine of these deified crew members rather than the full complement of ten—which led to the question posed to Shio. But in those days, there was a taboo on being taken prisoner, so the instructor's reply startled the students, and one of Kenji's friends whispered, "Do you think it is all right for him to say things like that?"

Shio was a Tokyo native, born and raised, and an author of books on stock-market investment. As mentioned earlier, he always dressed informally in a kimono and never wore the military-style national uniform. It is likely that from his knowledge of economic indicators alone, he was aware that the war was hopeless. Kenji recalls him saying at one point, "You're all going to forget the content of my lectures anyway— it's my random chatter you'll remember." And indeed, he would often discuss current events and other matters in the classroom.

Among the things he said that Kenji remembers best was the advice to "read the newspaper from the bottom." The mass media were strictly controlled, and the newspapers were filled with headlines giving the impression of a string of Japanese and German victories. But if you read the papers carefully, according to Shio's advice, a different perspective emerged: "It was especially true of the international news, where if you looked at the lead columns and the big front-page headlines, the stories were all about how Germany was winning. But if you took the trouble to look at the bottom of the page or other less prominent parts of the paper, there would be smaller articles relating news of German setbacks and difficulties. I think the reporters themselves were trying to get the truth across in this way. Shio-sensei used to say, 'Don't get fooled by the newspapers. Learn how to read between the lines.' And this habit never left me."

Shio ended up resigning from Waseda Jitsugyō in the summer of 1943, after Kenji had graduated. This was precipitated by a conflict between the Drill Squad—a student club with close ties to the officer serving as the military training instructor—and the Sumo Squad (as noted earlier, the clubs had been forced to reorganize as "squads").

The Drill Squad had deliberately invaded the Sumo Squad's ring—a sacred space—and touched off a fight. But the school authorities punished members of the Sumo Squad as the principal perpetrators of the incident, leading to a student strike in protest.

The members of the Drill Squad were widely resented by the other students, who saw them as trading upon the military authority of their instructor to lord it over the rest of the student body. The striking students stationed themselves along the route from the train station to the campus and persuaded others to join them. The result was successful: no one went to school. Such a development, particularly during wartime, enraged the training officer, who argued that it arose because Waseda Jitsugyō retained "a liberal atmosphere," and singled out Shio for specific attack. Consequently Shio was forced to resign.

For about six months after the outbreak of the war, news of Japanese victories continued. But in April 1942, Tokyo experienced its first air raid. A US navy aircraft carrier succeeded in slipping past Japanese defenses and into coastal waters to launch a squadron of twin-engine medium bombers. This attack later became known as the Doolittle Raid after its commander, Lt. Colonel James Doolittle. Sixteen B-25 bombers struck military facilities in Tokyo, Nagoya, Kōbe, and Yokosuka, and other targets. One plane whose intended target was the First Army Armory mistakenly bombed the campuses of Waseda Secondary School and Waseda Jitsugyō instead, killing two students at Waseda Secondary School.

The day of the attack was a Saturday, and Kenji had remained at school after morning classes as one of the students assigned to the cleaning detail. About 12:30 pm there was a terrible noise and a shock wave that broke all the windows in the building. An incendiary bomb had scored a direct hit on the school but luckily had not exploded. Piercing the roof and second floor, it had lodged in the ceiling of the first floor. A nearby hospital had been set afire by the raid, and Kenji and other Waseda Jitsugyō students were enlisted to evacuate patients and salvage equipment:

"When the school building was hit, I was on the first floor. I was startled but not hurt. If it hadn't been a dud, I would probably be dead. No one really expected an air raid, and there was no warning at all. The next day everyone had a bad case of nerves, and from morning onward there were numerous false alerts and air-raid warnings, though of course there were no more enemy planes coming."

The Doolittle Raid was quite small in comparison with the massive bombing attacks that would come late in the war, but it killed 87 people, wounded 466, and damaged or destroyed 262 buildings. And its psychological effect was even more profound. The Japanese navy, mortified that it had permitted this aerial assault on the imperial capital, launched the attack on Midway in an effort to expand Japan's defensive perimeter. This offensive resulted in a major defeat for the Japanese, including the loss of four of the navy's aircraft carriers. The official reports covered up the magnitude of this disaster, reporting one carrier sunk and one seriously damaged, but even among the students at Waseda Jitsugyō it was rumored that two carriers had been sunk.

In December 1942, Kenji was given an "accelerated graduation" from Waseda Jitsugyō—a year and three months earlier than normal. In order to meet the increased demand for labor and troops, the government was shortening the duration of educational programs. At the graduation ceremony none of the faculty, from the principal on down, made any particularly patriotic or stirring speeches.

After graduation, in January 1943, Kenji was hired by Fuji Telecommunications Equipment Manufacturing (forerunner of present-day Fujitsu, which adopted its present name in 1967), which was created in 1935 when Fuji Electric Company, a joint venture between Furukawa Electric Company and the German conglomerate Siemens, spun off its telecommunications equipment division as an independent subsidiary. Fuji Telecommunications was one of the innovative new industrial firms that had sprung up to supply the military. Many small-scale companies and their employees were being forced to merge into such war industries, and accelerated graduates of the secondary schools such as Kenji were assigned to work there until they were old enough to be called up for military service.

Kenji himself was not especially conscious of having been enlisted into the war effort: "Without much thought about it, I just responded to one of the recruiting notices posted on campus because a friend said it looked pretty good, and I got hired. About twenty others entered the company at the same time I did—twelve of them from Waseda Jitsugyō, five of them accelerated graduates like me. I just did what all my friends were doing. I regretted it later, because the commute was so long."

Yet the influence of government policy is undeniable. In response to the labor shortages and need for redeployment of the labor force following the outbreak of the Sino-Japanese War, the employment offices, which had previously been operated by local governments, were nationalized in July 1938, and corporate recruiting efforts and the recruiting notices sent to the schools came under the control of the central government.

Along with such efforts to control the distribution of the labor force, in March 1939 the government issued a Wage Control Ordinance, which was intended to deter exit from war-related industries and to inhibit the inflationary spiral of wages and prices caused by labor shortages and rationing of goods. Initially the controls targeted military-related mining and manufacturing firms with fifty employees or more, but from the second revision of the ordinance in October 1940 onward, almost all firms with ten employees or more, regardless of industry, were required to submit paperwork demonstrating their compliance with the wage controls. This, in fact, was the origin of the seniority wage system that would become emblematic of Japanese-style corporate management in the 1980s. And in January 1940, in order to finance military spending, the government followed the example of Nazi Germany and implemented what was then a new system of taxation—deduction at the source by employers from the wages of employees.

Under the provisions of the Wage Control Ordinance, starting wages as a secondary school graduate—regardless of industry—were set at ¥42 per month (about $1,500 today), with a raise to ¥45 from the second year. In this way the public-sector wage system, in which compensation was tied directly to academic credentials, was now spreading to the private sector as well. At Fuji Telecommunications, monthly wages were received in envelopes from the accounting department. There were no time cards, and while one could apply to receive overtime wages, no one Kenji knew seemed to be interested in working longer hours to make more money.

Fuji Telecommunications was located in the Keihin industrial zone south of Tokyo. Kenji, who had studied business and bookkeeping at Waseda Jitsugyō, was assigned to the bookkeeping section of the accounting department and worked in an administrative building next to the factory where switchboards and other telecommunications equipment were manufactured.

The monthly wage system modeled on the government bureaucracy applied only to the office workers in the administrative building, who had a secondary education or better. The factory workers, paid daily, generally came from the provinces and had no more than a higher elementary education. It was not the case at Fuji Telecommunications, but at many other companies in those days it was not only pay schedules that were different—office staff and factory workers even had to use separate entrances. Removal of such discrimination against factory workers would become one of the most important demands of the postwar labor movement.

According to Kenji, the office workers were also subdivided into three main grades, almost equal in total number: college-educated executives, secondary-school-educated male office staff such as Kenji, and female staff who had graduated from girls' secondary schools. (In prewar Japan, after elementary education the schools were divided by gender, and girls generally could not advance to a university education.) The chief of the accounting department was a graduate of Tokyo Imperial University; the head of the bookkeeping section, a Keio University graduate. Kenji remembers that his national uniform was the only clothing he had to wear: "When I got to work I changed into the company work jacket, but the college guys all wore business suits."

Since the factory was supplying the military, supervising officers from the army and navy each had an office on site. Says Kenji, "These military men couldn't have had any real understanding of the actual work and I think their supervision was just for show, but the company executives were careful to stay on their good side, visiting them frequently." This sort of collusion between officials and businessmen was a hotbed of wartime abuses such as diversion of military supplies into the black market, and also served as the template for postwar relations between government regulatory agencies and the business community.

Kenji had become the sole breadwinner for the Katayama family. He turned his entire monthly wage packet over to Ishichi, although the habitually taciturn Ishichi never displayed any outward satisfaction that Kenji was now earning a living. Still, Ishichi and Kochiyo were fond of the only grandchild they had reared to maturity, and called him by the nickname "Ken" that they had used since he first arrived in their household at the age of six. The first person in either the Katayama or the Oguma family to graduate from secondary school and earn a monthly wage, Kenji rose at 6:40 am, left the house carrying a boxed lunch that his grandmother Kochiyo prepared for him, and took a series of trams and trains to commute to work, a bit more than an hour away.

Kenji was one of the more capable members of the office staff. Had he not been turned out of Fuji Telecommunications after returning to the company from his internment in Siberia after the war, he might very well have been able to lead the life of a typical postwar Japanese office worker, or salaryman. As it was, his period as a company employee came to an end after a little less than two years, when he was conscripted into the army.

6

The month after Kenji joined Fuji Telecommunications in 1943, Japanese forces retreated from Guadalcanal—a turning point in the war in the Pacific. The retreat was officially announced as a "redeployment" (*tenshin*), which struck even the seventeen-year-old Kenji as a strange way of putting it. One radio commentator remarked, "Redeployment—now that's a handy word. If you fail your entrance exams, you can always 'redeploy' to another school."

In May 1943 the annihilation by US forces of the Japanese garrison on the Aleutian island of Attu was officially announced using the term for suicidal defense—*gyokusai*, or "shattered jewels"—that would become increasingly familiar in the late stages of the war. Beginning that summer, families in Kenji's neighborhood began to receive wooden boxes containing the ashes of men who had died in combat in Southeast Asia or the Pacific islands (or often, as the war entered its later stages, merely sand and gravel from the place where they had died). Kenji recalls one such war widow leaving the neighborhood with her three children to return to her family's home in the countryside.

Meanwhile, young men from the neighborhood were being conscripted into the armed forces with growing frequency. Already there were no more flag-waving send-offs courtesy of the white-clad members of the local chapters of the Women's National Defense Association. Kenji recalls: "They did that sort of thing during the war with China, but quit after the Pacific War started. People were spending all their time and energy just to get enough to eat, and there were too many guys getting called up. It was also becoming clear that they might not come back alive. And while it might make sense to make a show of sending off a young regular army recruit, by the time they started calling up older men with families and a life out in the world, neither the men themselves nor their families wanted to make a big deal of it. If you cried you would be branded 'unpatriotic,' so people refrained, but they weren't happy about it, either. Everyone knew this, so the send-offs just naturally stopped.

"In the fall of 1943, conscription deferments for university students in the humanities ended, and you would see groups of students making a great fuss sending off their friends at the train stations. When you were called up, you had to return to your family's official domicile to be enlisted into your unit. So these students were seeing off friends who were returning home to do this. When I would transfer through Shinjuku Station on my way home from work, I would pass groups of twenty or thirty of these students, formed into a big circle and raising a ruckus. They would sing military songs, and folk songs and ballads with risqué lyrics, trying to put up a brave and festive front. It was a kind of creepy atmosphere."

Eventually more and more men began to be called up, even from the Fuji Telecommunications factory. In the beginning there were farewell parties, but by late 1944 these had ceased. Neighborhood associations were no longer as active, and the fire and air raid drills had become perfunctory—even ordinary folks could see that it would be impossible to put out American incendiary bombs with buckets of water drawn from a well. Women who remained at home during the day were periodically called out to practice bucket brigades, but Kenji, who was away at work, never participated in such exercises.

Shortages of basic materials grew more severe. The rice ration was filled out with substitutes including barley, millet, and sweet potatoes, and eaten along with some sort of meager side dish. White rice was prohibited and brown rice promoted as superior in nutrition, but in fact this was mainly a way for the government to appear to be increasing the quantity of the rice ration without doing so. People had difficulty digesting brown rice, so every household used an improvised rice mill consisting of a two-liter bottle and a slender bamboo pole to polish the grains.

Sweets had completely disappeared. Kenji remembers one day in the summer of 1944 when he was on his way home from work with a friend and happened upon a vendor selling strawberry soda. But when they bought and drank it, they found it was just colored water, with no sweetener in it at all. They had just spent fifty sen out of their monthly wage of forty-five yen—the equivalent of about twenty dollars out of the starting salary of an average university graduate today. He also remembers spending fifty sen that autumn to eat a dried persimmon at a tea shop near Fuji Telecommunications.

Although distribution was tightly controlled, if you had connections with the military, it was a different story. Kenji remembers the excitement in the summer of 1943 when his family received some authentic Nara-zuke pickles from a neighborhood acquaintance who had such connections. The persimmon he ate at the tea shop had probably been procured in similar fashion.

Kenji (front row, second from right), dressed in national civilian uniform, at a farewell party for Fuji Telecommunications employees called up for military service.

The coal the family used to heat the bath in their house in Nakano was no longer available, and the local public bath did not have enough fuel to keep changing the water regularly, so if you went at night the water gave off an unpleasant smell. Kenji only had one summer dress shirt for work and could not buy another, so he wore it patched and mended. By the summer of 1944, even the university graduates on the Fuji Telecommunications staff had stopped wearing suits and had switched to the national civilian uniform with gaiters.

There was no way—and no leisure—to express whatever anxiety or discontent was felt at the way things were going. Kenji was still too young to vote, and he does not remember Ishichi ever voting. The only general election in the Pacific War period was held in April 1942; it was dubbed the "Yokusan election" because of official government approval given to candidates belonging to the Taisei Yokusan Kai (Imperial Rule Assistance Association)—created in 1940 to replace the political parties with a unified patriotic front—who were also backed by election subsidies paid out of the military budget. But Kenji does not recall anyone around him expressing any interest in that election.

Meanwhile, around September 1942 Kenji's father, Yūji, returned to his original home in Niigata, having resigned his position with the producers' cooperative in Hokkaido for reasons that Kenji recalls were rather unfavorable. Yūji had been successful in the cooperative, and he would get together with Kenji several times a year when he came to Tokyo on cooperative business. But in 1941 it was discovered that one of his trusted subordinates had been embezzling cooperative funds. Yūji made good the stolen amount from out of his own pocket, and took responsibility for the misdeed by resigning.

Even so, the sixty-year-old Yūji was able to relocate to Niigata with what could be considered adequate savings in those days, which he invested into a significant amount of Japanese government war bonds. But the runaway inflation of the wartime and immediate post-war years wiped out this nest egg.

According to Kenji, "Back then, if you were ordinary folk—not government bureaucrats or high-ranking military officers—there was no pension system for you. So you saved as much as you could for old age while you were still able to work. That was what my father and grandfather did. But the inflation laid waste to such planning. If my father had been able to anticipate this, he probably would have stayed

in Hokkaido. But there are very few people who can cope with historical changes as immense as the collapse of their country. Most people
simply think of things in extension of the life they are already living."

Difficulty in dealing with radical change was something everyone shared. Kenji would occasionally discuss the progress of the war
with his colleagues at Fuji Telecommunications, but no one expressed
much more than vaguely optimistic opinions.

In July 1944, the island of Saipan fell to US forces. The phrase
"shattered jewels" was used once more to describe the almost complete annihilation of the Japanese defense force, but the unusual
mournfulness of the radio announcer's voice in delivering this bulle-
tin conveyed the new urgency of the situation. The enemy was suddenly drawing closer to Tokyo.

Kenji did realize that the Americans could use Saipan as a base
for air raids against Tokyo, and Japan would be defeated. "But neither
I nor the people around me were able to think this through any further. We had neither the capacity nor the information. And we probably didn't want to think about it."

The newspaper continued to print optimistic articles on the war
situation. Even though the Tōjō Hideki cabinet (which had started the
war against the United States) collapsed after the fall of Saipan, "we
didn't have the background information, so no one knew what was
going on. It didn't even leave a major impression."

However, the newspapers did not always spout mere propaganda.
Earlier, in February 1944, the newspaper *Mainichi shimbun* had printed
a front-page lead editorial with the headline "Victory or Destruction"
and subheads that read "The War Has Come to This" and "Bamboo
Spears Not Enough," urging a major shift in wartime policy. The government had just commenced training civilians in the use of bamboo
spears in anticipation of an American invasion of the Japanese home
islands. This editorial is inscribed in modern Japanese history as the
most noteworthy example of resistance by the press in the face of the
rigorous censorship of the era; it enraged Tōjō, still prime minister at
the time, and the thirty-seven-year-old newspaperman who wrote it
was punished by being conscripted into the army.

The family subscribed to the *Mainichi shimbun*, but Kenji does
not remember having seen this article: "I may have read it, but at that
point it was all we could do to find enough to eat—there wasn't time

or energy left for anything else. And we didn't have the education to understand indirect modes of expression. Maybe the big shots with more leisure time read and thought about such things. . . ."

After the fall of Saipan, trenches began to be dug along the sidewalks on each side of the Ōme Kaidō highway in anticipation of air raids on Tokyo. But they weren't much deeper than a person could squat in, roofed over with boards and earth.

"Each household was issued a notice ordering them to dig their own air-raid shelters, but our house was rented and had scarcely any yard at all, so there wasn't any place to dig. We dug a pit under the living-room floor, and got ready to remove the mats and wooden floorboards in the event of an air raid. But if the house had really been firebombed, I imagine we would have roasted to death in that pit. Nobody really had any idea of what an air raid would be like—they just complied superficially with the orders that came down from above."

In October 1944, as US naval forces approached the waters off Taiwan, they were met with a counterattack by Japan's entire naval air force. Japan officially reported the loss of 312 airplanes, which effectively erased its capacity for naval air combat, while the Americans suffered only damage to two cruisers. Yet the Imperial Navy high command announced that eleven enemy aircraft carriers had been sunk, and news of the first great Japanese "victory" in some time was celebrated with lantern processions.

But soon afterward the supposedly vanquished American fleet appeared off the coast of the Philippines, landing US troops on the island of Leyte. The Japanese government and military loudly proclaimed this to be the golden opportunity for a "decisive battle" to annihilate the American forces. But the Japanese Combined Fleet dispatched to attack them was utterly destroyed in a one-sided battle, while the successfully reinforced Japanese ground forces were soon cut off from their supply chain and almost completely wiped out.

Kenji recalls that this was one of the times that the war situation became a topic of conversation at Fuji Telecommunications. The factory workers had been provided with a special ration of sweet potatoes, some of which made their way to the office workers as well. As he and his colleagues sat eating, their department chief, a Tokyo Imperial University graduate in his mid-thirties, commented that perhaps their forces had been tricked by the enemy.

"He probably didn't go so far as to imagine that the reports from the Imperial Headquarters were lies, but he seemed to think that we'd fallen into a trap set by US forces. In any case, at the time even ordinary folks thought there was something fishy going on.

"I didn't consciously support the war; neither did I resist it. I was just swept along by it. And I did think there was something strange about the fact that despite the victories being reported, the actual situation seemed to be getting worse and worse. But I wasn't in the habit of thinking more deeply about such matters, nor did I have the information to do so. I think most of us ordinary people were like that."

Kamikaze attacks by Japanese planes began during the Battle of Leyte. Kenji says, "I was neither for nor against this. I couldn't be critical when I thought of the feelings of the men who boarded those planes, but I also had a hard time accepting that the war situation had gotten so bad that such tactics were necessary. I'd been following Shio-sensei's advice to 'read the papers from the bottom,' so I was aware the war was going badly. Even so, there wasn't much decent information and I wasn't really in a position to judge things."

The later stages of the war went swiftly. On 1 November 1944, only ten days after the battle off Taiwan had been reported as a great Japanese victory, an American B-29 bomber appeared for the first time in the skies over Tokyo. Outfitted for reconnaissance, it had flown from the newly established US air base on Saipan to survey the city for the full-scale bombing raids to come.

The B-29s were massive four-engine planes, forty-three meters in length, capable of carrying nine tons of bombs, and equipped with pressurized cabins and exhaust turbines that enabled high-speed flight at altitudes of more than 10,000 meters (33,000 feet). The effective range of Japan's principal anti-aircraft guns was only 7,000 meters, and Japanese fighter planes took more than twenty minutes to reach the altitude of the B-29s. The B-29 reconnaissance plane completed its survey without even being challenged, returning to its home base.

Kenji remembers the reconnaissance flight: "I was at work at Fuji Telecommunications at the time. It was a clear day, and the B-29 was clearly visible at the head of its contrail. The air-raid warning sounded, but we all went out into the courtyard and stared up at the plane. We looked at it blankly, wondering why the Japanese military was unable to do anything about a single airplane. Someone said, 'Why don't they shoot it down?' but no one was equipped to think about it any further. I didn't really believe in the wartime slogan of 'the invincibility of the divine land,' but I also never imagined that Japan would lose the war."

Kenji had his conscription physical in April that year. He was classified B-2, which in normal times would have exempted him from being drafted. However, Kenji, who had had his nineteenth birthday on 30 October, was served with an induction order by the Imperial Japanese Army on 20 November 1944. A number of men had already been drafted from Fuji Telecommunications, and he had wondered when his own time would come. "'Well, finally,' I thought." Neither Ishichi nor Kochiyo had anything to say.

Kenji had only a secondary school education, so he could not seek a deferment like university students in science and engineering, or aim for the navy's reserve officer's training course as some other college students did. He had no option other than being drafted into the army at its lowest rank: private second-class.

His induction notice ordered him to report to the Komazawa Parade Grounds (now Komazawa Park) in Tokyo's Setagaya Ward at 9:00 am on 25 November 1944. An urgent telegram was sent to his father in Niigata, and Kenji barely had time to get ready and set his affairs in order; he did not even make the rounds of the neighborhood to say goodbye.

Special rations were issued to inductees, and so he took his coupons to the rationing station, where a set was waiting for him, including a Rising Sun flag and a liter bottle of saké. By this time shortages were bad enough that a Japanese flag could not even be found on the open market.

The bottle of saké was shared out among a few friends from Waseda Jitsugyō at a classmate's house. The Rising Sun flag was intended for friends and family to inscribe with messages of encouragement, but this custom had already died out among the people whom Kenji knew. There wasn't any real send-off party at Fuji Telecommunications, either. Kenji recalls, "There were only five days after I was called up. They went by pretty much as usual."

On 24 November, the day before his induction, eighty-eight B-29s engaged in the first full-scale air raid on Tokyo. After bombing the Nakajima Aircraft factory in Musashino in the western suburbs of Tokyo, the planes passed over the Katayama house on their way home, leaving contrails across the sky. Kenji remembers the mass of contrails as being strangely beautiful.

The morning of 25 November came. Under a leaden sky, a small group of relatives and friends, including Ishichi, Kochiyo, and Yūji, gathered to see Kenji off.

None of the neighbors bothered to come out; they were fearful of another air raid and simply benumbed to the almost daily occurrence of another young man being sent off to war. There was nothing at all stirring about Kenji's departure. He was not given a commemorative shoulder sash with his name on it, as had been customary earlier. Dressed in his drab khaki national uniform, he uttered the expected message, "I will do my best to serve my country!" then turned to his grandfather and grandmother and said quietly, "Well, goodbye for now."

His grandfather Ishichi was overcome with emotion. He had lost three grandchildren already to disease, and now the last he had raised was being conscripted into the army, likely never to return alive. Through the deaths of his grandchildren, the collapse of his business, and his own crippling stroke, Ishichi had endured, never uttering a word of complaint. But now, finally, he wept loudly. In those days it was unthinkable to weep at the departure of a family member for military service. Kochiyo said, "Ken, get going!" and bundled Ishichi into the house as quickly as she could.

After Kenji's induction into the army, a government order slated the family's home in Nakano to be demolished as part of a planned air-raid firebreak. In April 1945, Ishichi and Kochiyo were forcibly evacuated to their original home prefecture of Okayama, where they found lodging with relatives. Inflation wiped out their savings, and they had to live in a storehouse behind the family's farmhouse. Kenji would not be reunited with them for another four years, when he finally returned to Japan after forced labor in Siberia.

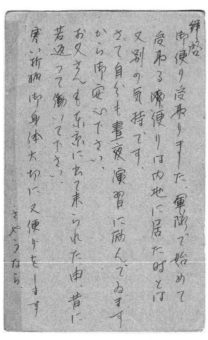

Postcard sent by Kenji to his father Yūji in February 1945.
Army censorship permitted little more than stereotypical content.
"I am training diligently night and day, so don't worry about me."

Chapter 2

In the Army

On 25 November 1944, Kenji presented himself at the headquarters of the Eighth Field Artillery Regiment in Tokyo for induction into the Imperial Japanese Army as a private second-class. Soon after his arrival, one of the veteran soldiers taking care of the new recruits told them, "You won't be here long. You're shipping out for Manchuria."

The army was another world. After he changed into the officially issued military uniform, all personal clothing had to be returned to his family. The new recruits handed over their civilian clothing and reluctantly bid farewell to their families in the yard in front of the barracks. Kenji's father Yūji and grandfather Ishichi had come to see him off. Ever since his stroke, Ishichi had been partially paralyzed on his right side. Kenji would never forget the image of him dragging his leg as he came to bid farewell to his grandson.

When his father heard that Kenji was bound for the much colder climate of Manchuria, he took off the vest he was wearing and tried to give it to Kenji. But Kenji, who had been instructed not to bring any items of civilian clothing, refused it. As he said his final farewells to his father and grandfather, Kenji nearly wept.

After several days in the barracks, on the morning of 3 December the recruits boarded a train at Shibuya Station, heading west. Four days previously, on 29 November, Tokyo had suffered its first night raid by US bombers.

1

The army transport train, with Kenji and several hundred other soldiers aboard, stopped briefly at Nagoya, where they were served hot tea by members of the Women's National Defense Association. Passing through Kōbe in the middle of the night, they arrived at the port of Moji on the evening of 4 December. After waiting for several days in barracks, they were loaded onto a transport ship, sailing for Busan on the Korean peninsula on 8 December.

Once at sea, they assembled on deck for an address by an army cadet. This date, the anniversary of the attack on Pearl Harbor and the imperial declaration of war on the United States and Great Britain, was observed throughout the Japanese empire with such ceremonies—though this would be the last year to be marked in this way. Eight months later, on 15 August 1945, Japan would surrender to the Allied forces.

Kenji recalls: "The young cadet was our transport officer. I suppose they were pretty short on regular officers at that point. The seas were rough, and as the bow of the boat rose and fell with the waves, this young cadet, who was right in the bow, bobbed up and down so violently that he could barely stay on his feet as he delivered his lecture."

Arriving in Busan on the evening of 8 December, they spent several nights in a school on the west side of the harbor before embarking for Manchuria on a train equipped with passenger cars. Military trains stopped frequently en route to meet the demands of the transport timetables. After spending days in transit, during which they slept aboard the train, they arrived on 28 December or so at the quarters of the Seventeenth Signal Regiment, stationed at Mudanjiang (now a city in Heilongjiang Province in China).

The new recruits with whom Kenji had been transported were from prefectures in northern Japan, including Niigata. In the Imperial Japanese Army, the conscription system was administered according to the family's official domicile. His father had kept Niigata as the official domicile for the family, so that was where Kenji was registered for the draft.

"Almost all my classmates from Waseda Jitsugyō were conscripted into Tokyo units the following year. That was true even of the group from the school that entered Fuji Telecommunications at the same time I did. They ended up serving a very short time in the home islands, digging trenches in preparation for the last stand against the American invasion, but Japan surrendered in August and after the war ended they were able to go home right away. Simply because I was registered in Niigata, I got sent to Manchuria and was then interned in Siberia. A person's fate can be determined by very trivial things.

"When the veteran soldier at our induction told us we were going to Manchuria, I think it was out of pity for us, and to let us say a last farewell to our families. The destination of any military unit was classified information, and ordinarily would not have been divulged. I think he sympathized with these poor nineteen-year-old recruits. After all, he'd had to say goodbye to his own family."

Arriving in Mudanjiang, Kenji and his comrades were in uniform but had no weapons or other equipment. All they had been given when they left Tokyo was a thick section of bamboo they were told to use as a mess kit and a canteen.

"When we arrived in Mudanjiang with these bamboo containers dangling from cords around our necks, the veteran soldiers there gave us some very strange looks. One of them said, 'Is that all there is by way of supplies back home these days?' That about summed it up. All we had was our uniforms. We were a completely unarmed unit."

The Seventeenth Signal Regiment, to which Kenji and the other recruits had been sent, was a unit of the First Area Army. This was an element of the Kwantung Army, which had once prided itself as being the cutting edge of the Imperial Japanese Army in North Asia, but its best units had already been redeployed to the fighting in the South Pacific. Sent as replacements for these seasoned troops, the young recruits were hastily trained and formed into units.

At the base, officers and noncommissioned officers were allocated separate quarters, but the common soldiers lived communally in barracks units (*naimuhan*). Their personal effects and letters were subject to inspection and censorship, and the only privacy they had was in the latrine. Normally the barracks unit would consist of a dozen or so men, with veteran soldiers charged with teaching a roughly equal number of young recruits. But with the wartime mass mobilization, the number of raw recruits had expanded dramatically. In the company of the Seventeenth Signal Regiment to which Kenji belonged, there were five barracks units of about forty men each—and about 150 out of the total of 200 men were greenhorns.

"Having sent its best troops to the South Pacific, the Kwantung Army was little more than a skeleton force. We were young conscripts, not older reservists who had been called up. Even so, like myself, many were not very robust physically."

By 1944, when Kenji was inducted, eligibility for service had been lowered to include individuals classified B-3 in the conscription exams. In addition, the maximum age for service had been raised from forty to forty-five, while the standard age for conscription was lowered from twenty to nineteen. Kenji had been called up as a result of these changes in the conscription system. Among the five barracks units in Kenji's company, the fourth and fifth had a large number of conscripts who were not in very good physical condition; Kenji was assigned to Unit Four.

In those days, upon induction into the Imperial Japanese Army, new recruits spent three months in a barracks unit undergoing basic training, and then would be classified for further service according to their performance in training and their prior educational level. Individuals who had completed secondary school or higher were eligible after three months to take officer candidate exams. If they passed, they would be promoted to private first-class. Then, on the basis of their performance during their next three months of service, they would be divided into Class A (officer) and Class B (noncommissioned officer) candidates, and at the end of their first full year of service they would be promoted to the appropriate rank.

Individuals with no more than a higher elementary school education could be promoted to private first-class if they performed with excellence during the three months of basic training, in what was called the "first cut." Then, three months later, the "second cut" determined who would advance to the rank of superior private, opening the way to promotion to NCO rank.

A fairly large percentage of soldiers who failed to be promoted after the first three months of basic training managed three months later to pass the "second cut" and advance to the rank of private first-class. And even those who failed both cuts would be promoted to private first-class at the end of their first year. But a soldier who had a poor work attitude or habit, or who was seen as a troublemaker by his superiors, might find himself a permanent private first-class who never saw another promotion. The institutional culture of the military not only valued academic achievement, but was also competitive with regard to performance.

As a secondary school graduate, Kenji was eligible to sit for the officer candidate exam, and when he was inducted in Tokyo he was placed in charge of six other new recruits. At Fuji Telecommunications he had been an efficient worker, but during the long period of train travel to Manchuria in the bitter cold of winter he developed a severe case of diarrhea that weakened him considerably. "As I lost strength, my judgment dulled and my thinking got cloudy. Although I'd initially been given a leadership position, I was slow to respond to orders, couldn't think quickly enough, and made a lot of mistakes. I was pretty worthless, as far as the army was concerned."

Kenji's performance was poor, but after completing three months of basic training he still sat for the officer candidate exam, in part because each company was competing with the others in terms of how many candidates it could field.

"When heading to the regimental headquarters to take the exam, we were made to stand in four columns in order of our performance ratings. I was about the fifth from the end of the line."

Almost inevitably, Kenji failed the exam. He also failed to make the second cut at six months, remaining a private second-class until the surrender. As only about a quarter of the men failed both cuts like this, Kenji must have been a very poor soldier indeed.

The barracks chief, an NCO, was nominally in charge of training the new recruits, but in fact it was the veteran soldiers who dominated the process. Life in the barracks unit followed an absolutely fixed routine—reveille, dressing, inspection, meals, training, cleaning and other chores, sleep—and if your reactions were slow or the maintenance of your rifle poor, or if one of the "vets" was simply in a bad mood, you would be punched or slapped. "There was never a day I didn't get hit. I often counted how many times it happened in one day." Such beatings by veteran soldiers were termed "unofficial punishment" and forbidden by regulations, but were actually endemic to the Japanese military at the time.

Prior to the Second Sino-Japanese War, the term of service in the army was two years, after which soldiers were demobilized. But with the expansion of the war effort, this became impossible, and the number of three- and four-year soldiers rapidly grew. Naturally enough, soldiers who had lost hope of demobilization and were confined to these barracks units grew restive and intractable. A culture developed honoring time in service over rank, and basic training began to take on the character of a hazing conducted by the seasoned soldiers.

According to Kenji, "Not all of the vets were violent. It seemed like the quickest to lash out were mostly guys who hadn't advanced as fast as their peers." The ones who stayed private first-class year after year reigned over their juniors regardless of rank, and were addressed not as "Private" but as "Sir Veteran Soldier" (*kohei-dono*). At the end of February 1945 a directive explicitly forbidding "unofficial punishment" was promulgated. But Kenji remembers that "the second- and third-year soldiers were running riot. The ban was completely ineffective." The expansion of the war and the deterioration of Japan's military position were factors in the rampant abuse, which could not be reined in simply through formal directives. In fact, it was this sort of petty bureaucratism, even more than the violence, that left Kenji with some of his strongest impressions of the Imperial Japanese Army.

"We had to memorize what were called the 'Regulations,' which included the Infantry Manual, the Operational Duties Manual, and the Imperial Rescript to Soldiers and Sailors. But they didn't care whether you understood the content or not—you simply had to parrot it back word for word. One of the 'vets' would say, 'The Imperial Rescript lists five precepts the soldier must observe and practice. What are they?' You couldn't simply answer, 'The five are loyalty, courtesy, courage, honesty, and frugality.' You had to say, 'One: The soldier should consider loyalty his essential duty. Two: The soldier must always observe proper courtesy...' and so on. And even with the Infantry Manual, which was about combat tactics, you had to answer with the exact wording of the original—it had to be 'maintain vigilance of your surroundings' and not 'watch out for what is around you.' It was all empty form; you had to make a show of doing exactly what your superiors told you.

"It was the same with equipment or supplies. Submitted paperwork had to be very precise about the numbers and amounts issued, but if the paperwork was in order and the numbers added up, that was all that mattered. If there were shortfalls in the barracks unit, somebody would be held responsible, so stuff got stolen from other companies to make up the difference. There was a lot of such thievery going on.

"For example, there was a drying yard where the new recruits would dry the laundry, and if a company did not mount a special guard over it, things would be stolen by soldiers from other companies. When you were washing dishes after mess, if you dropped anything and reached down to get it something else might be stolen, so you had to put your foot on what you dropped to prevent someone from getting at it, finish the washing up, and only reach down when you had called out to a buddy to keep an eye on everything.

"I had my shirt stolen, and one of the 'vets' helped me out by stealing someone else's. So I can't moralize about this, but no one was thinking about the big picture. All anyone cared about was not getting held responsible for anything by their superiors."

After entering the army, Kenji began to smoke the cigarettes that were issued as part of their rations. New recruits had absolutely no free time, and the few moments when they were in the latrine or given a break during training to smoke were the only times they could relax without fear of reprimand.

Midway through basic training, Kenji sent a photo of himself to his father, Yūji. "The army back then was very much concerned with keeping up surface appearances, so they had us send these pictures to our families to show that we were all healthy and happy and fulfilling our duties. Everything was censored, so of course you couldn't write to them about how you were being beaten every day." Kenji's letters home from the army went to Yūji, as his grandfather Ishichi had become too old and frail to entrust with any business that might need taking care of on Kenji's behalf.

After completing his three months of basic training, Kenji was assigned to the Second Air Signal Regiment, stationed at Ning'an, about twenty kilometers southwest of Mudanjiang. This was a unit of the Second Air Army responsible for wireless communications between the airfield and its planes, as well as ground communications within and out of the air base. Kenji, in poor physical condition and underperforming, remained a private second-class. He felt humiliated, because other secondary school grads who had entered with him and had, like him, been assigned as group leaders were now already officer candidates. In the Second Air Signal Regiment, the best soldiers were assigned to First Company—Kenji was put in Eighth Company.

Kenji's new barracks was on the outskirts of town about two kilometers east of the Ning'an rail station; the small airfield was located near the station. The three months of basic training had been extremely tense and terribly busy; after arriving in Ning'an he suddenly had a lot of time on his hands. There were no longer any airplanes in this area, so the Second Air Signal Regiment had nothing to do.

"I only saw one airplane the entire time I was there. Around May of 1945, a single-engine training plane touched down briefly and flew off again. That was it. We didn't have much by way of communications equipment, either. Since it wouldn't do to have the regiment completely idle, they'd send us off occasionally to do construction and maintenance work at the airfield, but most of the time there wasn't much to do. So we farmed a bit, or harvested edible wild plants.

"While we were loafing around like this, in April 1945 some of the other companies got a sudden influx of new recruits, who were subjected to brutal hazing. Like us, this batch seemed to have been shipped out purely to be taken prisoner by the Soviets and sent to Siberia."

The Second Air Signal Regiment was primarily composed of young conscripts who, like Kenji, were new recruits freshly dispatched from the home islands. There was a shortage of officers as well. Normally a company would be commanded by a captain, but Kenji's Eighth Company was headed by a young second lieutenant just out of accelerated training. The battalion commander was a superannuated major who had retired from service but had been called back to active duty.

"Once when I was out working in the fields I saw the elderly battalion commander ride up on a horse. It was the only time I ever laid eyes on him. And of course I never even saw the regimental commander."

Kenji was given basic instruction in code transmission and field medicine, but never had the opportunity to apply what he had learned. During basic training at Mudanjiang he had been issued a rifle of his own, but in the Second Air Signal Regiment there was only one rifle for every four or five men. The only weapon everyone had was a long bayonet nicknamed the "burdock knife." Kenji does not remember ever wearing a helmet.

In basic training Kenji was taught how to clean and service his rifle, but not how to shoot it, and right to the surrender he never had occasion to pull a trigger. The only time he ever fired a rifle was once in his third year at Waseda Jitsugyō, as part of the mandatory secondary school military instruction program. The first-year soldiers were not allowed to leave the barracks, so Kenji never went to visit the shops in Ning'an, never went to a comfort station, and never had any contact with the Chinese population.

As mentioned earlier, the Kwantung Army had been gutted to provide experienced troops for the South Pacific battlefront and the defense of Okinawa and the home islands and so, beginning in January 1945, a number of completely new units were created within it. Core personnel for the units were drawn from existing units, augmented by fresh recruits from Japan and veterans among Japanese colonists in Manchuria who were called up locally. But these new units were inadequate in both training and equipment.

The Second Air Signal Regiment was a long-established unit, but by the time Kenji joined it key personnel had been siphoned off and replaced with new recruits, so in reality it was in a sorry state, as Kenji discovered. Despite the tide of war clearly turning against the Japanese forces, nothing was done to prepare trenches or other defense works, nor did the soldiers receive any real training. Kenji explains: "The army was a bureaucracy. Orders came down to organize a unit and station it somewhere, and this would be done, at least on paper—but without orders, nothing would happen. From basic training we were beaten if we didn't follow orders to the letter, but we weren't taught to think for ourselves and no one expected us to. It never even occurred to us to think of what we would do if the enemy suddenly showed up."

Similar recollections are common in the postwar memoirs of other veterans of the Imperial Japanese Army. Even in the fiercely contested battlefields of the Pacific such as Saipan and Leyte, the troops were left to loaf about and did little to prepare for attack until the enemy was almost upon them. What Kenji experienced appears to have been far from unusual.

Meanwhile, the war situation continued to deteriorate. The Philippine front collapsed. American forces landed on Iwo Jima in February and on the main island of Okinawa in April. On 10 March 1945, a massive firebombing raid on Tokyo killed more than a hundred thousand people.

There was no way for ordinary soldiers overseas to stay informed of the enormity of what was happening. In March 1945, Kenji received a postcard from a former classmate at Waseda Jitsugyō saying,

"Recently carrier planes have been appearing in the skies over Tokyo." This was a reference to a raid from US aircraft carriers that had struck Tokyo on 15 February. Mail to and from the military was censored: "What he wrote was about as much as you could get past the censors at that point." In April, he received a postcard from Ishichi saying that he and Kochiyo had been forced to relocate to Okayama.

With ample leisure after being stationed with the Second Air Signal Regiment, Kenji had time to read the newspapers posted in the canteen—which no longer had food for sale. According to Kenji, about all that was left in stock was toilet paper. But he did go there to read the newspapers, which were full of stories of kamikaze raids off Okinawa sinking enemy carriers and battleships. Kenji was shocked to learn, after the war, that those had all been lies.

But the Japanese military was unable to see the situation objectively. The international news, which Kenji continued to follow as he had been in the habit of doing since secondary school, played up information that was even slightly favorable to Japan. In July 1945, a month before Japan's surrender, Churchill's cabinet resigned when the Conservatives lost the House of Commons election to the Labour Party. This news was written large on the blackboard in front of the officers' briefing room at Second Air Signal Regiment headquarters.

The massive 10 March 1945 air raid on Tokyo happened to coincide with Army Day, commemorating the Japanese victory in the Battle of Mukden during the Russo-Japanese War. Kenji and other first-year soldiers, who at that point were still undergoing basic training, were assembled in a lecture hall to listen to an address by the company commander, a captain in his late twenties who had graduated from the Imperial Japanese Army Academy. The gist of his talk: "When the end comes, we must die by our own hand rather than be taken prisoner. At that time, take a hand grenade, charge into the midst of the enemy, and take as many of them with you as you can!"

Nineteen-year-old Kenji was not in any better position to judge the situation objectively. Even when instructed in this way to carry out a suicide attack rather than surrender, the most he thought once he was back in barracks was, "I wonder if I could really do that . . . Probably not."

"It was a given that we were supposed to die rather than be captured, and I couldn't think beyond that. It seemed the only choices were to kill yourself, be killed by the enemy, or take a few of them with you in death."

In May they were told that Hitler had died in combat and Germany had surrendered. Hitler had of course committed suicide, but the German government had announced that he had died fighting Soviet forces in front of the Reich Chancellery. That was what was conveyed to Kenji, who says, "I thought, 'Hitler had the courage of his convictions.' What I didn't think about was what the German defeat meant for Japan."

On 26 July 1945 the Allies issued the Potsdam Declaration calling for Japan's unconditional surrender. Kenji read the newspaper report of this in the canteen. "The article was brief, but it mentioned that Japan would maintain sovereignty over the four main islands, and I thought to myself, 'At least they'll let us keep the territory we had up to the time of the First Sino-Japanese War.' Up to that point all I had been hearing about was the 'Anglo-American devils' and how they were going to massacre us all, so it seemed surprisingly generous to me that they intended to let Japan survive as a country."

Kenji's heretofore peaceful existence was shattered on 9 August 1945. At dawn that day, Soviet forces attacked across the Manchurian border.

2

The Soviet attack was carried out with overwhelmingly superior force. The German surrender had freed the Soviets to redeploy troops from the European front, allowing them to assemble a force of 1,580,000 men, 5,556 tanks and self-propelled artillery, and 3,446 aircraft. Against this, Japan's Kwantung Army was able to field only about 700,000 men and about 200 tanks and 200 airplanes.

The Kwantung Army was taken completely by surprise. Its leaders believed that the Soviet army had exhausted itself on the European front and that any plans it might have for advancing into Manchuria would begin in September at the earliest, or at latest in the coming year. Even so, on 10 July 1945 the Kwantung Army commenced an "all-out mobilization" of 250,000 men from among Japanese colonists in Manchuria to flesh out its troop strength, but the result merely expanded the number of nominal units, poorly equipped and trained.

Since the central command of the Kwantung Army had not anticipated the Soviet offensive, the front-line units were not combat ready. Some of these units had reported as early as 3 August that large Soviet forces were massing near the border, but central command did not change its assessment of the situation. As a result, the attack of 9 August was a surprise for the Japanese forces.

On that day Kenji was assigned to night watch. At 5:00 am he completed his shift, reported to his replacement that there was no unusual activity, and went back to the barracks to go to sleep. Suddenly, a trumpet sounded. It was actually an emergency warning, but he mistook it for reveille and shouted, "Everybody up!" Others took up the cry, and all the soldiers arose. They started heading to the barracks yard to form ranks for inspection as they normally would, but an order was issued that no one was to leave the building. They waited there, learning about 6:30 am that the trumpet had signaled an emergency and that the Soviet forces were attacking.

When orders finally came, they were to bring rations, signal equipment, and other supplies to the railway station at Ning'an. The enlisted men had no way to judge what was going on, and simply carried out the orders they were given.

"Every available cart and man was mobilized to load all the supplies and equipment onto freight cars. The army always wanted everything orderly, so you never set foot in the barracks in boots; you had to change into indoor shoes. But on the following day, 10 August, we were all running around the buildings with our boots on, so there was a real sense of emergency."

The train with Kenji and his unit on board departed for Mudanjiang on the afternoon of 10 August. The Kwantung Army had issued an order for withdrawal into South Manchuria. "The boxcars were filled with supplies and equipment, and the soldiers loaded in on top of that. I had neither a rifle nor a helmet. I think the officers rode in passenger cars."

As they approached the outskirts of Mudanjiang, a report came in that the city was under Soviet bombardment, and the train was halted. When they got down out of their boxcars to look around, they saw Soviet planes dive-bombing the streets of Mudanjiang. When the air raid was over, the train entered the station. It was raining, but the flames of the burning city lit the night as brightly as day.

There were some 60,000 Japanese residents of Mudanjiang, and the station was filled with Japanese civilian families seeking refuge. But the Imperial Japanese Army had no thought of using military trains to evacuate them.

"At any rate, no civilian refugees boarded our train. I think almost all of them were left at the station. At the time no consideration or thought was given to such people."

There were approximately 1.5 million Japanese colonists living in Manchuria then. The Kwantung Army was well aware that it would be impossible to stop a Soviet advance at the Manchurian border, and had developed a strategy to withdraw to a line of defense near the Korean border. Prior evacuation of civilians was rejected because it would give away this plan of operations. So even before the fighting started, a de facto decision had been made to abandon any attempt to protect the Japanese civilian population. Quite understandably, this

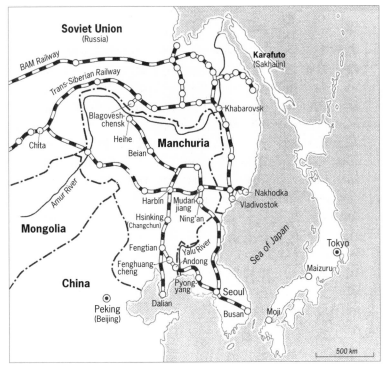

Map of main railways in Siberia,
based on map in Japanese Prisoners of War in Siberia by *Toshi Kurihara.*
(Iwanami Shinsho, 2009.)

became a source of great resentment against the army among former Japanese colonists in Manchuria.

After the Soviet incursion began, the Kwantung Army did engage in some evacuation efforts, but priority was given to the families of military personnel and government officials. There were about 140,000 Japanese colonists in Hsinking (now Changchun), the capital of the Japanese puppet state of Manchukuo, which, since its establishment in 1932 following the Japanese invasion of Manchuria in 1931, lay under the de facto control of the Kwantung Army and the large number of Japanese civilian bureaucrats dispatched to help administer it. The semigovernmental South Manchurian Railway Corporation (Mantetsu), founded in 1906 after Japan's victory in the Russo-Japanese War, also possessed significant influence in the region.

From before dawn until midday on 11 August, eighteen railway trains evacuated some 38,000 Japanese from Hsinking: approximately 20,310 were members of military families, 750 were family members of embassy and other government officials, and 16,700 were family members of employees of Mantetsu.* A bit of simple arithmetic suggests that fewer than 300 ordinary civilians were evacuated.

In cities like Mudanjiang that were closer to the Soviet border, the situation was even more dire, although there is little detailed information available. Mudanjiang was occupied by Soviet forces on 13 August, and there was a massacre of Japanese civilians. In *Akai tsuki* (Red Moon), a novel by Nakanishi Rei based on his personal experience as a civilian in Mudanjiang, military men and their families are evacuated from the city on a special train that ordinary civilians are not allowed to board without permission.† It is estimated that, of the approximately 1.5 million Japanese civilians in Manchuria, ultimately about 180,000 died.‡

The military train carrying Kenji and his unit passed through Harbin and arrived on 15 August in the city of Fengtian (now Shenyang). It was on this day that the emperor announced Japan's surrender to the Japanese people in an unprecedented radio broadcast. Kenji and his comrades did not hear the broadcast, but a rumor went

---

* Handō Kazutoshi, *Soren ga Manshū ni shinkōshita natsu* (Bungei Shunjū, 2002), pp. 231–32.
† Nakanishi Rei, *Akai tsuki*, vol. 1 (Shinchōsha, 2003), pp. 57–59.
‡ Handō, *Soren ga*, p. 354.

around that Japan had surrendered, which the officers roundly denied, calling it impossible.

Kenji and his unit spent 17 August in Fenghuangcheng, between Fengtian and Andong (now the city of Dandong in Liaoning Province), where they were finally informed of Japan's defeat. Kenji recalls his feelings at that time:

"When they told us, I was upset; I hadn't thought that Japan could lose. But after about twenty minutes I thought to myself, 'Wait a minute. This means I can go home and see my family,' and that made me happy. You couldn't let that show, so I kept quiet about it, but I think everyone felt that way."

The other thing that occurred to Kenji when he learned of the surrender was, "Hey, now I won't have to spend the rest of my life as a permanent private."

"In Japan in those days, the Imperial Reservists Association was a very big deal. In local society, your rank when you were in the army followed you around. Particularly in rural areas you'd often hear things like, 'He made superior private on the first cut. That's the kind of guy you want your daughter to marry.' A failed soldier like me would be stigmatized after being demobilized and sent home. But now that we'd lost the war, that seemed unlikely."

It seems that at times of radical changes in the social order, when people cannot see what the future holds, it is difficult for them to alter established patterns of thought. Given the changes that were in store for a demilitarized Japanese society after the defeat, Kenji's relief at not having to live under the stigma of being a poor soldier seems a bit wide of the mark, an example of not being able to see the future except as an extension of the social conventions of prewar Japan. Yet at the same time, Kenji was accurate in sensing the impending demise of militarism in Japanese society. If we look at history, the judgment of ordinary people may be wrong in some of the details, but it is frequently correct in grasping the broad outline of events.

The young second lieutenant who commanded Kenji's Eighth Company attempted to commit ritual suicide the following morning with his army sword, and failed. The human abdomen is well padded with fat and difficult to pierce with a blade, so disemboweling oneself is no easy matter. In the Edo period (1603–1867), when a samurai committed seppuku it was largely a formality—normally a second would be standing by to cut off the man's head as soon as the cut to the abdomen was made. Not knowing this, the young second lieutenant tried to disembowel himself, but ended up with no more than a wound that healed after a couple of weeks.

After being informed of the surrender, Kenji's unit was transferred to Andong, just north of the mouth of the Yalu River on the border with Korea, and split up among different billets. Kenji and his comrades stayed in a corporate dormitory that had been used by Japanese colonists. There was nothing to do, so they passed the time by talking with the Japanese who were still there. This was how they learned of the atomic bombing of Hiroshima and Nagasaki, and the nearly total destruction of the Combined Fleet. They were told of the terrifying destructive power of the atomic weapons, but did not understand much about them.

Kenji and the others continued to wait in the corporate dorm for further instructions. On 28 August or so, they were ordered by one of their officers to put their weapons away in a corner of the dorm. Kenji only had a bayonet, but he was now officially disarmed.

While they were awaiting orders, the men received their August wages from company headquarters. Soldiers' wages were ordinarily paid into national postal savings accounts, which the government then used to help finance the military budget. But now the postal service had broken down and they were paid in cash for the first time. Without anything better to do, the men spent the money buying things to eat from the Chinese.

"My wages were being paid into a postal savings account, but I'd never even seen the passbook for it, so when we got our pay this time, I realized for the first time that I was making about ¥15 [equivalent to about $500 today] a month. The army being a government bureaucracy, when it withdrew it had carted along all its paperwork, right down to our pay slips and the company commander's seal." Later, with the postwar inflation and the de facto writing off of government debt, the money in Kenji's account would be rendered practically worthless.

From the company dorm they could easily see the railway bridge over the Yalu River defining the border between Manchuria and Korea. But no trains were passing on the bridge. Over meals, the soldiers talked about this, saying, "When trains start crossing the bridge again, we'll probably be able to go home." A veteran first sergeant who was the company clerk warned the young soldiers spending their money on food, "You guys are going to have trouble coming up with the money for your return ticket." Kenji thought, "Since it was the government that brought us here, what is this talk about us having to pay for the return trip?"

After more waiting in Andong, they were loaded into troop trains again, which made typically slow progress with many halts for schedule adjustments, reaching Fengtian on 15 September or so. It was in the streets of Fengtian that Kenji first saw Soviet troops.

A few days later, around 20 September, Kenji and the other Japanese prisoners of war were assembled in a walled campus in the Beiling district of Fengtian. There had been a medical college and a normal school there, but Kenji is unclear as to which campus it was. Other units and individual Japanese military personnel from the area were sent there along with Kenji's Second Air Signal Regiment. "Orders were always given to us directly by our own officers. I imagine the Soviet forces intentionally maintained the Japanese army unit structure and gave orders for movement and assembly to the Japanese commanders."

Eventually the POWs were formed into battalions of about a thousand men each for transfer. "The organization was carried out by the Japanese officers, I believe. At the Beiling campus, Kwantung Army officers handled the administrative work. We thought they were getting us organized for the return trip to Japan. Nobody had any information, and among the troops there were never even any rumors of Siberia. Soviet troops were standing guard in the assembly camp, but the orders were being given solely by Japanese officers. No one even imagined we were going to Siberia."

The 29 August 1945 communication sent by the general headquarters of the Kwantung Army to the Soviets concerning the treatment of captured Japanese military personnel contained the following statement: "Until such time as they can be repatriated [to the home islands] we earnestly hope that you will utilize them in any way conducive to cooperation with your forces."* In fact, the "Outline for

---

* Kwantung Army General Headquarters, "Washirefusukii [Vasilevsky] gensui ni taisuru hōkoku," 29 August 1945. Cited in *Horyo taiken ki*, vol. 1, *Rekishi, sōshū hen*, ed. Soren ni Okeru Nihonjin Horyo no Seikatsu Taiken o Kirokusuru Kai (Soren ni Okeru Nihonjin Horyo no Seikatsu Taiken o Kirokusuru Kai, 1998), p. 371.

Peace Negotiations," drafted in July 1945 by former prime minister Konoe Fumimaro under orders from the emperor himself, earmarked Japanese army personnel and civilian auxiliaries in Manchuria to provide labor to the Soviet Union as part of a war reparations plan. The hope had been that by offering this bargaining chip, the Japanese government might have the Soviet Union serve as an intermediary in negotiations with the Allied powers.

However, the Soviet Union had already pledged at the February 1945 Yalta Conference to enter the war against Japan within two to three months after the cessation of hostilities against Germany, and in fact the Soviet attack on Manchuria took place almost exactly three months after the German surrender. After Japan surrendered, transport of Japanese POWs, planned in advance, was initiated by a top-secret order from Stalin dated 23 August 1945. The Japanese attempts to negotiate with the Soviets had been quixotic, but Kenji and his comrades had no way of knowing any of the background to what was happening to them.

Among the POWs at Beiling were many Japanese colonists drafted during the "all-out mobilization" that had taken place just before the surrender. Kenji recalls that one day around the middle of September a decidedly nonmilitary-looking group of Japanese showed up in Beiling, some of them still wearing wooden *geta* sandals.

"'Hey, the locals have arrived!' The word passed quickly among us. When we talked with the new arrivals, we learned that Japanese colonists who had been called up for military service had been demobilized and sent home immediately after the surrender. But then all former military personnel were ordered to present themselves at their local police headquarters to receive documents of demobilization. When they did, they were met by armed Soviet troops who escorted them to Beiling. I imagine that the Japanese military had been given a quota to fill by the Soviets, and had rounded out the numbers by calling these guys up again. In Beiling they were issued Japanese military uniforms that they were made to wear.

"Some guys had gone out to do a bit of shopping for their wives and stopped at the police station on their way home, only to wind up getting taken to the Beiling camp and sent to Siberia. They were bitterly resentful of the neighborhood and block association leaders who delivered the orders but didn't go themselves. Some of them said,

'When we get back to Japan, we're taking them to court!' Others had sensed something fishy about this summons, and simply ignored it, but not many. Your ordinary honest soul was the most likely to trust his superiors and fall into the trap."

Kenji told these local vets how his troop train had left the rest of the Japanese population behind when it withdrew through Mudanjiang. The men shrugged this off, saying, "That's the army for you," but they were worried about their families. "And for some of them that must have been a final farewell," Kenji says.

Most of the POWs, Kenji included, did not attempt to escape from the Beiling camp. "Soviet guards were stationed at strategic points, and at night there was sometimes gunfire. I think a few local veterans who could speak Chinese or had families in the area managed to escape. But I didn't know a word of Chinese. If I left my unit, how was I going to eat? So I just stayed with everyone in the battalion we had been formed into. I had no idea we were going to be sent to Siberia."

After about a week at the assembly camp, Kenji boarded another train for transport out of Fengtian. The Second Air Signal Regiment had already shipped out. But Kenji was weakened by diarrhea; he and about twenty others in poor physical condition were left behind. "The army was a bureaucratic organization. If you got in the way, you got left behind. It makes perfect sense that they didn't bother to protect civilians, either."

But in this case, Kenji was fortunate.

"Looking back on it now, it was one of the reasons I survived. If I'd been sent to Siberia with my original unit, with no fresh men coming in, in the labor camp I would have been treated very badly at the very bottom of the pecking order. I would have been last in line for food. I've read a bunch of memoirs of Siberia published after the war, and there are many examples of this sort of thing—the death rate was highest among new recruits. If I'd been sent with my original unit, given my clumsiness and my poor physical condition, I probably would have been dead that first winter in Siberia."

Kenji and the other stragglers from the Second Air Signal Regiment were incorporated into the newly formed Fengtian Fifty-Second Battalion. This was made up of a headquarters unit and six companies, amounting to about a thousand men altogether. Kenji was in Fourth Company, which had been cobbled together out of a number of smaller units, stragglers like Kenji, and "locals" drafted in the all-out mobilization of July and August.

"The 'locals' were men in their thirties and forties and treated us stragglers from the Second Air Signal Regiment like children. But they'd been civilians until only recently, and the customs and prerogatives of the army meant nothing to them. Because of this, even after we were sent to Siberia, at least in the camp I was in, former officers were not able to get away with overt attempts to pull rank or cheat on food distribution. This is another reason I was able to survive."

Around 25 September, Kenji and the rest of the Fengtian Fifty-Second Battalion were loaded into a freight train departing from Huanggutun Station in the northern part of Fengtian. The train, pulled by a steam locomotive, was made up almost entirely of boxcars. There were only two passenger cars with standard seating, and the headquarters staff rode in these; everyone else was loaded into the boxcars, which had been divided into two levels with plank flooring to hold about a hundred men per car. There was a plank walkway along the roof of each car, and this was where the Soviet guards rode. The full moon was on 23 September that year; Kenji recalls thinking how beautiful the moon was, seen from the former campus on the eve of their departure.

When the train with Kenji and the others aboard departed from Fengtian, they all still believed that it was taking them home to Japan.

3

After leaving Fengtian, the train headed north. If they were being taken to Japan, it should have been going south. But the POWs still did not imagine they were being sent to Siberia.

"When the train headed north, we figured it must be going to the port of Vladivostok by way of Harbin. But we passed through Harbin, and were still going north. Then a rumor went round that the railway bridge had been destroyed in the fighting and we were going to Vladivostok by way of Blagoveshchensk. People never want to believe the worst. They always want to hold onto optimistic projections."

The POWs squatted in more or less random groups on the two levels inside the boxcars. They had been thrown together so quickly that military organization had not really taken hold. "You just bunched together with familiar faces."

Numerous other trains were carrying prisoners on the same track, forcing Kenji's train to halt time and again when trains were backed up ahead. During the waits the train would take on coal and water. Most of the stations looked to be in the middle of nowhere, surrounded by flat plains. When the train halted it might be hours before it moved again; but once it started up again it seemed as if it would go on forever.

The boxcars had no toilets, so the men either waited for the next stop or did their business through holes in the floorboards. As long as the train was running, it was impossible to cook meals. Each man had been given about two kilos of Russian black bread, but it was so sour-tasting that everyone rejected it, preferring to eat the rice and other grains they had first been supplied with.

"When the locomotive stopped for water we'd have time to cook the grains or rice in the Japanese fashion—but this required lighting a fire. I'd never encountered Russian black bread before. It seemed pretty convenient, since you could survive on bread and water alone. When the train wouldn't stop, we started out eating the grain raw, then finally started chewing on the bread."

The train would stop without warning, precipitating frantic efforts to stock water and cook food. At each stop, there would be a tank of water for resupplying the locomotive. As they had no buckets, the POWs used their mess kits to collect water, which would have to last until the next stop.

The biggest problem with cooking during these stops was finding an adequate supply of fuel. Since formal unit organization was not functioning, groups of buddies would scour the surrounding area for dry grass, burnable wood, and threshed straw to feed the cook fires. Often they would find the immediate area had already been picked clean by earlier POW trains. With nothing left near at hand that would burn, they had to range farther afield, where some were waylaid by local thieves. When the train signal sounded, there was a great panic not to be left behind.

It might seem odd to be so afraid of being left behind by a train that was taking you to internment in Siberia. But these men had very limited information on which to judge their situation. "I had no idea of what was going to happen to us. With no knowledge of the local languages, running away seemed futile. I just tried to keep up with everybody else."

Many memoirs of Siberian internment recall that Soviet guards lied and answered "Domoy" (home) when asked where the trains were going, and that this was why there was so little resistance to being shipped to Siberia on the part of the Japanese troops. But Kenji says, "I heard rumors of the guards saying such things, but I never heard anything like it directly. At the time, everybody desperately wanted to go home and all sorts of hopeful rumors were flying about, so I think it likely that this was rumored more often than it was actually said."

According to the postwar newsletter published by surviving members of Kenji's Fengtian Fifty-Second Battalion, no more than a couple of dozen members escaped after departing Fengtian.* Kenji's recollection is that most of the escapes happened immediately after the train left Fengtian, and that the last occurred at Beian (now part of the city of Heihe in Heilongjiang Province).

"The Soviet soldiers on the roofs of the boxcars were equipped with submachine guns. I heard gunfire in the night on at least one occasion, so I think there were men trying to escape. The ones who did were probably guys who had been locally drafted and knew how to speak Chinese."

When they stopped, local people would approach the train to barter with the Japanese POWs. Kenji traded his military-issue leather belt for food. Such trades were usually for ready-to-eat items such as boiled corn-on-the-cob and steamed buns. Some of the colonists who had been drafted into the battalion at Beiling and outfitted with uniforms traded their civilian clothes for food.

For Kenji, who had been abandoned by his original unit and was weak from diarrhea, the train trip was arduous. "When we stopped to

---

* "Hokuryō [Beiling] kara Maizuru made," *Chita-kai kaihō* 3 (1982), pp. 29–32. According to the appended note, this chronology (which covers from September 1945 to August 1948) was compiled at a 1981 meeting of the group based on a draft by Kenji recording his own recollections, which the other members worked together to expand.

get water and such, it was no problem for the guys who were smart and fast on their feet, but I was always slow off the mark. Since the unit had just been thrown together, there was no sense of group solidarity—if you couldn't fend for yourself, no one was going to help you."

Eventually, after passing through Harbin, the train pulled into Beian, where it stopped. The POWs spent a week waiting there, still on the train.

"In Beian, I saw that a Japanese war memorial in the central square had been knocked down. When I think about it today, it only makes perfect sense. The memorial was a symbol of the period of Japanese rule. Of course the local people wouldn't just leave it standing in the middle of the city square."

Then, on about 10 October, the train proceeded to Heihe, on the Soviet border, where Kenji and the other prisoners disembarked. At Beian they had passed a train full of Japanese civilians headed south, but in Heihe there were no longer any Japanese. The streets of the city had been damaged by Soviet artillery fire. On the other side of the Amur River was Blagoveshchensk, administrative center of the Amur Oblast of the Soviet Union.

The POWs were put to work loading river barges hauling goods the Soviet army had looted from Manchuria, mostly foodstuffs such as soybeans and sorghum. The prisoners carried bags weighing around fifty kilos apiece across gangplanks onto the barges, which were manned and operated by Russians. This work continued for about a week, at the end of which the POWs were ferried across the river in the same barges. Kenji remembers it as 17 October, because one of his fellow POWs said it was the date of the local festival back home.

It was raining when they arrived in Blagoveshchensk on the other side of the Amur, but no lodgings had been prepared for them. The POWs spent a night sheltering under the eaves of a building, and the next day dug trenches in the middle of a field. Using the tarps they carried as part of their field kit, they roofed these over, dug drainage ditches around the perimeter, and sheltered there from the rain—if not the cold. For about another week in Blagoveshchensk they were put to work unloading barges they had loaded on the other side.

From Blagoveshchensk there were trains running to join the main line of the Trans-Siberian Railway. After the men had worked for a total of more than ten days on both sides of the Amur River, the Fengtian Fifty-Second Battalion was loaded onto a train on the evening of 25 October, departing Blagoveshchensk in the middle of the night.

The next morning the POWs looked at the direction of the sun and debated whether the train was running northeast or southwest. The train shifted direction so many times that it was difficult to tell for sure. But that afternoon, the direction of the sun made it clear that they were westward bound, deeper into Soviet territory. Kenji recalls, "After that, everyone was pretty downcast, and no one had much of anything to say."

Having entered the Soviet Union, they were now more stringently guarded, and not permitted to disembark except to relieve themselves. A kitchen car had been coupled to the train to which they had been transferred in the Soviet Union, and large metal pots of porridge were distributed to each of the cars carrying the prisoners, who no longer cooked outside. The black bread they had been issued in Fengtian was long gone, and even those who still had some mixed grain had no way of cooking it—though when something interfered with the food distribution, they would nibble on it raw.

At least one soldier who, like Kenji, had been left behind by the Second Air Signal Regiment continued to decline physically during the long journey and eventually disappeared from the train.

"I think it was about the third day after we left Blagoveshchensk. It was a fourth-year soldier who was one of the 'permanent privates.' To remain a permanent private you either had to be a problem in terms of your thought or behavior, or else really be incompetent as a soldier. The reason for this guy was that he was somewhat mentally retarded. A person like that was a burden to a unit, which was why he had been left behind. He was always on the losing end of food distribution, work assignments, and so on.

"He couldn't fetch water, or collect firewood, or cook, and it got to the point where all he did was lie in the boxcar. Some of his buddies looked after him for a while, but when things got tough, everyone was basically looking out for themselves. In the end, he became a kind of phantom no one even thought about anymore, and he just disappeared. I imagine that he was put off the train on the pretext he was going to a 'hospital,' but we were passing through quite desolate territory without any towns in sight that might have had a hospital. There

74

wasn't any system set up for helping someone like that, and I doubt he survived."

The same was later true in Siberia, but Kenji did not directly witness anyone's death. "This was true of most of us. It wasn't like the movies or novels. People simply vanished at some point."

On the afternoon of 28 October, about a month after departing Fengtian, the train passed through the central railway station of a major city and arrived at a switchyard outside the city. After being made to wait for an hour or so in the boxcars, the POWs were ordered to disembark in the darkness. They were divided into three groups: the first consisted of First and Second companies, the second of battalion headquarters and Third and Fourth companies (Kenji's unit), and the third of Fifth and Sixth companies.

When they passed through the central rail station the POWs realized the city was Chita. Chita was the administrative center of the Chita Oblast of the Soviet Union (now Zabaykalsky Krai in the Siberian Federal District), and in the nineteenth century had been known as Tsarist Russia's "City of Exiles." Japanese military maps had shown no towns of any consequence west of Blagoveshchensk until Chita, so the prisoners realized from the scale of the city alone that it must be Chita.

After they disembarked from the train, a steam whistle sounded, indicating it was 5:00 pm. Kenji recalls what a truly mournful sound it was for these men who had no idea what was going to happen to them next. That day there had been a breakfast ration, but nothing afterward. The hungry men were ordered to start walking in the cold dusk; there was a hint of snow in the air. By this point, all that Kenji possessed was his mess kit and canteen, a tattered military blanket, and a rucksack containing a few other items of daily use.

After a month aboard trains, it was tough being made to march hungry and cold through the evening dark. One of the Japanese officers shouted, by way of encouragement, "It's only a few kilometers more!" The men in one group carried on their shoulders the corpse of one of their number who had died aboard the train.

"They were probably made to carry the corpse to make sure the numbers worked out. The Soviet army transport officer had no doubt been ordered to deliver the entire number of prisoners to the camp. So he would have to deliver them, dead or alive, get the numbers checked by the camp commandant, and receive proper papers in acknowledgment. The military was like that—Soviet army, Japanese army, it was all the same."

The avenues of this sprawling continental city were broad and empty—apart from an occasional streetlight, there were few signs of cars or people. The prisoners passed by concrete buildings and colossal bronze statues of figures they did not know, arriving after about two hours at a cluster of wooden structures. It had been a trip of about five kilometers, but at the time seemed terribly long. Kenji's group stopped there, but the other groups were sent on farther. Kenji never saw them again.

Night was now fully upon them. The exhausted prisoners were in no state to think of what might come next. Relieved simply to have arrived somewhere, they decided who would sleep where in the huge three-tiered bunks and swiftly fell asleep.

For Kenji, this night was the beginning of three years in Twenty-Fourth District Camp No. 2 in Chita.

Chapter 3

Siberia

On 28 October 1945, the 500-plus officers and men of the headquarters and Third and Fourth Companies of the Fengtian Fifty-Second Battalion arrived as prisoners of war at Twenty-Fourth District Camp No. 2 in Chita. Two days later, Kenji turned twenty.

The prisoners carried the body of one of their number who had died aboard the train on the way to this POW camp in Siberia. Everyone watched as the body was wrapped in a straw mat and loaded onto a cart to be taken to the graveyard. Later, when hard labor and starvation had taken their toll, funerals were accorded even less ceremony. As the autumn deepened, it was rumored that the bowl of rice left out as an offering for the dead had disappeared overnight. The bitter cold and hunger of the Siberian winter had already begun.

Barracks at a camp in Nakhodka in the Soviet Union. (Courtesy of Mainichi Shimbunsha.)

1

The exact number of Japanese military and other personnel—employees of the South Manchurian Railway, civil and police officials of the state of Manchukuo, civilian auxiliaries of the military, etc.—forcibly transported to the Soviet Union at the end of World War II is the subject of dispute, but is thought to be in the neighborhood of 640,000.* They were sent to prisoner-of-war camps and certain special camps for high-ranking officers or war criminals in Siberia, Outer Mongolia, Central Asia, and European Russia. These camps extended from the vicinity of the Kamchatka Peninsula in the east to the Dnieper River in the west; from the shores of the Arctic Sea in the north to the western foothills of the Pamir Mountains in the south.

As a result, the POWs suffered a variety of environments. In Siberia, there was brutal −45°C cold; in Central Asia, broiling 40°C heat. In humid climes there were swarms of biting insects; in deserts, persistent thirst. Amid constant hunger, they were put to backbreaking manual labor: digging in mines, laying railway track, building roads, logging.

Chita was the administrative center of the Chita Oblast and an important transportation crossroads. In Tsarist Russia it had been a place of internal exile; the Soviet Army made it the headquarters of its Zabaykal Military District. During the civil war following the Russian Revolution, Chita was occupied for a time by the White Russian armies, and at one point was attacked by Japanese troops during the Siberian Intervention (1918–22) against the Bolshevik regime. On the outskirts of Chita, Kenji saw a monument erected by the Fifth Division of the Imperial Japanese Army at the time of the Siberian Intervention; in a pine forest on the outskirts of town were two buildings said to have been the consulates of Japan and Manchukuo.

---

* On 12 September 1946 the Soviet Union reported a total of 594,000 Japanese prisoners, but many researchers believe that the actual number was almost certainly higher. See, for example, Soren ni Okeru Nihonjin Horyo no Seikatsu Taiken o Kirokusuru Kai, ed., *Horyo taikenki*, vol. 1, chapters 2 and 3; and Tomita Takeshi, *Shiberia yokuryū* (Chūōkōron Shinsha, 2016), p. 95.

"They were elegant and Western in style, and we used to pass them often on our way to labor assignments. I heard that they had been the consulates after walking by them for about a year.

"After returning to Japan, I read a memoir by someone who had served in the Japanese consulate. He mentions that just before the surrender, he had looked out of the consulate windows with binoculars to monitor the troop trains headed east along the Trans-Siberian Railway for the invasion of Manchuria. During the war, when they went by car into Chita to collect information, a Soviet car would tail them, acting in an intimidating manner and at one point even sideswiping them on a gravel road. The center of Chita was paved with stone, but by the outskirts the roads were gravel, and I remember we had a hard time walking on them."

The POW camps were divided by district; in Chita and its environs were the Twenty-Fourth District (Chita) and the Fifty-Second District (Kadala). According to statistics published by the Japanese Ministry of Health, the thirty-four camps of the Twenty-Fourth District contained more than 10,000 prisoners, an estimated 3,200 of whom died.* Of the approximately 640,000 Japanese transported to Soviet territory, more than 60,000 are thought to have died in captivity, but other estimates exist and accurate figures are unavailable.

Life for Kenji and the others in Twenty-Fourth District Camp No. 2 began with reveille at 6:00 am, which was sounded not by ringing a bell but by beating with a hammer on a railroad rail hung in front of the guardhouse.

After reveille and breakfast, from 7:30 to about 8:00 am, the prisoners would form up in five columns just inside the prison gate to be sent off on their work details. In the Siberian autumn and winter, it was quite cold and dark at this hour.

"We were made to form up in front of the guardhouse, where the guards would count us to make sure everyone was there. But the Russians appeared not to have learned their multiplication tables, and instead of multiplying by the number of columns, they added us up in groups of five. If the guard lost count, he'd start over again from

---

* Eguchi Toshikazu, "Jo ni kaete," in *Horyo taikenki*, vol. 6, *Zabaikaru [Zabaykal] chihō, Mongoru [Mongol]*, ed. Soren ni Okeru Nihonjin Horyo no Seikatsu Taiken o Kiroku-suru Kai (Soren ni Okeru Nihonjin Horyo no Seikatsu Taiken o Kirokusuru Kai, 1988), p. viii.

scratch. It was terribly cold, and they made us stand there forever, stamping our feet to keep warm. At times like that I thought what a stupid lot they were."

After that, they would be divided into work crews and head out to perform that day's labor. Their first assignment was to complete the construction of the camp itself. Despite the large number of prisoners now living inside the wooden buildings, the finishing touches had yet to be done. Outfitting the kitchen, fixing up the bunks, building the perimeter fence—the work continued.

"Our first job was to build the fence that would enclose us. We were surrounded by frozen wasteland and weak with hunger, so with or without a fence, escape was unthinkable. After the war I read accounts by people who escaped from the camps. They must have been blessed with exceptional circumstances and been in good physical condition— but none of them made it back to Japan. They were all recaptured."

After about twenty days of this construction work, the prisoners were dispatched from the camp for a variety of tasks.

"Work assignments were communicated from the Soviets to the Japanese battalion headquarters, and from there on down the chain of command—company, platoon, squad. Squad leaders would form smaller groups from the twenty or so men in the squad, and assign them to specific tasks. Today you will go here and do construction; tomorrow you will go there and do farm work. They sent us all over the place, doing all kinds of labor."

The camp operated something like an independent profit center dispatching temporary labor to various local enterprises, which would use quotas and norms established by the Soviet authorities to calculate their payments to the camp. In turn, the camp paid wages to the prisoners, after deductions for the costs of food, electricity, fuel, medical services, and so on. But these deductions were quite substantial, and only a select group of prisoners with special skills actually received payment, beginning in 1947.

The Soviets drew upon forced labor not only from Japanese and German POWs, but also from domestic political dissidents and prisoners incarcerated for ordinary crimes. Japan had made use of prison labor from the Meiji period onward; it has been said that road construction in Hokkaido and the development of coal mines would have been impossible without the use of prison labor.* Even so, forced labor in the Soviet Union took place on a much greater scale than in any other country; it has been estimated that in 1949 more than 10 million "prison laborers" were at work there. Kenji and his compatriots became part of this vast system.

Such treatment of POWs was exceptional, but the officers and soldiers of the Japanese army were ignorant of international law and conventions. They had been taught that they should die rather than be captured—not what their rights should be after being taken prisoner. Kenji and others unable to fulfill their quotas were treated as substandard workers, and they never expected to be paid anything.

"Some work was terribly hard, and some was easy. Logging, road work, and construction work on the open plains—these were tough. But compared with memoirs of other camps where the prisoners had to mine coal or lay railways, I guess we were fortunate.

"The easiest work was anything indoors, where it was warm. And farm work gave you the chance, if you were lucky, of receiving some food, like potatoes. One good job was disposing of the frozen wastewater that accumulated behind the houses of the Soviet army officers. Chita didn't have running water or sewers. Liquid wastes were disposed of by being thrown behind the house, where in winter they would freeze into a mountain of ice. So before the spring thaws when it would start to stink, we would break up the ice and dump it in the river. It was fairly easy work, and the officers' wives would feed us. Everyone wanted to do work like this that had some sort of payoff.

"The Russians who were kind enough to give prisoners food were mostly women, particularly older women. I imagine a lot of them had lost sons or husbands in the war. They would always ask, 'Skolko let?' [How old are you?]. And when I answered, 'Dvadcat' [Twenty], in my broken Russian, they would shake their heads sadly and say, 'Molodoy' [So young] and 'Papa, mama, est?' [Do you still have your papa and mama?]. At that point I would recall my grandma in Tokyo and feel very sad and lonesome."

---

* Daniel Botsman, *Punishment and Power in the Making of Modern Japan* (Princeton University Press, 2005), chapter 7.

The Japanese battalion commander at the camp, Uenae Komao, and his adjutant, Kumabe Kai, were captains, since officers of the rank of major and above had been sent to the camps where superior officers were housed. Kenji belonged to Fourth Company, Second Platoon, commanded by Captain Urayama and First Lieutenant Tashita, respectively.

Only about half of the battalion officers were regular active-duty officers. The remainder were reservists called up from among the Japanese colonists in Manchuria in the "all-out mobilization" immediately before the end of the war. Until the outbreak of the Second Sino-Japanese War in 1937, the Japanese army had had a limited budget; the standing army, which was relatively small, was staffed by officer graduates of the Imperial Army Academy and by Class A soldiers. After two years of active service, soldiers were demobilized. Class B-2 conscripts—those in poorer physical condition, like Kenji—were not drafted until the war turned against Japan, when demobilized soldiers and retired officers were called up once again to augment Japanese forces. These were older men who had been living normal civilian lives.

In the Fifty-Second Battalion, the commander and his adjutant were both active-duty captains who had been attached to an army air base battalion. But Lieutenant Tashita, in command of Second Platoon, was a Japanese colonist in his forties who had been called up from the local reserves after serving during the period of defense cutbacks in the 1920s as a volunteer short-term officer.

Captain Urayama, the commander of Fourth Company, was a former English instructor at a girls' school who had served as an administrator of a POW camp run by the Japanese in Fengtian. The commander of First Platoon was, like Tashita, a locally mobilized Japanese colonist. The commander of Third Platoon was a regular active-duty lieutenant, but the commanders of Fourth and Fifth Platoons were second lieutenants, barely twenty years old.

With Japan's surrender and acceptance of the Potsdam Declaration, all Japanese army personnel at or below the rank of colonel were formally advanced one rank. This "parting gift" from the Imperial Japanese Army to its personnel meant little to enlisted men and NCOs, but for higher-ranking officers, it added to their military pension, which was determined by their final rank. The platoon commanders had all been promoted in this way; such officers were called "Potsdam lieutenants" and "Potsdam captains." And even Kenji became a private first-class at last.

The Fifty-Second Battalion, thrown together hastily in Fengtian, organized itself more thoroughly upon arrival in the camp. Kenji's squad of twenty or so men was led by a veteran active-duty sergeant with combat experience named Takahashi who had been transferred with his unit from North China to Manchuria. At the surrender, he had been temporarily demobilized like many of the local soldiers drafted in the "all-out mobilization," but appeared to have been called up again in Fengtian and then shipped off to Siberia.

Corporal Maruya was a local Japanese colonist. Around him gathered a group of five or six other local recruits who seemed to have been friends in the Fengtian Japanese community before being mobilized. There were also two local recruits who had been reporters for the *Manshū nichinichi shimbun*, a Japanese-language daily paper published in Fengtian.

A soldier in the squad named Sahashi had actually been a lieutenant but was passing as a private first-class. After deserting his unit in the confusion following the surrender, he had been staying at the home of the corporal, his former subordinate.

Then there was Private Iizuka, a Japanese-American Nisei and former interpreter who had worked in the same POW camp in Fengtian as Captain Urayama of Fourth Company. Born in Los Angeles, he had been visiting his parents' original home, Hiroshima, when the war broke out. Unable to return to the United States, he had been drafted into the Imperial Japanese Army, where he was pulled out of a regular unit and sent to the Fengtian camp to serve as an interpreter for the Allied POWs there, though there were nuances of Japanese he did not understand. The POWs he interpreted for at the time included Lieutenant General Arthur Percival, the British commander in Malaya and Singapore; and Major General Jonathan M. Wainwright, the American commander in the Philippines, both of whom had been captured by the Japanese at the beginning of the war and later sent to Fengtian. Iizuka described Percival as "small-minded."

In the battalion headquarters there was also another former interpreter named Kawamura, a somewhat older corporal originally from Hawaii who was now the mess captain. Captain Urayama had been both Iizuka's and Kawamura's superior officer at the Fengtian

POW camp. An interpreter between Japanese and Russian named Motoyama, who had joined the group during their period of labor on the Amur River, served as liaison with the Soviet army. He was rumored to be fluent in Russian as a result of having worked in Manchuria with a trading company or some such business. About fifty years old, he had a calm and steady personality and was regarded as a man of integrity.

"Interpreters were in a position to tell the Russians what they wanted to hear without fully communicating what the prisoners wanted to say. But Motoyama-san did right by us. How the interpreter did his job could have a major impact on meals and working conditions. Motoyama-san was mild-mannered, but when the Soviets were being unreasonable or overbearing, he would gently talk them down, always firmly arguing for what was right. He never blustered or exaggerated, but everyone respected him for his strength of character."

All of this information on the background of the other prisoners in the camp was gleaned by Kenji from camp gossip, and may not be fully accurate. How Sergeant Takahashi was rounded up in Fengtian, or why Sahashi, the former lieutenant, had chosen to conceal his identity and pretend to be an enlisted man remain mysteries.

"Things like what a person did before entering the army would pop up sometimes when we were chatting. But the most popular topic of conversation was food—stuff like 'What do you want most to eat when we get home?' Even this was mostly from the spring of 1946 onward when things got a bit easier; that first winter we were all so exhausted we just fell into our bunks to sleep."

The Soviets investigated the background of the prisoners and kept particularly strict watch over men believed to have been connected with Kwantung Army intelligence units. Kenji says, "With ordinary soldiers, I don't think they really cared much even if we were posing as a different rank or whatever, as long as it didn't interfere with camp operations." Kenji himself was called in only once for interrogation about his background, and no follow-up was done during his time in the camp.

Since the Fifty-Second had been hastily thrown together, it contained individuals from a variety of backgrounds. Its heterogenous nature seemed to soften the normal hierarchies of rank. Many of the Japanese residents of Manchuria drafted on the eve of the surrender knew one another, and though some might nominally be NCOs or officers, when it came to dividing food rations or assigning work, they did not abuse their authority. "There was easy work and hard work, work that had some reward or privilege attached and work that did not, but our squad leader made a point of being fair in making assignments."

In the camp the Japanese officers were assigned to separate housing and received special treatment. This was in accordance with the 1907 Hague Convention, ratified by the Soviet Union, which provided for separate treatment for officers and enlisted men and forbade the use of officers for labor.

"I knew nothing about international conventions and treaties at the time, so it seemed unfair, but aside from that there was no discrimination by rank in the camp where I was. And that was very fortunate. In other camps, the first-year troops were put at the very bottom of the list for food distribution and work assignments, and many died as a result."

Even so, human relations in the camp could be harsh. Even within the same squad, the men did not spend the day working together, and were not all that friendly with one another. And because relationships were not so strictly defined by rank or unit, incompetent or slow workers could be seen as excess baggage.

"For example, in the summer of 1947 we were sent into the hills for about three months to do some logging. We worked in pairs using two-man crosscut saws. The saws varied considerably in quality, and the ones that hadn't been sharpened properly cut poorly. The guys who knew their tools and had strength and skills wanted to work together. Guys like me who were clumsy, weak, and unskilled had to team up with other 'rejects.' I ended up with another first-year soldier from the Second Air Signal Regiment who, like me, was weak and clumsy. The more capable teams would somehow manage to meet the quotas given us by the Soviets, but he and I struggled every day and still couldn't make our quota. When we got back to the camp after three months, people said, 'You really lost some weight.' I think if that had been the first winter, I would have died."

After the first winter, prisoners with knowhow and experience found positions as skilled workers—electricians, carpenters, barbers. These were mostly indoor jobs, and since the Soviet Union had

a shortage of such skilled labor they were treated well. It was also easier to meet quotas doing skilled rather than unskilled physical labor; at
least from 1947 on, some of these workers received enough in wages
to be able to buy things at the bazaar in Chita.

Even without prior experience, many prisoners who were clever
and good with their hands were able to become what were called
"Siberian craftsmen" by learning on the job. "And in the camps there
were a fair number of guys who had worked in various trades before
the army as plasterers or carpenters or farmers." Such skills were useful in camp life. Around March 1946, a ration of unhusked rice the
Soviets had taken from Manchuria was delivered to Kenji's camp. The
Russians had no idea of how to husk and mill rice, so they left the processing to the prisoners. The men with farming and carpentry experience made a milling mortar out of a large round of pine and built a
hand-cranked fan for blowing away the chaff. The prisoners were able
to conceal the actual yield and keep the surplus, eating close to their
fill for about three months.

Kenji, however, had only just turned twenty, and had been a low-
level office clerk. He had no special skills, had never worked in farming or construction, and was not at all quick on his feet.

"In the spring of 1947 we were sent to deliver fuel to a bread factory. This was the kind of desirable work that got assigned on rotation
within the company. The factory workers were mainly middle-aged
ladies, and the pushy, clever guys would go in shouting, 'Madam, davay
[come on]!' and the ladies would throw them pieces of bread. But I just
couldn't bring myself to do this. Everyone back at camp was hoping you
would bring back some bread or flour as a 'souvenir' from the factory,
but I never managed to take back more than a couple of slices, hidden
in my shirt—maybe enough to share with two other guys."

"There was one guy who packed away an entire two-kilo loaf,
hung in a bag round his neck, under his overcoat. In the body search
when he got back to camp he flipped the bread up along with the
overcoat to keep it concealed from the guards. Someone else stole
flour and hid it in his cap so he could cook and eat it back at camp.
Scroungers with street smarts were resourceful."

The inexperienced Kenji made many mistakes. While doing
outdoor work in May 1946 he came across a patch of edible greens
growing in a field and cooked it in his mess tin with some rice saved

from breakfast, but it was so bitter he couldn't eat it and, practically in tears, he ended up throwing it out. Anyone who had grown up in the countryside would have known that you had to first boil away the bitterness.

Naturally enough, the prisoners' motivation to work was far from high, and their efficiency was poor. In November 1946, for example, they began working on a brick apartment building, but they were starting from scratch in a potato field, using almost exclusively manual labor, and only two floors had been completed by the time Kenji returned to Japan in the summer of 1948.

"I saw a story on television about an opera house that had been built by Japanese POWs in Russia, but I find that hard to take at face value. Some Japanese may have worked on it, that's all. I imagine what happened is that later on, when Japan became renowned for its economy and technology, the Russians started saying that the Japanese had built it."

In any case, it was only from the spring of 1946 that conditions improved to the point that prisoners could relax a bit and even show some sense of humor. "The first winter was really tough. Almost all the deaths from malnutrition happened then."

2

It was not only at Kenji's camp that the winter of 1945–46 was the worst for the prisoners—almost all memoirs of Siberian internment agree on this point. We can cite several reasons for this.

First of all, the Soviet economy itself was in dire straits in the immediate postwar period. Soviet loss of life in the war against Germany has been estimated at 15 to 20 million people. The population of the Soviet Union went from 195,970,000 in 1940 to 173,900,000 in 1946—a drop of nearly 11 percent. By comparison, Japan's war dead were about 3.1 million, or about 4 percent of the 73,060,000 who resided in the home islands as of 1940.

Moreover, the industrial heartland and granary of the western USSR had been occupied by the German armies and then ravaged by scorched-earth battle tactics. So the Soviets had won the war but were left with a ruined economy. Casualties had been horrific; in many villages hardly any men returned from the war. On the kolkhoz collective farms, the ratio of males to females, which had been 1:1 in 1940, had fallen to 1:27 by 1945.*

This was one reason why the Japanese POWs were put to use by the Soviets as a labor force, and why so many Russian women sympathized with young POWs like Kenji. As Kenji recalls, "In December 1946, I was sent with a small number of other prisoners on a work project, during which we stayed in a Russian home with a woman who appeared to be a war widow and her two children. I was amazed to see that all they had was the clothes on their backs—there wasn't a stick of furniture. It was bitterly cold, but there wasn't even a bed in the earthen-floored house. When they went to sleep they just lay down and pulled their overcoats over themselves. There was a wood stove and a cookpot and a few dishes, and that was it—about as marginal an existence as one could imagine. In Japan I never saw anything like it, before or after the war."

Such dire economic conditions meant that supplies intended for the POWs were siphoned off by the Russians. By the time they reached the prisoners, already meager rations of food and fuel had been depleted even further.

"We were vaguely aware that fuel and food being sent to the camps were getting misappropriated. The paperwork would say that so-and-so many tons of food or fuel were being delivered, but along the way the railway workers and truck drivers were picking off goods for their own families, and we only got whatever was left.

"Once in the spring of 1947, I was forced to assist in such looting. A Russian truck driver used us to unload coal at his own house and those of his buddies. When the truckload reached the factory, as long as the amount of wastage wasn't too obvious, no one would say anything. Wartime Japan was like that, too. In a controlled economy, when basic goods become scarce, everyone begins to loot and thieve."

The Soviet government had directed that POWs be provided with a specified daily food ration,† but the reality, as we can see, was widely different. Indeed, the Soviet state itself had looted large quantities of materiel in the brief war against Japan. In March 1946, Kenji and a

---

* Shirai Hisaya, *Kenshō Shiberia yokuryū* (Heibonsha, 2010), p. 83.
† Viktor Karpov, *Sutōrin no horyotachi*, trans. Nagase Ryōji (Hokkaido Shimbunsha, 2001), pp. 105–8.

crew of other prisoners were sent for about a three-month stint sorting goods in a Soviet freight depot.

"There were mountains of looted goods. Military materiel from the Kwantung Army like electrical cable, aluminum conduit, and telephone receivers had been brought in by freight cars and lay piled where they had been flung off the trains. One time I was astonished to find a shipping box full of twenty or thirty of the metal door pulls used on the fusuma [sliding paper doors] in Japanese houses. They seemed to have just grabbed anything that came to hand.

"We pilfered some of the aluminum and made spoons from it. Eventually an order came down from the POW leaders to bring more aluminum to the camp, where a prisoner who had been a metalsmith melted it down and made plates and dishes from it. It was a society in which thievery was the norm—for us, for the Russians, it was all the same.

"As we worked our way through sorting these mountains of goods, someone said, 'This must be why they were able to beat the Germans.' The Soviet soldiers were crude in their methods, but really powerful. When an order came down, they would execute it by brute force. In the Japanese army the superior officers would issue absurd and impossible orders, but the lower ranks didn't have the drive to see them though."

The discrepancy between the extreme poverty of civilian life and the strength of Soviet military power made a lasting impression on Kenji. The Soviet tank unit garrisoned to the east of the city of Chita was equipped with enormous, long-gunned T-34s. "In breaks during work I had a chance to see them up close. Wow, I thought. Japanese tanks were much smaller, with the armor plates riveted on—there was no way they could have won out against something like this."

Soviet military power was reinforced by aid from its World War II ally, the United States. "The first time I saw a Soviet army truck, in Fengtian, I was amazed they were using trucks that big. The trucks had two front wheels and four double-tired rear wheels, and they could really move up a slope. They were completely different from Japanese trucks. I came across a lot of them in Chita, and when I saw they had USA STUDEBAKER written on the front, I realized they were American military assistance. The prisoners often used to say, out of spite, that without US aid the Soviets would have been beaten by the Germans."

This contrast between the poverty of civilian life and wealth of military resources was apparently a source of resentment for the

Soviet people but something they could not openly discuss. "I think it was in the summer of 1946 when a pale, unhealthy-looking Russian came up and started talking to us while we were working. 'Stalin ne khorosho' [Stalin is no good], he said. We weren't particularly friendly with him or anything, but I imagine he said such things to us because he couldn't say them to other Russians. In Stalin's era, if you were reported for such talk, you'd go straight to the camps."

Another reason for the poor conditions suffered early on was that the Soviets were unprepared for the sudden influx of POWs. Many memoirs by Japanese POWs report that, as in Kenji's case, their first work was finishing construction of their camp. And although at Kenji's camp the prisoners were issued winter clothing, it was looted Japanese army cold-weather gear and boots that were useless against the Siberian winter.

"Japanese army cold-weather gear was really inferior to that of the Soviet army. For example, though the winter boots had hobnails to prevent slipping, they were run straight through the sole and transmitted the cold directly to the feet. The Soviet winter cap had a double layer of material at the forehead; Japanese caps, only one. The Russians used to say that in Siberia it was fatal to let your forehead get cold. I can't believe we intended to fight the Soviet army with cold-weather gear like ours. The Japanese army seemed to have learned nothing from the lesson of the Siberian Intervention of 1920; I can't imagine what they had been thinking. The Soviets seemed to be unaware of this problem with the gear. Everyone wanted Soviet cold-weather gear for the next year."

According to Kenji many suffered frostbite doing outdoor work that first winter. But the second winter, if the thermometer read at or below $-35\,^{\circ}$C at 6:00 am the guards would cancel outdoor work details, and the Soviets gave repeated frostbite warnings to the prisoners. "I don't think the Russians had realized that the Japanese soldiers would be so vulnerable to the cold, or that so many would fall victim to it."

The lack of preparedness and poor living conditions further degraded prisoner morale and work efficiency. According to Soviet Ministry of Internal Affairs statistics, the profit from prison labor did not fully cover the cost of maintaining and managing the camps; in 1946 a 33 million ruble deficit had to be supplemented from the federal budget.*

To note such circumstances, however, is not to completely vindicate Soviet actions. Even if we set aside blame for using POWs as slave labor, to transport some 640,000 prisoners without adequate preparations for their housing or longer-term treatment can only, at the most charitable, be termed incompetent management. The result was a travesty twice over—a humanitarian disaster that was also an economic failure. Even if there was no malice on the part of individual Russians, the state itself cannot evade responsibility.

Some Russian historians have argued that the treatment of Japanese prisoners by the Soviet Union was far more humane than the abuse inflicted by German forces on captured Soviet soldiers, or that, since the Soviet Union was not a signatory of the 1929 Geneva Convention, there was no obligation to observe its provisions on the treatment of POWs.† And it might also be allowed that the central government did give instructions for prisoners to be provided with a standard food ration, that it paid them wages, and that some prisoners were even able to buy goods in local bazaars. But none of this is grounds for denying that the Japanese prisoners were essentially held under conditions of slavery.

Russia is not the only country that has used such excuses to legitimize the harm it has inflicted on other countries. Colonial rule over Korea by the Japanese Empire may have been a losing proposition financially, but that is no basis for arguing, as some conservatives in Japan do, that it was altruistic. And the looting of goods and materiel from local populations across Asia by the Imperial Japanese Army was the outcome of incompetent management that underestimated the considerations of logistics and supply—ultimate responsibility for which resided with the Japanese government for expanding the battlefront beyond the limits of its capacity as a nation. Even if there was no

---

* Elena Katasonova, *Kantōgun heishi wa naze Shiberia ni yokuryū sareta ka*, trans. Shirai Hisaya (Shakai Hyōronsha, 2004), p. 54.
† Shirai Hisaya, "Nihonjin horyo to Shiberia yokuryū," in Katasonova, *Kantōgun heishi*, pp. 350–51.

malice on the part of individual Japanese soldiers, the state itself cannot evade its responsibility. We would do well to ask if there are not, in regard to war responsibility, counterparts in today's Japan to the arguments of the Russian historians cited above.

3

Placed as they were at the lowest rung of a Soviet society under considerable strain, the prisoners led a life of extreme deprivation. According to Kenji, "It was like the Stone Age." When he arrived at the camp, Kenji was wearing an Imperial Japanese Army uniform and had nothing more than a mess kit, a canteen, a tattered army blanket, and a rucksack with a few other items of daily use—but no toothbrush, drinking cup, dishes, or change of underwear.

"I don't remember exactly what I had, other than army-issue socks and a sewing kit that my grandmother Kochiyo had given me when I was called up and that really came in handy later on. Since I didn't have a change of clothes, I had to mend any rips or tears myself. In the −40°C Siberian winter, not having wearable clothing could be fatal. When I ran out of thread, I unraveled the socks, which were no longer wearable anyway.

"Sewing needles were particularly valuable. From the summer of 1946 on, clever prisoners made their own flints for starting fires, and some guys tried to make sewing needles out of some wire they'd gotten ahold of. They succeeded in figuring out how to straighten the wire and sharpen it to a point, but trying to drill a hole through it for inserting the thread was really difficult. Fortunately, I already had needles.

"Scraps of cloth were precious as well. If your clothing was torn, you had to put a patch over the rip or it would only tear again. But material for patches was hard to come by in the camp. So while out on work assignments you'd grab scraps of cloth and anything else that looked like it might be useful."

Among the few other items in Kenji's rucksack was the Rising Sun flag specially issued upon enlistment in the army. Kenji says that on the way to Siberia he used it as a makeshift carrying bag.

"About ten days after we arrived in the camp, that Rising Sun flag was confiscated by one of the camp guards. The Soviet troops imagined that the Japanese soldiers were carrying valuables, and possessions were frequently confiscated in what were called 'inspections.'

"But the Soviets were also poor—they didn't have anything more than the prisoners. We discovered while out on work details that the people of the Soviet Union didn't seem to even have decent clothes to wear. I saw women wearing Japanese army uniforms shipped from Manchuria. I don't think my Japanese flag was taken for any ideological reason—the soldier probably wanted to use it as a neckerchief or something.

"Memoirs by Japanese officers often mention Soviet soldiers stealing their wristwatches, but I never had anything like that in the first place. A recruit didn't have the leisure to be consulting a watch."

Kenji's camp consisted of two wooden structures. The barracks in which he and the other enlisted men lived was a high-ceilinged single-story building, similar to a warehouse, that held approximately 500 men. The other building was slightly smaller and contained the headquarters unit, the kitchen, an infirmary, a dining hall, and Soviet administrative offices. Yet when Kenji and the others first arrived, this second building "looked like a junkyard" and was barely functional. The dining hall was not usable, so porridge was brought in large wooden buckets to the barracks and distributed there.

The barracks was illuminated by only a handful of small, bare lightbulbs. Three shelves of large, unseparated wooden bunks ran down either side of the building, accommodating a company of men—some 200 individuals—in each half. These were where the prisoners slept and lived, crammed in with barely enough headroom on each level to sit up cross-legged. Vertical posts divided the shelves into units sleeping seven to eight men, giving each man a space only about fifty centimeters in width. This was too narrow to sleep shoulder to shoulder, so the prisoners alternated head to foot.

The horizontal surfaces of the shelves were unmilled timber, which chafed against the back. They were merely laid on, making them creaky and unstable. When someone turned over in his sleep, it would disturb those around him. The men all laid their blankets out as a bottom layer, and, in the unbearable cold of winter, pulled their overcoats over themselves. Kenji started out sleeping on one of the top platforms and eventually moved to a bottom one, where there was an intermittent rain of dust and wood debris from above.

In the cold of the Siberian winter, when temperatures might drop to −45°C, life without the Russian wood stoves called *pechka* was impossible. There was a *pechka* in the camp barracks, but it was small and there was never enough fuel. During the first winter, each man had only a single thin blanket and an overcoat to sleep in, and the prisoners relied on the body heat of the men lying on either side of them to keep warm.

They wore the same clothing constantly; there was nothing to change into. The first winter Kenji cut arm and leg holes in leftover paper cement sacks and wore those as extra protection against the cold. Paper does have an insulating effect, so this helped a bit. Socks went to pieces fairly quickly, but Kenji was able to stave off frostbite by wrapping his feet in rags and whatever pieces of cloth came to hand.

There was no running water in Chita, so even the Russian population drew water from the river flowing to the south of the city. This river water would be put in large wooden barrels and loaded into carts pulled by two horses going around to individual households. In the camp, too, there was a large storage barrel for water. The Russians threw their wastewater into the backyards of their houses, where in winter it immediately froze.

Thus water was precious. There wasn't enough of it for the prisoners to even wash their faces; they only drank it in soup for breakfast and dinner. During the first winter they neither shaved nor cut their hair. Kenji says that the following summer, when conditions had eased a bit, they were occasionally able to wash underwear and such in the river south of Chita, but does not recall ever doing this during the first winter. Somewhat fortunately, however, the air was dry, so they did not sweat much, and their metabolisms were slowed by malnutrition, so they did not become that dirty.

Still, wearing the same clothing all the time bred lice. Sunday was the only day the prisoners did not have work details, and so the first thing on the agenda Sunday morning was picking lice. In Kenji's camp there were no outbreaks of typhus, which is spread by lice, but in other camps such infectious diseases killed many prisoners.

One night in early November 1945, not long after they had arrived in camp, the prisoners were all suddenly ordered outside. Trembling with fear, they were led to what proved to be a public bath. There was a large steam disinfection chamber where their clothing was sterilized while they washed themselves with a trickle of hot water from taps. But because the sanitary conditions at the camp did not change, this delousing had no more than a temporary effect. And when they returned to camp, they found that their belongings had been rifled by the Soviet guards and that items of value such as fountain pens had been stolen. "I doubt that there was very much to steal, but they certainly made a mess going through our things."

Kenji was mildly nearsighted and in the military had been outfitted with eyeglasses. But they were broken in Siberia, and he had to do without. "That was the least of my problems. I imagine there were guys with eyesight worse than mine, but I don't recall ever hearing anybody complain. Not having glasses was not going to kill you."

For the first two months or so in the camp, the prisoners mostly ate thin *kasha* (porridge) made with sorghum. Other foods were rice and millet. "Mainly 'spoils of war' from Manchuria, I believe. I loaded enough of it onto barges at the Amur River." In the following year they would occasionally have a stew of mixed grains with salt-cured fish, or soup using canned corned beef sent as foreign aid to the Soviet Union by the Americans, but during the first winter there was nothing like that.

Around the beginning of 1946, in addition to the breakfast and dinner porridge they began to be issued a ration of black bread to eat at lunch on their work details. But breakfast was usually so meager that most of the men ate the bread in the morning, too. Even if they were trying to save it for later, they were so hungry that one bite would make them want to finish it off.

The porridge was cooked by a kitchen detail of prisoners, and ladled into each man's mess kit. The Soviets provided no dishes or utensils, so the prisoners used the mess kits they had brought with them, supplemented with spoons fashioned from aluminum or pieces of wood stolen from job sites. Some of the more skillful prisoners made quite decent spoons that were good for getting the very last drop of gruel from the bottom of the mess kit, but Kenji's was not much more than a sliver.

"Your mess kit was your life. You might throw almost anything else away, but you held onto the mess kit no matter what. I was still carrying it with me when I finally made it back to Japan. Some guys held onto theirs for quite a while afterward. The second year, when canned American corned beef began to be distributed, we used the empty cans as dishes. Empty cans also frequently turned up when we were clearing out the frozen wastewater from behind the Russian officers' houses, so lots of guys picked them up and used them for tableware."

There were two standard types of Japanese army mess kit—a "single," which had only one compartment, and a "double," which had two nested compartments. They held different amounts, and even a server who was trying to dole out equal portions had difficulty being fair. Other memoirs of Siberian internment note that many prisoners would knock out the bottom of their mess tins to enlarge them so that they might get even a little more food from the servers.

At mealtime, rather than serving into each man's kit as they passed down a line, all of the mess kits were collected, filled with porridge, and then redistributed.

"When the food was being doled out, everyone was all eyes watching. Everyone's mess kits were collected in one place, where they were filled from tubs of porridge sent from the kitchen detail to each platoon. The servers did their best to be fair, but with everyone watching so intently there were bound to be complaints about who got too much or too little. So there was always trouble over the food distribution. When we worked together to make dishes out of pilfered Soviet aluminum in the spring of 1946, the idea was that unless we all had the same type of dish and started receiving the food directly from the servers, there would be no end to these disputes."

Even so, since the prisoners in Kenji's camp belonged to a relatively newly formed mixed battalion, the distribution of food was fairly equal. In other camps where original units preserved their command structure, the officers and NCOs controlled the food distribution, and enlisted men—particularly first-year soldiers—were at the end of the line. This was one of the reasons for the emergence of a "democratic movement" among the prisoners, something that will be discussed in greater detail in the next chapter.

4

As mentioned earlier, one prisoner who had died aboard the train on the way to the camp was seen off to the graveyard by all the inmates. But after that, no one had the time or energy for such ceremony.

As the bitter cold deepened, the men were set to work at a thermo-electric power station digging out the ice clogging the inflow and out-flow channels that circulated river water for conversion to steam to run the turbines. About 300 of the 500 prisoners were mobilized from January to March 1946 for this work outdoors.

"We worked near the riverbank using steel rods to break up the ice. But it was a frozen mass of ice, gravel, and dirt—hard as concrete, and no matter how hard you worked you could only dig about ten centimeters in a day. At −45°C, even with hardly any humidity the water vapor would freeze instantly into diamond dust. It was hard work in biting wind and cold, and between hunger and malnutrition and hypothermia and exhaustion, people were dying right and left."

The prisoners were so desperate that they started adding salt they had somehow managed to procure to their paltry porridge, trying to enjoy their food by flavoring it as much as possible. But that only led some of them to develop edema from the combination of malnutrition and overindulgence in salt.

On the way out to their work details, the prisoners often passed by a restaurant in downtown Chita where pieces of bread lay frozen in the icy wastewater filling the gutter from the kitchen. Kenji felt miserable when several of his fellow prisoners broke ranks to go after these bits of bread, and were shouted back into line by the guards.

Among these awful conditions, one of the most unpleasant was elimination of bodily wastes. There was no toilet in the barracks, and even in the middle of the night the men had to go outside about fifty meters to an outdoor latrine—really nothing more than a long slit trench.

"Malnutrition makes you pass water more frequently. Then you get diarrhea. And in the end, you are leaking on your way to the toilet. Everyone got up frequently in the middle of the night to urinate. Sometimes when you were lying there, piss from guys with malnutrition would trickle down from the upper sleeping platforms through the cracks between the logs.

"There were times when I had to get up and go to the latrine more than once an hour. At night one of the prisoners would be assigned to keep watch beside the wood stove with a wristwatch provided to him by the Japanese headquarters unit that had survived being looted. I asked him, and that was how I knew less than an hour had passed since the last time I'd gotten up.

"When you went outside at night in −40°C weather, you didn't feel cold, you felt pain. But when you dropped your pants in the latrine, your buttocks would not get frostbitten because they were rounded. What got frostbite were smaller pieces of you—nose and fingers—that stuck out. If your nose got red, you had to be very careful to warm it up slowly, or it could fall off.

"The waste in the latrine froze immediately. Before long there was a frozen mountain of it that would block the opening, so then people would start relieving themselves on the floorboards, which also became choked with frozen excrement. There were also icy streams of frozen urine from those who couldn't make it all the way to the latrine; men in weakened condition would often slip and fall on them. Malnutrition also caused night blindness, increasing the chances of falling."

There was no toilet paper. "But perhaps because what they ate was so different the Russians didn't seem to use it anyway. Our stool got harder, too, and we stopped wiping. And it wasn't just the camps—at the time Russian toilets were all outhouses." Still, "The first winter was really tough. People with diarrhea wiped themselves with whatever they could find—bits of clothing, rags, and so on."

In these conditions, many died from malnutrition and exhaustion. "Sometimes we would get up in the morning and find someone had died in the middle of the night. But the only funeral was for the first guy who died. After that everybody was completely occupied with keeping alive and didn't have time to think about anybody else."

Kenji and the other prisoners greeted the New Year of 1946 in the camp. According to a memoir written for the newsletter of the Chita-kai (an association of veterans of Kenji's camp) by a prisoner assigned to administrative work, on the morning of New Year's Day the inmates assembled in the courtyard to bow in the direction of the imperial palace and shout a chorus of "Long live the emperor!" But Kenji says he has absolutely no memory of anything like that.

"The officers might have had the time and energy for such things, since even when they did go on outside work details it was just to supervise. But I wouldn't read too much into it, anyway; I imagine they were just homesick for Japan and simply continuing prewar customs, like going to a temple or shrine at New Year's. Certainly from the next year on there was nothing like that."

What Kenji does remember vividly from that first New Year is visiting the sickbed of his friend Kyōsaka Kichiji, who had fallen ill from malnutrition. Kyōsaka had been stationed with the Eighth Air Signal Regiment in Hsinking (now Changchun); like Kenji, he had been called up in Tokyo in December 1944 and sent directly to Manchuria. He and Kenji had become friends in the camp, as they were similar in age and experience in an environment dominated by older men who had mostly been Japanese colonists in Manchuria.

Kenji has written almost nothing of his experiences in Siberia, except for this brief reminiscence of Kyōsaka that he published in the 1980s in the newsletter of his neighborhood association in Tokyo:

August 1945. I was a first-year soldier stationed on the outskirts of Mudanjiang in eastern Manchuria. Following the unconditional surrender to the Soviet Union, in late October I was transported as a prisoner of war to a camp in Chita in eastern Siberia.

There, some 500 men were packed into three-tiered sleeping platforms like those familiar to anyone who has seen pictures of Auschwitz.

The psychological strain of not knowing what was going to happen next; near-starvation rations, despite being forced to do hard labor; the almost terrifying cold, slightly worse each day as a harbinger of the even more bitter temperatures to come; homesickness, hunger, cold. The only thing that kept us going every day was the faint hope that someday, somehow we would return home.

By the end of November many men had already died, and many dozen more seemed likely to follow. My friend Kyōsaka, another first-year soldier, began to show symptoms of malnutrition. He had become night-blind, and after the work details were formed up in the early morning darkness, I would hold his hand on the snowy trail to our work site. Otherwise he would have slipped and fallen.

Probably because his legs were swelling, he began to complain sadly that he couldn't get his boots on, and a number of times I helped him shove his feet in to make it to morning formation. Soon he became incontinent, and around the middle of December he was relieved of work duties and hospitalized in the camp infirmary. But of course he was not given any treatment; he was just left to lie there.

New Year's Day, 1946, was a holiday in the Soviet Union as well, and in the afternoon I went to visit Kyōsaka in the infirmary. There were perhaps seven or eight beds. The stove was weakly burning a bit of coal, but it did little to heat the room; spilled water had frozen on the floor and the triple-paned glass windows were completely iced over except at their very center, from which I peered outside. A Russian family trudged by. Smoke rose from the chimneys of houses. Home and hearth—they seemed a very distant world from where I was that day.

Kyōsaka's condition had deteriorated terribly; anyone could tell he had only a few more days to live. I don't remember what I said. There wasn't really much of anything good that we could talk about, and I imagine all I did was utter some stale words of encouragement.

But when with a faraway look in his eyes he whispered, "Today they're celebrating New Year's back home with rice cakes, aren't they?" and "I wish I could eat some with them too," those words were lodged into my memory.

He died several days later. Perhaps because of the hard labor and the cold, at the time I myself was weak from a four- or five-day bout of diarrhea. What time on what day in January did he die? How did I find out? Who told me? I have no memory of it. The news probably simply drifted to me somehow. I think everyone in the camp had lost the human empathy that allowed them to care about news of others. Of course there was no wake or funeral. The life we were living cannot be called a human one.[*]

As noted here, Kenji himself began to have diarrhea, a symptom of malnutrition. During the work digging out the channels for the electric power station, he fouled his underwear on at least one occasion. He used the warm water from the station's exhaust channel to wash out his soiled garments.

In February the diarrhea grew worse, and a Soviet army medical officer gave him an exemption from outdoor labor. Still not sick enough to be hospitalized, he was left behind in the barracks, where a prisoner in similar circumstances invited him to join in a scavenger hunt—by which he meant rifling through the belongings of the other prisoners to find any food that they might be hiding. Kenji agreed, but

---

[*] Oguma Kenji, "Aru wakamono e no tsuioku," *Shiyō* 2 (1986).

as it turned out, no one in the barracks had any surplus to conceal. Even so, Kenji felt terribly guilty for this attempted raid.

"I didn't think anything about stealing food or materials from the Soviets, but I regretted having picked through the belongings of fellow prisoners who were starving just like me. It was something I shouldn't have done. I think I'd lost my conscience as a result of the cold and hunger and malnutrition."

The exemption from outdoor work was only temporary, and Kenji was soon called out to work at ditch-digging once more. If this continued, it seemed likely that he would meet the same fate as Kyōsaka. But here Kenji encountered a stroke of good fortune: reforms came early to Twenty-Fourth District Camp No. 2.

In the middle of December 1945, Lieutenant Akhmadullin was appointed as the third commandant of the camp. According to Kenji, "The first commandant was relieved of command in mid-November, the second in the middle of December. I think they were dismissed over irregularities in the camp administration, including misappropriation of materials. One of the prisoners said he'd seen the previous commandant being led off in handcuffs. Akhmadullin addressed the prisoners through an interpreter, saying that the previous unjust state of affairs would now be corrected. And certainly, after that the food situation improved. In fact, to make up for earlier shortages, for a time they gave us more than the prescribed rations.

"There were two reasons I survived. The first was that I was in a mixed unit so that there was no discrimination on the basis of rank. The second was that reform of the camp administration came early on. I think this was because the camp was in Chita, the headquarters of a Soviet military district. In camps located farther from the large cities, there probably were more deaths."

So Kenji attributes his survival to this coincidence of objective conditions—not to his own good judgment or attitude, or the strength of his will or spirit, or the protection of gods or buddhas.

"I don't believe there was anything particular about the people who died during this period. I don't think things like weakness of will or what a person did before he went into the army had any effect on whether he lived or died. The officers didn't have to do hard labor, so it's obvious why more of the enlisted men died—but death was only natural to anyone in that environment."

In written accounts by other Siberian internees, one often comes across passages recalling the frustration felt at wasting their youth in such circumstances, or despair at the terrible fate that had befallen them. But Kenji says, "I didn't think anything like that. I was too busy trying to stay alive. People who thought in such abstractions must have been especially high-minded to begin with, or else they were officers who got by without having to do outdoor labor."

War memoirs—not only those of the Siberian internment—tend to be written by people blessed with education or status: conscripted university students, reserve and regular officers, and the like. Such records are valuable, but they are also written from a particular perspective. Ordinary people—hard-pressed by life and often not as articulate—tend not to leave their own historical testimony.

The number of prisoners who died in Twenty-Fourth District Camp No. 2 is unclear. According to the Chita-kai newsletter, by 31 March 1946 there were about forty-five deaths.* Kenji says, "I think the number was probably somewhat smaller," but if we accept that figure, it would be slightly less than 10 percent of the total population of prisoners.

Some 640,000 Japanese were interned in Siberia, of whom about 60,000 are believed to have died in captivity. That would suggest that a death rate of about 10 percent was the average, and that perhaps Kenji's camp was not as fortunate as he describes it being.

In March 1946, as the winter came to an end, so did the work at the power station. The prisoners were shifted to somewhat less demanding work assignments, such as sorting goods commandeered in Manchuria by the Soviet army or cleaning up the wastewater in the backyards of Soviet officer housing. Their treatment in the camp itself also gradually improved. In the summer of 1946 new barracks were built by the prisoners, the sleeping platforms were redone with two tiers rather than three, and living conditions got a bit better. At the same time, security at the camp was heightened, with a triple fence of barbed wire and a new watchtower equipped with searchlights. But after this time, no one died in the camp.

As conditions eased somewhat, hopeful speculation concerning repatriation began to spread. One man reporting he had seen

---

* "Hokuryō kara Maizuru made."

trucks carrying prisoners while out on work detail was enough to start a completely groundless rumor that the trucks were being used to begin the process of transporting them home. In fact, however, more than two more years would pass before Kenji would be able to return to Japan.

Daily life among the Siberian internees. (Courtesy of Mainichi Shimbunsha.)

Chapter 4

Political Indoctrination

In the spring of 1946, conditions began to improve for the prisoners in Twenty-Fourth District Camp No. 2. In September of that year, a second barracks building was constructed, and the three-tier sleeping platforms were converted into more generous two-tier structures. Meals were now served in a mess hall. That summer an outbreak of bedbugs led the prisoners to sleep for a time on the piles of lumber stacked up for the new construction, but the period of extreme cold and hunger had passed.

The infestation of lice from the previous year was also conquered by having the prisoners strip and boil all their clothing in a huge cauldron in the yard of the camp. The twice-daily porridge of mixed grains began to be supplemented with salt-cured fish and tins of American corned beef sent as aid to the Soviets. The mess crew was even able to carefully save up sugar provided by the Soviets to make a special sweet chestnut porridge for New Year's.

However, Kenji recalls, "In contrast to the first winter, which was a struggle with hunger and cold, from the second year on a different sort of suffering began." This was the so-called "democratic movement"—a movement of mutual criticism among the prisoners based on communist ideology.

1

Before discussing this "democratic movement" among the prisoners, I want to sketch how the Soviet people and administrative system appeared from Kenji's perspective, as this is important for understanding why the movement took the form it did.

Japanese internees fell under two different jurisdictions within the Soviet system: (1) camps run by the Chief Directorate for Affairs of Prisoners of War and Internees (Soviet acronym GUPVI) of the People's Commissariat for Internal Affairs (NKVD, renamed the

Ministry of Internal Affairs, or MVD, in 1946); and (2) labor brigades under the authority of the Soviet army (Ministry of Defense). Kenji's camp belonged to the first. Along with Border Guard units, the NKVD had Internal Guard units charged with security at key locations and management of prisoners; both were organized according to a system of ranks like that of the military. The camps under the NKVD were the responsibility of the Internal Guards.

At Kenji's camp, the commandant and a dozen or so other officers and NCOs commuted to duty from quarters located nearby. The guards also lived in a barracks nearby but separate from the camp, from which they would come to escort the prisoners to and from their work details.

In the middle of December 1945, Lieutenant Akhmadullin was appointed as the third commandant to serve at the camp, after two predecessors had been relieved of command, apparently for misappropriation of supplies. Akhmadullin had black hair and a round face, and seemed to be of Central Asian stock.

In this regard Kenji says, "Nobody made much of the fact that Akhmadullin looked Asian. I don't think there was any particular significance in the Soviets assigning someone like him there. I never sensed any racial discrimination in the Soviet Union, maybe because they were such a mixture themselves." Remarks on the absence of racial prejudice in the Soviet Union are common to almost all memoirs of Siberian internment, regardless of their stance on other aspects of the Soviet system.

In Kenji's camp, the de facto representative of the Japanese prisoners in negotiations with the Soviets was Captain Kumabe Kai, adjutant of the Fifty-Second Battalion. According to a reminiscence Kumabe wrote after returning to Japan, Akhmadullin was a man who liked to go by the book, and while he put an end to the siphoning off of camp supplies and improved the treatment of the prisoners, he was also a stickler for achieving the labor quotas.

The most popular of the Soviet officers among the prisoners was Second Lieutenant Sestakov of the guards. Kumabe says Sestakov told him that "he could understand our suffering because he had been taken prisoner by the German army, but even beyond that he was generous in his treatment of us Japanese in every respect. The days when he was on duty there was never any trouble, and he never made any unreasonable demands."* Kenji recalls how he spent from New Year's Eve 1946 into New Year's Day 1947 on a work detail under Sestakov loading lumber into freight cars. "It was freezing in the freight cars on the way back to the camp, so Sestakov ordered us to wrestle with one another to keep warm, and joined in just like everyone else."

During World War II approximately 5.7 million Soviet army personnel were captured by German forces. Of these, approximately 1 million were released for use as auxiliaries by the Germans, but another 3 to 3.3 million were either massacred near the front lines or died from maltreatment in POW camps—a death rate of about 60 percent.

Conversely, of approximately 3 million members of the German armed forces captured by the Red Army, about 1 million are believed to have died, for a death rate of about one-third. The death rate for Japanese in the Siberian internment is said to have been approximately 60,000 out of 640,000, or about 10 percent. The death rate for United States and British Commonwealth POWs captured by Japan was roughly 27 percent.

Red Army officers and soldiers who survived imprisonment by the Germans were later treated brutally by the Soviet Union itself. In August 1941, after the commencement of hostilities between Germany and the Soviet Union, Stalin issued Order No. 270, which proclaimed that to surrender to the enemy was "the violation of an oath and a betrayal of the motherland" punishable by death.† Even when liberated after the war, former POWs were regarded with suspicion as collaborators of the Germans, and were sent to reeducation camps or penal brigades, where large numbers of them died. The details of their fate are still largely shrouded in mystery.

According to Kumabe's memoir, Sestakov had been an elite officer but after his capture his fate was reversed; "He said he didn't and couldn't hope for much." Kenji says that although Sestakov was a second lieutenant, among the guards he was called "Major," which seemed to have been his former rank. His wife also worked at the camp. A number of other memoirs by Japanese POWs similarly mention camp administrators who, like Sestakov, were officers who had been demoted after having spent time in German prison camps.

---

* Kumabe Kai, "Afumadorin to Sestakōfu," *Chita-kai kaihō* 2 (1976), p. 1.
† Karpov, *Sutārin no horyotachi*, p. 72.

Kumabe writes of Sestakov, "He really was an extraordinarily humane man who helped restore my faith in the people of the Soviet Union." Kenji recalls him as "a second lieutenant of about thirty, always smiling, a really good guy. When we prisoners passed him we would salute, and he would give a small smile and lightly raise a clenched fist in response." The prisoners, in their broken Russian, called him *khorosho leytenant*, the "good lieutenant."

Kenji remembers a few other Russian personnel—a paymaster lieutenant; a tall lieutenant and his wife, a major, both in the medical corps; a lanky, long-faced NCO the prisoners called "Praying Mantis."

"A prison camp in Siberia was not exactly a plum assignment for them, either. We saw them almost every day, so even without talking to them, we got to know what sort of people they were. Some of them were good people, and some were not. The second lieutenant in charge of the work details was the kind of guy who would push the prisoners to work harder all to advance himself."

In Kenji's camp, the prisoners were not required to salute the Soviet officers. Sestakov would return a salute, so the prisoners would salute him in passing, but this was not obligatory. Nor did any of the guards physically punish or abuse the prisoners.

Kenji recalls, "I thought the Soviet army was better than the Japanese army. When they were off duty, the officers and men of the Soviet army were relaxed and personal with each other. On holidays such as May Day, they would bring their families to the camp and celebrate with dances and such. On those days the married medic couple would walk about holding hands, and because the wife was of higher rank, we used to say, 'Boy, I bet she really wears the pants in the family.' The officers never resorted to violence in dealing with the troops, and if they had just cause, enlisted men could protest the actions of their superiors.

"To relate something from my own experience, around June of 1946 a dozen of us were sent to work in a small fur factory. Next to it was a place for tanning sheepskins, where an old Russian furrier cuffed me on the head. I'd been needling him, humming while I was working, so it was partly my fault. But because we'd been told to report any time we encountered violence at work, I did—and my protest was successful. Captain Kumabe, the Japanese interpreter, and Commandant Akhmadullin went with me back to the workplace. The old man said his piece, but in the end admitted he was wrong in hitting me. I heard that later Akhmadullin was angry with Captain Kumabe, saying, 'It's all because of that prisoner's bad attitude,' but I still doubt that a POW of the Japanese army could have done what I did.

"This was the only time in Siberia that I was ever hit by a Russian. Though in the spring of 1947 I came close: We were sorting cabbages that had been allowed to freeze for preservation during the winter, getting rid of the ones that were spoiled, and I tossed some of the good ones to my buddies for them to take. A guard saw me and was about to beat me, but I fell to my knees and clasped my hands and apologized, and in the end he let me off."

Other accounts of Siberian internment also record instances of prisoners being allowed to protest their treatment. There were even cases in which personnel were transferred after their mistreatment of prisoners was reported to visiting central government inspectors.* In this respect, Kenji was not the only one who had the impression that the Soviet army was preferable to the Japanese army.

Even so, the Soviet Union did possess a fearsome secret police apparatus. This began after the Russian Revolution with the Cheka (Emergency Committee, 1917–22), followed by the State Political Directorate (GPU), which, after a variety of changes in organization and nomenclature, evolved into the Committee for State Security (KGB) in 1954, following the death of Stalin. During Kenji's internment, the secret police, like the labor and internment camps, lay under the jurisdiction of the People's Commissariat for Internal Affairs (NKVD), which was reorganized into the Ministry of Internal Affairs (MVD) in 1946.

In the Soviet army, so-called political commissars wielded considerable clandestine power. After the revolution, the Soviet Union employed former Tsarist military officers in its efforts to build up its defenses, but because their loyalty was doubted, political commissars from the GPU were embedded in the army. Particularly after the Stalinist purges of the Red Army, the political commissars came to possess greater authority than the strictly military officers, and often created confusion by meddling in tactical operations.

Political commissars frequently visited Kenji's camp. One who arrived in the spring of 1947 had such a fearsome countenance the

---

* Wakatsuki Yasuo, *Shiberia horyo shūyōjo* (Simul Shuppankai, 1979), p. 163.

prisoners nicknamed him "Kondō Isami," after the dreaded leader of a secret police unit in the last days of the Tokugawa shogunate. There appeared to be a mutual antagonism between the political commissars and the camp staff. In his memoir, Kumabe portrays both Akhmadullin and Sestakov quite positively, while calling the GPU commissars "all quite unpleasant individuals" whose "devious ways were sickening."

Of course the prisoners had no way of knowing the fine points of the Soviet chain of command. In addition to the Internal Guards units of the MVD charged with camp administration, officers of the GPU and GUPVI were also dispatched to or stationed in the camps. At this point, it is impossible to confirm the organization to which "Kondō Isami" belonged and other such details, and the following discussion is based on this necessarily limited perspective.

2

In Kenji's camp, the "democratic movement" commenced in the latter part of 1946. But other forms of self-organized activity among the prisoners emerged from an even earlier date.

In August 1946, as life in the camp finally escaped the abysmal conditions of the first winter, the prisoners built a drum tower in the yard to celebrate the Japanese midsummer festival of Obon with singing, dancing, and other entertainments. The principal organizer of this event was a former sheet-metal worker who knew how to fashion buckets and other practical items. As noted earlier, prisoners with such special skills were generally assigned indoor work, got better food, and had both the time and energy for something beyond mere survival.

In September, to commemorate the first anniversary of their departure from Fengtian, the prisoners formed a fraternal organization, the Isoji-kai. By this time, rank in the Imperial Japanese Army had ceased to determine relationships among the prisoners, and they had stopped referring to one another by their former ranks. This facilitated the formation of the social group.

According to Kenji, the Isoji-kai was "basically about getting together on long autumn evenings to reminisce about our homes and how we missed them." A list was drawn up sorting the members by place of origin, and prisoners from the same prefecture got together to share a sense of local solidarity. Kenji went to a meeting of the Tokyo group, and then to one of the Niigata group (his father's home prefecture, in which he was officially registered), but didn't feel very comfortable in either.

"Before the war ended, I'd received a letter from Grandpa telling me that he and Grandma had been forced to evacuate to their home village in Okayama and the house in Tokyo had been torn down. So I knew I had no home to return to in Tokyo. If I did go back, it would be to Niigata, where my father was. I figured some connections would be useful if I was going there, which is why I went to the meeting of the Niigata group. But I had never lived there, so I didn't have any reminiscences to share."

Kenji had already become a man without a home.

Kenji says that after a couple of sessions, the group stopped meeting. "I think it was because the Soviets were concerned about prisoners forming their own associations and put pressure on it to disband." Certainly, the Soviet system imposed very strict prohibitions on the formation of voluntary associations. Yet as we shall see, later on in the democratic movement the Japanese POWs tended to excessively self-adapt to the perceived will of the Soviets, and so in this case, too, the extent of actual Soviet involvement in the termination of the Isoji-kai remains unclear.

In the winter of 1946–47, the prisoners organized a theater troupe. As mentioned earlier, starting from December in this second winter of their internment, the prisoners were exempted from outdoor labor when the temperature dropped to $-35\,°C$ or below at 6:00 am, giving them free time indoors. Initially this troupe, called the Dawn Performing Arts Company, performed Japanese popular melodramas. Central figures in the troupe were a drama-loving NCO, a music-loving college-educated young officer, and a first-year soldier who had been an *onnagata* (male actor specializing in female roles). In early 1947, as communist indoctrination began to make itself more felt, the troupe changed its name to the People's Theater, but the content of its performances did not change much at first.

The official voice of the "democratic movement" among the Japanese internees in Siberia was the *Nihon shimbun* (Japan News), first issued on 15 September 1945 under the guidance of the Political Directorate of the Red Army (PURKKA). Published with the participation of Japanese POWs interned in Khabarovsk, it ran for 662 issues before it shut down in December 1949 (averaging about three issues a week), and at its peak is said to have had a circulation of 800,000 copies. The democratic movement began with the Soviets distributing this paper to the camps and organizing reading circles among the internees.

Kenji first encountered the *Nihon shimbun* in October 1945, while at the Amur River border between China and the USSR on his way to Siberia, when he overheard one of the other POWs say "Odin davay" (give me one) to a Soviet officer who was carrying some copies. "So that's what you say when you want something—*Odin davay*," Kenji thought. The prisoners passed the paper around, but it was merely news of the great victory of the Soviet forces written in awkwardly worded Japanese, and they discarded it without really reading much of it.

The second time Kenji saw the paper was in January 1946, when the prisoners passed around some copies that a Soviet officer had brought to the camp. Many dismissed it as "propaganda" and ignored it, but there was no other source of news about Japan. The first article from this newspaper to leave an impression on Kenji concerned General Tōjō Hideki's failed suicide attempt and his arrest by Occupation forces in September 1945. In January 1941, as minister of the army, Tōjō had issued the "Instructions for the Battlefield," famous for its injunction "Do not suffer the shame of being taken prisoner while alive." He had been prime minister when the decision was made to go to war against the United States.

"When this article was passed around to me, I felt enormous contempt. We had been taught that rather than being captured we should kill ourselves while taking along as many of the enemy as possible, and that sense of things stayed with us, though we figured that since we had surrendered and become prisoners at the order of the emperor, we were justified in living on. But when I heard that the general who had commanded us never to be taken prisoner had bungled his suicide and been taken prisoner himself, I was filled with scorn. If he'd stuck the pistol in his mouth and pulled the trigger he would certainly have been able to die. My feelings were all the stronger since I'd heard that Hitler had gone down fighting."

Another article that left an impression on Kenji was the news of the imprisonment of Prince Nashimoto, a member of the imperial family, for his involvement in the war. In copies of the paper that made their way around the camp in February 1946 there was also a story about a former Japanese army air base in the Inland Sea being converted to peaceful use as a salt pan. Both would have been unthinkable in prewar or wartime Japan.

Kenji says, "Until 1946 I had never heard the word democratization, or thought about it. 'Democracy' I had heard of, but didn't think was compatible with Japan's national character." But Kenji, who had been skeptical of the wartime Japanese press, read these articles and thought, "The world has changed. There may be more to this newspaper than mere propaganda."

In the spring of 1946, an article in the *Nihon shimbun* on the terrible postwar inflation in Japan reported that salmon were selling for several hundred yen each. "A prisoner from Hokkaido said, 'That's ridiculous. It's just propaganda.' But I'd learned about the German inflation after World War I in secondary school, and I thought the story could very well be true."

In July 1946, the prisoners made a wall newspaper using paper and ink, which, though hard to come by, had suddenly been provided for their activities. Up to that point the prisoners had never been given paper of any sort, to the extent that they had been resorting to using grass or rags when they went to the latrine, but the new supplies, as Kenji says, probably came "through some route involving the political commissars."

The wall newspaper was of course subject to censorship by the Soviets. Initially, however, it featured mostly haiku and other literary efforts by the prisoners, and was relatively unrestricted. The first edition in July ran an article praising Sestakov as the *khorosho leytenant* ("good lieutenant") that had been written by the prisoners of their own accord. "I heard that afterward Sestakov said to Kumabe-san, 'This sort of thing is going to get me into trouble. Please don't do it anymore.'"

The climate definitely began to change later in 1946, with the deepening of tensions between the Soviet Union and the Western allies foreshadowed by Churchill's famous "Iron Curtain" speech in March, though at first daily life in Kenji's camp remained much the same. The *Nihon shimbun* had begun to feature articles with an anti-American slant, writing of the oppression of the Japanese people under the "reactionary Yoshida cabinet" and of popular protests against the Allied Occupation, but they only succeeded in turning off most of the prisoners, who preferred to use the paper to roll cigarettes rather than to read it.

Beginning in the second winter, cultural enrichment programs were held when it was too cold to work outside, all of them relatively innocuous—lectures on agriculture by a prisoner who had been a professor at Hokkaido University, or classes in elementary Russian. With its second edition, the wall newspaper took on a more propagandistic coloring, but after a few more issues it folded. The theater troupe gave performances of works based on stories about popular resistance by prewar Japanese Communist Party writers, like *Kani kōsen* (The Cannery Ship) by Kobayashi Takiji, but no one was taken to task for being indifferent to their ideological content. In the early summer of 1947, copies of a Japanese-language introduction to Marxism and Leninism were provided, "but you had to read it where it was set out, and there was only one copy for each company, so mostly they just sat there unread."

According to Kenji, "The democratic movement got underway little by little beginning in autumn 1946, but it still wasn't too bad. From the summer of 1946 to about the middle of 1947, work ended at 5:00, dinner was at 6:00, and after that was free time when we would play cards or Japanese board games like go or shōgi. Those months were the most relaxed of my life in the camp." But in the autumn of 1947, the situation would take on a far darker cast.

3

Judging from a number of memoirs and reminiscences of the Siberian internment, the "democratic movement" among the prisoners resulted from a coming together of multiple factors. One of these, of course, was instigation from the Soviet side—but certain conditions among the prisoners also made them ripe for a response.

One factor on the Japanese side was the continued existence in the camps of the hierarchy of the Imperial Japanese Army and the "unofficial punishments" customary to it. Inequities in food and work allotments and the use of soldiers as personal orderlies by officers were common. In the early days of the democratic movement, calls for equality in food distribution met with enthusiastic applause.

The situation in different camps varied immensely, so generalization is difficult. In Twenty-Fourth District Camp No. 2, where Kenji was interned, there was not much discrimination by rank even at the beginning, and by the summer of 1946, ranks were not even being used as a form of address. At the other extreme was the camp in Ulaanbaatar known for the "Dawn Prayer" incident, in which the senior Japanese officer had a number of men who did not meet work quotas punished so severely that they died. (The men were left tied to stakes so that when dead they looked as though they were praying with heads bowed to the sun, hence the name.) Even in November 1947, the Japanese officers of this unit were witnessed upon arrival at the port of Nakhodka for repatriation wearing immaculately shining leather boots as they ordered a squad of emaciated ordinary soldiers to carry their luggage.*

Accordingly, in many camps the early phases of the democratic movement took the form of an "anti-militarist struggle," including the elimination of officer privileges, saluting, and insignia of rank as well as the termination of discriminatory treatment with regard to food and work. The democratic movement seems also to have been inspired, at least in part, by the example of the Soviet army with its absence of unjust discrimination by rank. Moreover, for many of the younger prisoners— including officers, conscripted college students, and the members of the young colonists' brigades sent to Manchuria and Mongolia†—who had grown up on a steady diet of militaristic propaganda and education, the democratic movement was the first encounter they had with communism. The stimulation of their intellectual curiosity regarding the workings of society led some to passionate participation in the

---

* Eguchi, "Jo ni kaete," p. vii.

† The young colonists' brigades (Manmō Kaitaku Seinendan) were civilian units organized by the Japanese government from 1931 to 1945 following a proposal by the Kwantung Army. Their purpose was to populate areas bordering the Soviet Union with Japanese settlers so as to strengthen Japanese influence in the region. At the end of the war they numbered about 270,000 people, of which about 47,000 young men were conscripted into the Kwantung Army on the eve of the Soviet attack. The retreating Kwantung Army abandoned the remaining women, children, and elderly, many of whom eventually made it back to Japan, but only after heavy losses along the way.

movement. Others who joined voluntarily had been involved in the communist movement in Japan before the war.

In many cases, a number of these factors were at work simultaneously. For example, the prominent activist Asahara Seiki, one of the editors of the Nihon shimbun, had been arrested for his involvement in the communist movement during his student days at Tokyo Imperial University. He claimed in a statement published after his return to Japan that his participation in the movement in Siberia had begun with a letter he sent to the paper exposing discrimination in food rationing by rank in his camp.*

Thus, some researchers in Japan argue that even though the democratic movement began under Soviet influence, it also involved a certain spontaneity and even inevitability. Certainly this belief is marked in the memoirs of Asahara and other former movement activists. But Kenji is critical of such a point of view.

"In that first winter, when it was a life-or-death situation, I can understand how camps where there was discrimination by rank must have been terrible. But that wasn't when they began their anti-militarism struggle, was it? It would have been great if they had organized the struggle when it was really needed—but for the most part, it began the following year when living conditions had eased a bit, and at the instigation of the Soviets.

"I can't trust what those guys have written in order to justify themselves. Asahara claims he sent a letter to the Nihon shimbun that first winter, but there is no way an ordinary prisoner in the camps could have posted a letter. It's an unbelievable story, unless he approached a Soviet political commissar and got him to deliver the letter to the editors. And that would have been possible only for someone with special connections."

In fact, the democratic movement is said to have boosted a fair number of prisoners into the "privileged ranks," which up to that point had included the officers, who were exempted from labor by the Hague Convention, and others with special skills (carpenters, barbers, performers, etc.), who received special consideration in food rations or did not have to engage in outdoor work—factors that at times could mean the difference between life and death. Some prisoners seem to

---

* Asahara Seiki, "Dema, chūshō ni kōshite," Chūō kōron 70:11 (October 1956), pp. 160–70.

have seen participation in the movement as a vehicle to secure indoor work and more food.

Internee memoirs give differing accounts depending on the author's own position. Those critical of the democratic movement portray the activists as enjoying special privileges and lording it over the other prisoners. Memoirs by participants, while acknowledging that some joined cynically with an eye toward gaining privileges, relate how their eyes were opened by new knowledge, firing their passionate engagement in the movement. There is probably truth on both sides.

Even so, the majority of memoirs are critical of the democratic movement. And even memoirs by participants frequently mention time indoors engaged in cultural activities, editorial work, and so forth, as well as time spent in schools the Soviets established to train activists for the movement. It is not difficult to imagine how this fostered envy and resentment in prisoners—the majority—who were forced to labor outdoors in the bitter cold.

At any rate, as we shall see a bit later, the democratic movement among the prisoners tended to run out of control, exceeding even the intentions of the Soviets. Both memoirs for and against the movement tend to agree on this point. Kenji's recollections of it should be read in this light.

As mentioned earlier, Kenji's camp had already experienced a degree of democratization. Thus the democratic movement there contained no element of spontaneous anti-militaristic struggle, and was more or less entirely initiated by the Soviets. Based on Kenji's recollections and a chronology compiled by the Chita-kai—a post-repatriation organization of camp veterans—the movement developed as follows.*

First, in October 1946, a Soviet major named Ivanov began coming to the camp almost daily to call for the formation of a chapter of "Friends of the *Nihon Shimbun*," a reading circle also established in many other camps. Three prisoners responded to this appeal: Nishida, Kurata, and Yoshikawa. All three were enlisted men. Nishida, a forty-something Manchurian colonist originally from Osaka, did administrative work and had served along with Captain Kumabe as an officer of the Isoji-kai prisoners' group mentioned earlier. Back in Japan

---

* "Hokuryō kara Maizuru made."

117

Kurata had been imprisoned in the March 15 Incident of 1928, a government crackdown on socialists and communists. Yoshikawa was an intellectual—he had been an assistant professor at a university in Japan. The Soviet strategy then, it is said, was to center the democratic movement around members of the intelligentsia.

"By October it was already cold. Nishida-san had been assigned to indoor work from the start, so he had it fairly easy. I don't know by what channels Kurata and Yoshikawa came to participate, but it gave them a chance to work inside. And that could be a matter of life or death."

Slightly earlier, around the end of summer 1946, the battalion's top staff including Captain Kumabe had been transferred to another camp. Of course there was no farewell party. "At some point they just disappeared."

"It seems that they were shipped off one day when we were out at work. Even when we got back, we didn't realize at first what had happened. It was like, 'Oh, now that you mention it, I haven't seen them.' Later, when there were other transfers, it was the same thing."

In November, a Japanese activist in the democratic movement named Tsuchita arrived as the "commander" of the camp prisoners, and the remaining officers were put to work alongside the enlisted men. To do so was in violation of the Hague Convention, which did, however, stipulate that officers could engage in light labor if they requested it. The result was that many officers worked, at least nominally, as volunteers.

In any case, the officers and men of the Imperial Japanese Army were essentially ignorant of international treaties and conventions. Kenji himself had thought the preferential treatment given to the officers to be unfair. In this environment, it appears that at least some of the younger officers actually did "volunteer" for labor duty, as they felt guilty for being idle when the ordinary soldiers were being forced to do heavy labor.

In 1947, the internal order of the camp changed significantly. As a first step toward "democratization," in January the military nomenclature of battalions, companies, platoons, and so on was abandoned in favor of "work teams," "subteams," and the like. Nishida was named team leader.

Almost all of the officers had been transferred out of the camp by about the middle of 1947. They were replaced by movement activists of worker or farmer background brought in from elsewhere over the summer and autumn. Top-level policy for the democratic movement had shifted: instead of intellectuals and younger officers, leadership positions were now being allotted to soldiers of more politically correct origin.

Perhaps as a result, Kurata (the former communist) and Yoshikawa (the former assistant professor), who along with Nishida had initiated the democratic movement in Kenji's camp in the autumn of 1946, fell from favor in the early summer of 1947 and were returned to outdoor labor. Tsuchita, the activist "commander," was transferred to another camp.

In the autumn of 1947, selected individuals from the camp began to be sent off to school for training as activists. One enlisted man, a farmer from Fukushima, was sent to a school for the Chita region, returning three months later. But according to Kenji, "He was too honest to be much use as an agitator. And since he couldn't cut it as a 'fighter,' he just sort of dropped out of sight after a while."

It was not only officers who were transferred. In April 1947, a mass transfer of sixty-six men arrived at the camp. Because they were all outfitted in *manfuku* ("Manchurian dress," the Japanese term for black cold-weather clothing common in northeast China) that had been commandeered by the Soviets, Kenji and the other prisoners nicknamed this new group "the crows."

"Transfers became more frequent, and I would say that by the time I went home in August 1948 only about a quarter of the original group of 500 POWs was left in the camp."

The frequent transfers both into and out of the camp produced a change in atmosphere. "In the group I came with from Beiling there were a lot of settlers who already knew each other before being drafted. And since we'd been through a lot together, there was a certain sense of reassurance about one another, if not solidarity. But with the new guys coming in, this was absent."

The intensification of the movement in this climate bred mutual distrust and paranoia. "From the summer of 1947 on, you really had to watch what you said, for fear of letting something slip that would lead you to be branded a reactionary. Before, you could skip the reading circles and such if you came back from work and felt too tired to bother. But not anymore. The frequent transfers prevented us from

119

developing any solidarity. Later when I read books like Solzhenitsyn's *Gulag Archipelago* I realized this was a standard administrative tactic, not just in the POW camps, but in the camps for Soviet citizens as well."

At some point the intellectual-led "Friends of the *Nihon Shimbun*" was dissolved. From 1948, "anti-fascist committees" began to be formed in accordance with policies laid down by the Soviet Ministry of Internal Affairs in December 1947. Concurrently, activists recently installed in the camp spearheaded the removal and replacement of the Japanese in leadership and administrative positions.

"What really surprised us at that time was the removal of Kawamura-san, the chief of the mess. An NCO in his late twenties, he was a Hawaii-born Japanese-American who had served as an interpreter at a camp in Fengtian for POWs of the Japanese army. He was widely seen as a man of integrity who was honest, fair, and able to keep private concerns separate from official duties. He'd been appointed mess officer for two years running. There were lots of perks associated with that position, and although everyone said only an honest guy like Kawamura was fit for the job, he was reassigned to general labor.

"Not only was Kawamura-san honest, but his command of English had allowed him to master Russian quickly. So he could negotiate with the Soviets about supplies, working on our behalf to prevent us from getting ripped off. But he was an American Nisei, and with the Cold War getting underway maybe the Soviet commissars had their eyes on him. Everyone was shocked when he was dismissed, but no one had the courage to protest. Going up against the activists would be equated with resistance to the Soviet Union, and people were afraid they would never make it home again."

4

The daily routine had been reveille at 6:00, breakfast, roll call at 7:30, work, lunch at noon at the worksite, end of workday at 5:00, dinner at 6:00, free time. However, from the latter half of 1947, the period from dinner until 10:00 pm was turned over to "exposure of reactionaries," a kind of kangaroo court. By 1948 sessions would begin right with morning reveille and even encroach into the noon lunch break.

The prisoners would sit in groups of ten or so, find some grounds for accusing one or another of their group of being reactionaries, and censure them with increasing ferocity. This would go on for two or three hours after dinner, until finally the leaders declared, "Today we have fought a successful struggle against reactionaries," and everyone would conclude by singing a revolutionary anthem.

In Kenji's estimation, "The exposure of reactionaries resembled the hazing of first-year soldiers in the Imperial Japanese Army. In the old barracks units, after the evening meal they would find some suitable pretext—you hadn't cleaned your rifle properly, you'd been disrespectful—to say that you had a 'bad attitude' and beat you or force you to apologize. The so-called democratic movement was the same thing all over again.

"Anything could be used as a pretext. One of the songs we had to sing was 'The Communist Marseillaise.'* The activists were calling it 'The Communist Party Marseillaise,' and one time a guy who had graduated from the Tokyo University of Foreign Studies murmured that it wasn't the 'Marseillaise' of the party, but the 'Marseillaise' of people who are communists. This got him exposed and condemned as a reactionary, even though I doubt he intended to be critical of the activists or had any other deep motive for saying what he did." Memoirs of the Siberian internment tell of speeches or lectures given by activists of worker or peasant origin who mangled terms like "the Tokugawa shogunate" or "historical materialism" because they were only semiliterate.† Anyone who pointed out such errors ran the risk of being labeled a reactionary.

In accounts from other prison camps, many of those "exposed" as reactionaries had attracted resentment previously as members of privileged elites within the Japanese empire: officers, military police, special services units, the Manchukuo national police. In Kenji's camp this did not seem to be the case, probably because the camp had had a mixed composition from the beginning, and because of the process of democratization that had taken place even before the movement got underway. Even so, "Since I had been at Fuji Telecommunications, I

---

* The Japanese title of "The Workers' Marseillaise," the Russian revolutionary anthem set to the melody of "La Marseillaise."
† Wakatsuki, *Shiberia horyo shūyōjo*, p. 179.

could have been exposed as a reactionary who had worked in military manufacturing. Any excuse would do."

In other camps sometimes the "exposure of reactionaries" took place en masse in the mess hall, or suspects were tied to pillars and subjected to group assaults that left them close to death. This type of corporal punishment did not occur in Kenji's camp, but the psychological suffering was intense.

"The 'democratic movement' did not involve beatings, but it was harder to take psychologically than the physical abuse in the Japanese army. In the barracks units the soldiers would beat the new recruits, but after they hit you, it was over, and the new recruits had nothing to fear from each other. But with the democratic movement, once you were branded a reactionary, the label followed you everywhere in your daily life. And you never knew when or by whom you might be accused. There was no way of telling who was an activist.

"In the army, both the guys dealing out the punishment and the ones receiving it actually knew it was stupid. But in Siberia, if you were blacklisted as a reactionary you might never be able to go home, so you had to either totally keep your mouth shut or make a big show of agreement. I was not particularly enthusiastic, and just shouted along with the rest of the crowd—but if you didn't participate at all you'd become a reactionary.

"The guys who'd been together since Beiling still tended to go easy on each other. But as more transfers took place, this ended. Around April 1947, when everybody in the camp still knew each other, if you went to work at the bread factory it was a matter of course to steal some bread to bring back and share with the others, but by the end of the year the atmosphere had grown to be like, 'Who are the reactionaries stealing the resources of the Soviet Union, homeland of the workers?'"

The activities of the democratic groups seemed almost totally meaningless. In mid-1947, the prisoners were forced to take turns making what were called "street-corner speeches"—rehearsals for agitation among workers and farmers that they were expected to carry out upon returning to Japan.

"If you didn't participate you'd be labeled a reactionary, so I made a speech that was just a string of clichés, nothing eloquent, of course. I just followed the form they wanted, all the while thinking there was no way I would be doing this when I got back to Japan."

On May Day 1948, the prisoners were ordered to stage a march—within the confines of the camp—demonstrating against capitalism and imperialism.

"It was like kids playing soldier. One young activist cut across the line. The demonstrators made way for him, in deference to a great leader. But then one of the older activists reprimanded them, saying they should never let anyone cut across a demonstration. Nobody knew—or had any basis for judging—which of them to please, and it threw the whole thing into complete confusion."

In the winter of 1947, Kenji came dangerously close to being accused as a reactionary. In his sleep he muttered, "This democratic movement stuff is limited to Siberia," and was overheard by one of the rank-and-file activists in his democratic group. The next day, the activist waved him over, and when they were alone, warned him, "It's all right because I'm the only one who heard what you said, but you've got to watch it. You need to work on a more positive attitude."

Kenji recalls, "This guy was an ordinary factory worker from Tokyo who sincerely believed in Marxism on the basis of his own experience. Some of the activists from worker or peasant backgrounds said they now finally understood why they had been so poor despite working so hard all the time. He was one of them, and we had a normal human relationship with each other, so I had a lucky break. He could have won points for exposing me as a reactionary, but chose not to. I was grateful, and terrified when I thought of what might have happened if it had been one of the more hard-nosed activists.

"The people who got actively involved in the democratic movement fell into several types. First of all were simple, straightforward guys from farmer or worker backgrounds who accepted Marxism without question because they honestly believed that it gave them a way of understanding their situation. A lot of them were young. I've also read that there were many of this type among the younger officers and the settlers who had come out of the Japanese youth brigades for the colonization of Manchuria and Mongolia.

"Among the pamphlets I read in the camp, one on imperialism left an impression. I learned a lot of new terms—'financial oligarchy,' 'export of capital,' 'partitioning of the globe'—and felt like I'd gained a different perspective on the world. I think it had been written by an intellectual prisoner who'd been studying Marxism since before the war. The lectures by the activists were totally boring, and though I pretended to listen, I didn't pay much attention. But occasionally there was something to learn, and I imagine there were some people who participated sincerely because of that.

"Still, many were not like that. Activists were excused from labor duty, and there were lots of other perks. Once they got people under their sway into the mess team, they could even control the food supply. And they might be sent outside the camp to a training school, which was like a dream for your ordinary prisoner. So there were guys with an eye to the main chance who used the democratic movement to advance themselves. Then there were the guys who were simply bullies. So there were a lot of completely different types. And one's true face comes out in such circumstances."

To what extent were the Soviets involved in the movement? While they did indeed initiate it, it would appear that overadaptation on the part of the Japanese prisoners had some role in the way it played out. The Soviets are said to have prohibited corporal punishment in the movement, and to have been concerned at excesses impairing the efficiency of the work teams.

"As far as my camp was concerned, I think the Soviets took a hands-off attitude toward the movement. When the exposure of reactionaries went on too late at night they would step in to halt it, saying it would interfere with the next day's work. In any case, I don't think the camp administration was at all interested in it, although I don't know about the political commissars.

"In the spring of 1948, when the activists revived the wall newspaper, there was a bit of a tussle between them and the camp authorities. The paper carried a cartoon showing a prisoner getting caught trying to smuggle bread from his work site into the camp in his cap. A reactionary traitor to the homeland of the workers, in other words. But the cartoon also showed a Soviet army officer standing in the background, and Commandant Akhmadullin found this problematic. The activists who had created the cartoon pushed back, arguing, 'We cleared it in advance with Hakamada-san' [Hakamada Mutsuo, a leading prisoner-activist in the Chita region]. This infuriated Akhmadullin, who snapped, 'Kto hozjain?' [Who is in charge here?]"

At least in Kenji's camp, the idea that participation in the movement would influence one's chances for repatriation turned out to be unfounded. When repatriation commenced in April 1948, individuals who had been labeled as reactionaries were among those selected to go home.

"Once repatriation began, everyone started to realize that participation didn't seem to make any difference. But we remained paranoid and hedged our bets, and continued as before with the democratic movement and the exposure of reactionaries.

"Nobody ever said anything like that to me, but I imagine that sometimes if the Soviets didn't like someone's work attitude they might have threatened, 'Keep that up and we're not sending you home to Japan.' For them it would just be a way to spur us on, but for us it would be truly terrifying. The activists took advantage of this fear, and borrowed the authority of the Soviets to lord it over everyone.

"Men who had been activists never came to meetings of the Chitakai camp veterans' organization after we got back. Nor did I ever hear of any of them participating in the communist movement in Japan. They had done terrible things. I think it's because they were ashamed of what they had done that after they returned home some of them tried to present it as exposure of class discrimination or a struggle against militarism."

As noted earlier, the situation was different in each camp, and it is impossible to generalize from a single case. For example, one often reads in memoirs from other camps that prisoners suffered because food rations were linked to work quotas. In Kenji's camp this system was introduced at the beginning of 1947, but did not function very well and was abandoned after a month or so.

"With some jobs like logging, the work load could be accurately measured by number or volume, but there really wasn't any systematic way to measure quotas for many other tasks. And skilled tradesmen like carpenters or electricians were able to achieve ridiculously high quotas. Trying to reflect this in how much food each of us was given became so unfair that everyone resisted, especially seeing as it was a life-and-death matter. The mess crew were all our people, so when the Soviet guards were around they'd make a show of serving out bonus food for exceeding work quotas, but then take it back when they left. In my camp, the Soviets as well put on a show of enforcing the policy since it had come down from above, but I don't think their hearts were in it."

Thus, too, the degree to which participation in the democratic movement influenced selection for repatriation remains unclear. It is said that in some prison camps the activists had a hand in drawing up the repatriation rosters, but details remain murky. One thing upon which all memoirs of internment agree, however, is that the movement among the Japanese prisoners exceeded even the intentions of the Soviets.

Also in 1947, around November, a single prisoner called Kurehashi Shūgō was transferred into Twenty-Fourth District Camp No. 2. He was rumored to be a former Japanese army soldier of Korean origin who spoke excellent Russian. Kenji would see him from time to time—never imagining that he would encounter him again a half century later.

5

Returning home was the most fervent hope of the Japanese POWs. In autumn 1947 the prisoners in Kenji's camp got their first concrete confirmation that repatriation had begun, in the form of an article in the *Nihon shimbun*. About the same time, the prisoners were permitted to send postcards to Japan, and in the latter half of the year, replies began to be delivered. These letters from home were virtually the sole source of information, aside from the propagandistic *Nihon shimbun*, that the prisoners had.

One prisoner was startled to learn from the address on a reply postcard that one of Tokyo's wards had been renamed. Another was puzzled by a letter from home reporting that everyone was busy with preparations for the summer festival—which contradicted articles in the *Nihon shimbun* depicting the Japanese people as groaning under the tyranny of American imperialism. The prisoners also learned that the majority of veterans from their hometowns who had been in the theaters of the Pacific, Southeast Asia, and China had already returned home.

Kenji sent postcards to Ishichi and Yūji a couple of times but received no response. The post was censored; letters in envelopes were forbidden and only text in katakana allowed so they could be easily read by Soviet censors. Only about half of these communications are thought to have gotten through. Some memoirs of the period relate that because of censorship and the democratic movement, about the only message one could write was something along the lines of "Dear Mother, I hope this finds you well. I am very well myself, and thanks to the generous concern of Marshal Stalin, I lack for nothing in my daily life.'"[*]

Kenji says, "I think I only wrote this sort of formulaic stuff myself. Part of it was the atmosphere of the camp, but even before, in the army, it was no different." From the time they had been inducted into the Imperial Japanese Army, every letter Kenji and his fellow soldiers had written was censored, and they had effectively lost the habit of writing freely.

"People receiving this sort of letter could guess what was going on. So when they replied, they also wrote only what they thought would make it past the censors. In March 1945 when I was still in the army I received a postcard from an old school friend that read, 'Recently carrier planes have been appearing in the skies over Tokyo.' He couldn't say straight out that there were air raids by American forces, so he put it that way. Everybody was used to doing stuff like that."

In the summer of 1947, Kenji was reassigned to the mess crew. He had spent time on the crew doing kitchen cleanup from January to March that year, when he and several others determined by the Soviet camp medics to be in weakened condition were assigned to indoor work to prevent the kind of deaths suffered by prisoners during the first winter.

But this time the reason was different. "I think it was because I was apolitical and had a reputation with my subteam leader and others as a diligent and conscientious worker." Mess crew work was easier than working outdoors, with better opportunities for food than the other prisoners, so it was difficult to get assigned to it.

The mess crew ran a twenty-four-hour schedule in two shifts. If you were on the night shift making breakfast, you would sleep the following day. The meals were one-pot affairs—after rinsing, grains were cooked over a fire in a large covered cauldron and then stewed together a bit longer with seasoned meat and vegetables. Bread for the noon meal would be sliced and set out to be distributed along with breakfast. In the latter half of 1947, soup and a side dish were added to dinner. One couldn't be especially creative in the kitchen: the materials were too limited and there were too many men to be fed.

---

* Wakatsuki, *Shiberia horyo shūyōjo*, p. 69.

127

In April 1948, the first group from the camp was selected for repatriation. The second group departed in June. Wearied by the increasing momentum of the democratic movement, Kenji waited anxiously to be chosen.

"About a hundred men were chosen for the second group. A Soviet and a Japanese representative read out the names of those to be repatriated in the camp courtyard, confirmed their identity, and formed them into groups. I'd been up all night working the mess crew night shift and had just eaten breakfast when someone mistakenly said to me, 'You're on the list,' so I went outside and stood in line. But my name was never called. I was devastated. I recall getting angry at one of the mess crew guys who teased, 'You must have dreamed it.' I got quite depressed, stopped caring about my work, and got yelled at by the crew chief. Not long after that I was relieved of my mess hall duties and reassigned to general labor."

Toward the end of July 1948, a third group was selected for repatriation. On the day the roster was to be announced, all the prisoners gathered in the yard and waited for the names to be called.

"My name was called by the Soviet officer. When I realized I was going home, I was overcome by joy. No one was jumping up and down, out of consideration for the guys who would be left behind, but they all must have been pretty happy. I have scarcely any memories of what happened after that. I was too happy to care."

As a result of all the transfers, not many men were left who had been in the camp from the beginning, so Kenji had few he could speak with openly, and no one asked him to take any messages back to Japan. Preparation for departure was simple. Taking Soviet currency out of the country was prohibited, and the prisoners had almost no possessions anyway.

"It didn't occur to me to take home some sort of souvenir of the Soviet Union. But my mess kit and the sewing kit Grandma had given me were essential for survival, so I didn't let go of them until I got to my father's home in Niigata."

As noted earlier, the degree of one's participation in the democratic movement does not seem to have been a determining factor in the selection of prisoners to be repatriated. However, the two Japanese-Americans—Iizuka and Kawamura, the former mess captain—were passed over all three times. The other prisoners sensed that they were being held back out of suspicion that they would cooperate with the American military when they returned to Japan.

The day of departure came several days after the selection was announced. When the prisoners formed up to leave, the Soviet staff saw them off at the camp gate.

"I think they felt good about seeing the Japanese they had been living with all this time happily returning home from Siberia. Praying Mantis had been transferred out of the camp. Akhmadullin was still commandant, but he happened not to be there that day. Sestakov had been transferred once before returning again at the beginning of 1948, but I heard a rumor just before we left that he had been arrested on some charge or another. His wife stood at the camp gate to see us off, though."

After leaving the camp they were, as before, made to wait for about two days in the marshaling yard at Chita due to the railroad timetable. Meanwhile orders came down from somewhere or other to decorate their train for the trip home. So the prisoners found a large board, painted a slogan like "Long Live the Friendship of the Soviet Union and the Japanese People!" on it, and fastened it to the side of one of the freight cars.

The train made good progress to the port of Nakhodka on the Sea of Japan. On the way, the prisoners pledged allegiance to the Communist Party and sang revolutionary songs like "The Internationale," "The Red Flag," "The Workers' Marseillaise," and "Bravely, Comrades, Let's March." They also sang a song written by prisoner-activist Hakamada Mutsuo with lyrics that included the line "Rise up, farmers and workers, against Hirohito who enslaved you . . ."

"We all just wanted to get safely home. I didn't seriously think that I would be kept back if I didn't sing revolutionary songs, but if it was going to get me home I would sing and cheer and do whatever they wanted."

Upon reaching Nakhodka, the prisoners were shifted to three different camps in brief succession as they waited their turn to leave. At the final camp they went through exit processing and headed for the harbor, where they found the prisoners from the second repatriation group working on the docks as longshoremen. Among them were Lieutenant Sahashi, who had pretended to be an enlisted man, and the first-year soldier with whom Kenji had teamed during his stint as a logger. When asked what had happened, they said that they had been held back and ordered to work. And in fact they were not released from labor in Nakhodka until the following June.

Kenji and the other members of the third group boarded the Japanese repatriation ship without further incident. "When I saw the crew my first thought was, 'Japanese are really small.' We'd been so long in Siberia where everyone except the prisoners was so big that it seemed strange to see ordinary people who were so small."

He did not weep at seeing the Rising Sun flag flying on the boat, or experience any real upsurge of emotion.

"After the end of the war in 1945 I'd used my Rising Sun flag as a carryall. I hadn't had room for anything other than survival. Besides, ever since we'd been told we were going home, we'd been making our way closer bit by bit, so I don't recall suddenly experiencing any strong emotion upon seeing the ship. Returning home had been such a dream for so long that it was hard to respond to it actually happening. I think that was true for all of us, not just me. Reality is different from the movies or novels."

Even after boarding the ship, the prisoners had difficulty adjusting to their changed conditions. Soviet propaganda had told them that they were unable to return home because the Japanese government did not send ships to bring them back.

"On the ship the crew members told us that wasn't true, but we all had a hard time believing them. Some guys said what the crew were saying was a pack of lies.

"But that was the extent of our indoctrination. The people who were held over until the following year sometimes fought with the crew members or engaged in 'class struggle' with them. There was even an instance [the so-called Kyoto Incident of 4 July 1949] in which a group of returnees transported by special train from Maizuru [the Japanese port where the repatriation ships landed] clashed with police upon arrival at Kyoto Station. I read news of things like this with a heavy heart. If the returnees could just be given a little time back in Japan, they'd get over their indoctrination and everything would be fine, so I wished the Japanese people could welcome them back with a bit more patience."

After two days aboard ship, Kenji's group arrived at Maizuru on 20 August 1948. In the harbor, the masts and prows of ships that had been sunk during the war protruded dismally from the surface of the water. "I was happy to be seeing Japan again, but the landscape seemed like a miniature. In contrast to the vast landscape of Siberia, it felt so tiny."

They spent about four days in a processing center at Maizuru. There was a US army interrogation by a Japanese-American Nisei officer, who showed Kenji an aerial reconnaissance map of Chita and asked him to locate his camp and provide information about Soviet military facilities in the area. Kenji told him what he could remember.

Upon release from Maizuru, each man was given a free ticket to his hometown and a lump-sum payment of several thousand yen from the Japanese government for the wages due him as a soldier. But the precipitous postwar inflation had reduced its value to about a hundredth of what it would have been before the war.

Kenji took the train from Maizuru to Kyoto and then transferred to another line for Niigata. He still held fast to his mess kit, his "lifeline" in Siberia. After four years away from Japan he felt disoriented, but the station attendants and student volunteers of the Repatriation Assistance Association helped him find his way. The landscape passing by outside the train window still looked tiny to him.

He finally transferred to a local line, arriving at Ogikawa Station. There, he was met by his father and his sister Hideko, the youngest child, who had been raised in Saroma after their mother's death by Yūji and his new wife. But it was not an emotional reunion, perhaps because they had never really lived together as a family.

"I had parted from my father and sister when I was sent to Tokyo from Saroma at the age of six. I saw my father occasionally when he came to Tokyo, but I'd met my little sister and my stepmother, my father's new wife, only once, when I visited Saroma in 1939 while in secondary school. We had nothing in common, and none of us knew how to handle the situation. I think it would have been different if I had gone back to Grandpa and Grandma and the house in Nakano, but I no longer had any home to return to."

So there was no dramatic and tearful reunion. They walked about thirty minutes to reach his father's village, but Kenji had only been there once prior to his induction into the army, and he knew none of the villagers they passed on the way.

At the house they sat down to dinner. "It was a totally ordinary meal. That was a disappointment, too. It was a country village, so I hadn't expected any great feast, but there was nothing special at all about what was put in front of me. I thought to myself, 'So this is the homecoming I dreamed of for so long.'" After a fleeting moment of happiness at returning to Japan, Kenji was plunged into the difficult realities of postwar life.

Chapter 5

A Hardscrabble Life

In August 1948, Kenji finally returned from the war to a muted reception at his father's home in Niigata. Now twenty-three years old, he was soon plunged into an uncertain life drifting from one job to another in defeated Japan.

1956. Kenji is dressed in his best suit for this photo commemorating his release from the tuberculosis sanatorium.

1

Kenji's father had grown up in Niigata Prefecture in the Warino district of the village of Ryōkawa, located on the Echigo Plain in Nakakanbara-gun; the village was absorbed by the city of Niigata in 1957. Warino lay along the Koagano Canal connecting the Shinano and Agano rivers. The nearest rail station, Ogikawa on the Shin'etsu Main Line, was about a thirty-minute walk, crossing over the canal on a railway bridge. If there was an oncoming train, pedestrians would wait patiently on either side of the steel bridge to let it pass.

Yūji had left Warino for Hokkaido in 1901, not returning until 1942. The house he built there was assembled from the pieces of his house in Hokkaido, dismantled and shipped to Niigata. It was a small, single-story affair with little more than a bedroom, a living room, and a kitchen. The walls were roughly plastered with earth mixed with straw. One could tell at a glance that he was poor.

The evening meal on the day of Kenji's arrival was totally ordinary, with no feeling of special welcome or hospitality. But food was meager in rural Japan in those days. And though Yūji had saved up sufficient funds in Hokkaido to envision a comfortable retirement in Niigata, the terrible wartime and postwar inflation was daily eating away at his savings. Kenji didn't have the heart to ask his father about his economic situation.

"Meals in Warino rarely included any meat. Traveling vendors would come through with fish, but they stopped only at rich people's houses, so it was pretty rare for us to eat fish, either. Every day it was pickles and miso soup and vegetables and rice—and every once in a while, dried fish. It was a farming village, so even right after the war nobody starved, but it seemed worse to me in some ways than my life in Siberia, where the food, at least, had gotten better in the last year or so. In Siberia I'd dreamed of eating sweet red-bean soup with rice cakes, but I couldn't bring myself to say that to my father. Maybe if it had been Grandma and Grandpa, I would have."

Nearby was the house of the main branch of the Oguma family, which had passed to Yūji's younger sister—Kenji's aunt—who in turn had retired the headship in favor of her eldest son. They were not very close to Yūji; after all, he had left for Hokkaido at the age of eighteen and not returned home until he was sixty. Kenji's aunt would sometimes slip food or other essentials to Yūji when she could escape the notice of her daughter-in-law, but otherwise there was no assistance.

When Kenji returned to Japan, Yūji was already sixty-five. After resigning from the producers' cooperative in Hokkaido and moving back to Niigata, he had been pressed by wartime inflation to begin a business wholesaling medicinal herbs from Hokkaido to Tsumura Juntendō (the present-day Tsumura & Co.), a chain of pharmacies specializing in traditional medicine. But by the time the war was over, so was this line of work.

Without a job, Yūji began operating a small lending library out of his home, specializing in comic books for neighborhood children.

Niigata Prefecture

From paper recyclers who bought up used comics in four-kilogram lots, he would procure copies for around five yen each and rent them to kids at two yen a time, for some profit. But this was no more than a minor side business, and never brought in any significant money.

Realizing how hard life had become for Yūji, Kenji immediately offered to find work. Before the end of the month, through the good offices of a neighborhood carpenter, he was hired as an apprentice foreman for a contractor in Niitsu. It was a small shop, with about five men in all, including the owner.

"I commuted to work in Niitsu with the carpenter who had given me the introduction. We walked as far as Ogikawa Station over the railway bridge—quite a distance, and no buses. When I complained to my father about how far it was, he just said, 'Everyone around here walks it.' I thought to myself that these country folks were a tough lot, but actually very few of them were commuters, and most people stuck pretty close to the village in their daily lives. They farmed, or worked in the local government office, or were barbers, or what have you."

This was a period of decline in the urban population in Japan. According to government statistics, before the war the percentage of the population living in urban areas had increased rapidly from 24 percent in 1930 to 33 percent in 1935 and 38 percent in 1940. But by 1947, this figure had fallen once again to 33 percent. Around the time Kenji had first moved to Tokyo in 1932, rural areas were suffering from the growth of a national market economy and the worldwide economic depression. The attendant migration of population to the cities was sustained over the next years by the rapid development of heavy and chemical industry in the wartime mobilization. But the air raids then destroyed Japan's industrial base, and this, together with the evacuation of urban residents to the countryside and the food shortages immediately after the defeat, combined to bring urban populations back down again to about the levels of 1935.

In addition, some 6,880,000 Japanese—about 3,670,000 military personnel and auxiliaries and 3,210,000 colonists, plus other civilians—returned from overseas after the war, a number representing more than 9 percent of the total Japanese population at the time. This influx could not be absorbed by the bombed-out cities, and flowed into the countryside. Japanese war deaths, meanwhile, totaled approximately

3.1 million (of which about 800,000 were civilians), or about 4 percent of the total population.

Such was the situation when Kenji returned to Japan in 1948. Rural areas did not have the industrial base to absorb the influx of evacuees and refugees from the cities. In Warino, there was little work available offering a steady income. This surplus working population, along with the baby boom generation who began to be born at this time, would flow back into the cities from the 1950s onward and form the labor pool that supported Japan's decades of high economic growth. But that was all still in the future. Meanwhile, Kenji had to make a living.

Kenji was twenty-three. He'd done construction work in Siberia, but had no experience whatsoever as a foreman; despite his new job as "apprentice foreman," making the rounds of the work site was about all he could do. Then, after about a week, a letter came from his grandfather Ishichi in Okayama, to whom Kenji had written shortly after arriving in Niigata informing him of his return to Japan.

"I'd been away from Japan for so long that I was still pretty out of it, but now I suddenly realized I wanted to see Grandpa and Grandma. And I wanted them to see me. I decided to go right away."

He told his boss about the letter, and left immediately for Okayama. It was a small company, "without any fancy policies about extended leave and so forth," so this meant he was quitting his job. And naturally enough, he received no pay for his week or so as an apprentice.

Having just returned from Siberia, Kenji had no money. The few thousand yen he had received upon repatriation had been given to Yūji for safekeeping as soon as he arrived, but it was not enough for the trip to Okayama. So in the end, Yūji helped out with the travel expenses. "My father understood my relationship with my grandparents, and probably realized that I might end up staying with them for good, but he was kind enough to let me go anyway."

It took Kenji an entire day and night of train travel, from Ogikawa via Kyoto, to arrive at Ishichi's place in Okayama. Past Kyoto, vast swaths of Osaka and Kobe were still burned-out ruins from air raids. Prior to this the only cities Kenji had seen since his return had been Niigata and Kyoto, neither of which had been bombed, so this was Kenji's first exposure to such devastation.

"The Osaka-Kobe industrial belt was totally destroyed, with nothing left but a mass of twisted steel framing, and I thought wow, this is terrible. Still, I'd already read in the *Nihon shimbun* in Siberia that Japan's cities had been bombed into ashes. So really my main response to it was, well, I guess that's what happens in a war."

After getting off at Seto Station on the San'yō Main Line and walking for another two hours, Kenji finally made it to the Yoshida household, his grandmother Kochiyo's childhood home. He'd been there once before with Kochiyo, in 1940, and memories of that time helped him find his way.

Ishichi and Kochiyo were both from Okayama originally, and when they first evacuated back from Tokyo they had stayed with Ishichi's family. But the head of the household, Ishichi's nephew, was having a hard time of it financially, so they moved in with Kochiyo's family. The government had ordered mandatory evacuation from urban areas, but left the evacuees completely on their own in finding places to live.

The Yoshida home was a fair-sized farmhouse, but it was now crammed with three families—a total of ten people in all. There was the eldest son (Kochiyo's elder brother), up from Kyoto; Kochiyo's younger sister and her daughter, who were living in a shed on the property; the eldest son's daughter, a widow who had fled from Yokohama with her four children when the bombing began; and Ishichi and Kochiyo, who lived behind the main house in an old plaster storehouse with an interior about the size of an eight-mat room.

Ishichi and Kochiyo, who had not seen Kenji for four years, greeted him warmly. After arriving in early September, Kenji spent about a month living with them in their storehouse. They still fondly called him "Ken," and he felt much more at home there than in Niigata. But life was hard. In the storehouse were the small dining cabinet and family Buddhist altar Kenji remembered from the house in Nakano, but not much else. These few furnishings were all that they had been able to transport from Tokyo with the allotment given them by the government at the time of their evacuation after the great air raids of March 1945.

Ishichi was seventy-two, Kochiyo seventy-one. And Ishichi was paralyzed on one side as a result of his stroke. Inflation was daily eating away at their paltry savings, and they could not expect any financial support from Yūji. They couldn't afford to replace their old footwear when it wore out—instead, Kenji helped Ishichi beat straw to soften and weave sandals from it.

Food was rice and vegetables, occasionally with other condiments. The farmhouse kitchen had a wood-fired stove. There was no gas or running water. There was electric lighting in both the main house and the storehouse, but aside from that there were no modern appliances. The bath was a *goemon-buro*, a large round tub filled with twenty or thirty buckets of water carried in from an outside well and heated from underneath with a fire made from straw and collected leaves and twigs. Since eleven people including Kenji were using it, by the end the water was pretty dirty.

"Bureaucrats and high-ranking military men, even after Japan had lost the war, could sit back after the peace treaty was signed and collect their pensions. But the savings ordinary folks had put away when they were working were wiped out by the postwar inflation. I felt like the bunch who had started the stupid war, gotten so many people killed, and put my father and grandparents in such dire straits should take responsibility for what they had done."

In 1953, the year after the San Francisco Peace Treaty ended the Occupation and Japanese sovereignty was restored, military pensions—which had been suspended during the Occupation—began to be disbursed once more. The amount of the pensions was determined by rank and length of service, and high-ranking career officers might receive substantial amounts. But no pension at all was paid to conscripted enlisted men like Kenji, whose length of service was deemed to be too brief. (For further details, see chapter 9.)

Kochiyo was upset at her inability to get in touch with her second daughter, Midori. Her first daughter, Yoshie (Kenji's mother), was already dead of tuberculosis, so Midori was her only living child. In the early 1930s, Midori had emigrated to Brazil with her husband and two children. Around the time of the 1936 Berlin Olympics, she had sent a letter saying that they intended to visit Tokyo for the Olympics scheduled in 1940. But Tokyo forfeited the Olympics due to the outbreak of the war, which also interrupted further communication. After the war was over, no reply came to numerous letters sent to Brazil.

"Before the war I remember using the Latin alphabet I had just learned at Waseda Jitsugyō to help Grandpa address a letter to Midori: Assaí /

Santa Catarina / Paraná / Brasil. Paraná was the state; Santa Catarina was a rail line, and Assaí was the name of a town where a lot of Japanese immigrants had settled—I was told it comes from *asahi* [morning sun]."

The two sons of the Yoshida family were critical of Midori, saying, "How can she not reply to her parents' letters when they are in such a state?" The eldest son headed the Yoshida house, while the younger son had opened a store in the neighborhood selling and servicing radios and had done quite well for himself; radios were a luxury item at the time, and such a business had been a smart choice for a rural youth who lacked higher education but was clever at fixing things. This man's only son worked in the Okayama branch of the Bank of Japan, and Kenji visited him in the city, which was still in the process of rebuilding the damage suffered in the air raid of June 1945.

During the month or so he spent living with his grandparents, Kenji thought about his future. Whom should he live with—Ishichi and Kochiyo in Okayama, or Yūji in Niigata? For all of these elderly people, Kenji was the only able-bodied worker in the family. As mentioned earlier, Yūji seemed to have been worried that Kenji might end up staying in Okayama. Kenji himself was ambivalent about the decision, until an apparently casual remark by the normally taciturn Ishichi helped him make up his mind.

"Grandpa said, 'It's all right,' and I decided it was only right for me to return to Niigata. Grandpa and Grandma were at least living with relatives. But my father was on his own. And at the time there was also the expectation that even if they had never lived together, a child should care for his aging parent."

At the beginning of October, Kenji left Okayama, reluctantly bidding farewell to Ishichi and Kochiyo in front of their storehouse. It would prove to be the last time he ever saw Ishichi.

Yet, if he returned to Warino there would be little chance of decent work, so Kenji headed straight for Tokyo, where Fuji Telecommunications was obligated to make good on the promise it had made when he was drafted to preserve a position for him upon his return to Japan. The wages he would have made during his absence— albeit with no adjustment for the postwar inflation—had been sent each month to his father.

At the time, Tokyo was experiencing food shortages and the government wanted to limit the influx of population into the city, so that rice-rationing booklets would only be issued with evidence of employment there. Without a booklet, one would be forced to subsist on black-market rice at inflated prices. The rationing booklet was thus a de facto form of identity papers. If Kenji could be restored to his post at Fuji Telecommunications, he would be able to get a rationing booklet—or at least this was his hope when he boarded the San'yō Main Line for Tokyo.

After passing through the burned-out streetscapes left by the bombings of Kobe, Osaka, and Nagoya, he arrived in a Tokyo that was also still in ruins. He stayed at the home of a niece of Ishichi's to whom Ishichi had written in advance of Kenji's visit. It was a two-story townhouse in Nakano similar to the one in which Kenji had lived in Kōenji; they let Kenji stay in the room on the second floor. The niece's husband was an affable electrician who seemed to be doing pretty well for himself, given the demand produced by the post-war reconstruction of the city.

Kenji stayed with them for about two weeks. Though only distant relatives, they treated him quite well, even when he woke in the middle of the night and ate up all the sweet potatoes that had been steamed and left to cool—he'd been back from Siberia less than two months and could not shake the habit of eating anything and everything in sight, still fearful of going without.

The first thing Kenji did in Tokyo was go to have a look at the house in Nakano that he had lived in prior to his induction into the army. But the entire neighborhood had been bombed out.

"The cleanup had scarcely begun. It was still very raw. Anything at all that might be useful, like unburnt lumber, had already been scavenged, so that all you saw scattered about was worthless scrap. Even the big Nakano public market had been obliterated, leaving only a burned-out lot. I was overcome with emotion—my old home was completely gone.

"Even so, my barber from before the war had set up shop again in one of the sheds hastily constructed amid the ruins. It brought back memories of old times and somehow cheered me up. It occurred to me, as it had in Siberia, that folks like barbers and electricians, who possessed essential skills, were in a strong position."

Then Kenji went to see Kōenji, where he had lived while in elementary school. The neighborhood had been spared in the air raids and a number of familiar shops remained.

"When I visited the tailor shop next door to our old house, I was surprised to find that the daughter had grown up into a beautiful young woman. More than ten years had passed already since we'd left Kōenji."

Ishichi's niece was a pleasant woman a little past forty, but she and Kenji had their differences. One day she asked him what he thought about the emperor, and Kenji replied, "I think at this point he ought to abdicate." She became quite upset, and told him, "I wish you wouldn't say things like that."

Kenji comments, "I'd been in the army, so I naturally felt that the emperor, as the supreme commander who had issued the declaration of war, ought to take responsibility for the defeat. Everything seemed to have changed as a result of the surrender, and at the time a lot of people were arguing that he should abdicate. But older people felt differently. The phrase 'Siberian returnee' had begun to be used to refer to those who had been exposed to communist indoctrination and had come back as 'reds.' If you weren't careful what you said, some people might take it the wrong way and you could get in a lot of trouble.

"In the countryside, even after the war people would display a portrait of the emperor along with photos of their ancestors, and older folks maintained a simple reverence for him. Even so, people didn't fly the Rising Sun flag anymore on national holidays. Ordinary people were having a rough time just getting by, and didn't care much about such things one way or the other."

Kenji's feelings about the emperor were not especially rare among veterans. Younger soldiers and lower-ranking officers in particular had been thoroughly indoctrinated that it was shameful to be captured alive and that a captain should go down with his ship. For such men, it was only natural to feel contempt for Tōjō Hideki, who had botched his suicide attempt and been taken prisoner, or to think that the emperor, who had issued the declaration of war, should take some kind of responsibility for his actions.

For example, the political scientist Kamishima Jirō, who had fought in Luzon as a lieutenant in the army, and Watanabe Kiyoshi, who had served as a marine aboard the battleship *Musashi*, both wrote after the war that at the time of the defeat they had believed the emperor would take responsibility by committing suicide.* Former

---

* Oguma Eiji, *"Minshu" to "aikoku"* (Shin'yōsha, 2002), pp. 109, 118.

lieutenant Onoda Hiro'o, an Imperial Japanese Army holdout "discovered" on the island of Lubang in 1974 who was later noteworthy for his right-wing activities, remarked in an interview the year after his repatriation that the emperor should have taken personal responsibility.*

Among people who had lost family members to the war, there was also a certain amount of critical sentiment toward the emperor, if one slightly different from that harbored by veterans. On his way to Tokyo from Okayama, Kenji had stopped in Kobe to see his great-aunt (Ishichi's younger sister), whom he had visited once before as a child in 1940, when he had played with her three boys.

"Of those three boys, the eldest had been killed in the war and the second had died of tuberculosis. The third son was the sole survivor. I was told the eldest son had died when his troopship had been sunk by an American submarine on the way to the Philippine battlefront.

"My great-aunt's husband was a former policeman, and though he retired after the war, they had trouble making ends meet so he went back to work as a department-store security guard. While I was talking with him during my visit in front of a photo of the eldest son, a news program came on the radio about the emperor. He grimaced and spat out, 'I wish they'd shut up about that guy!' Not surprising, considering he'd lost his eldest son to a war that began with an imperial command. And if it hadn't been for the malnutrition brought by wartime shortages, his second son might not have died of TB."

Eventually Kenji embarked on the main purpose of his trip to Tokyo, and headed out to the Fuji Telecommunications plant. The factory had escaped the bombings, and he met a number of his old colleagues and superiors. But he was unable to regain his position at the company. He was interviewed by his old boss in the bookkeeping section, now head of the personnel department, who slipped in a few pointed questions about his Siberian internment and the "indoctrination" he had received there. Later, he was told that there were too many veterans returning to work and the company could not reinstate him at the present time; they would continue to send him wages, and he should wait at home until they could recall him.

The fact of the matter was that Kenji and the personnel department chief had gotten into an altercation before the war.

---

* Kikuchi Ikuzō, "Burajiru no Onoda Hiro'o Nihon-koku musekinin ron o kataru," *Asahi Journal*, 3 October 1975.

"Back when I worked under him in bookkeeping, this guy was the type who liked to curry favor with superiors. He would check up on his staff after regular work hours to make sure none of them went home before the department chief did. I was an efficient worker and would get my work done in time to go home, so then he would bring me a pile of new tasks about a half hour before quitting time. Being young, one time I confronted him outside the office to protest. He dodged me by saying something like 'I just wanted an outstanding worker like yourself to do a bit more,' but I imagine he thought I was a troublemaker.

"When I got back from Siberia, he turned out to be the guy in charge of interviewing former employees who wanted to come back to the company. The rule was that returning vets were supposed to be reinstated, and I'm sure that the guys returning earlier from other battlefronts were. But you never know how things are going to go in life. Even the wages they promised to send were what I had been making before I got called up, which had been so devalued by the postwar inflation that it was impossible to live on them."

Many Siberian internees report that after their return to Japan they were subjected to police surveillance, faced discrimination in their communities, or had difficulty finding employment. Kenji now found the path to a career in a major Japanese corporation effectively closed to him. His itinerant life from job to job and place to place had begun.

2

Kenji had no choice but to look for work in Tokyo, and the electrician he was staying with gave him an introduction to a well-digging company looking for office staff. He succeeded in getting the job on the basis of his secondary-school education, his bookkeeping experience at Fuji Telecommunications, and the fact that the company president, whose son was also a Siberian returnee, was sympathetic to his situation.

The company was small, with about thirty employees. Although he had been hired to do office work, soon after he joined he was ordered to go help dig a well somewhere on the outskirts of Yonezawa in Yamagata Prefecture, some three hundred kilometers north of Tokyo. At the time rail service on the Ōu Main Line between the prefectures of Fukushima and Yamagata was being converted from steam engines to electric power, and a railway tunnel through the Ōu Mountains between Fukushima and Yonezawa, near the prefectural border, was being electrified. But this was high in the mountains, with no accessible water for the construction project; hence the order for a well.

When Kenji arrived, he found the site to be close to the summit of the range, beside the tunnel entrance. For three months, from October through December, Kenji lived with the project foreman and his wife in temporary lodgings near the worksite, fulfilling various tasks including monitoring the operation of the gas-powered digging rig. At this juncture, however, he received a letter from Yūji advising him to return to Niigata.

"After I found that job, I wrote to my father to let him know what I was up to, and we exchanged several letters. I believed I'd found office work with a Tokyo company, but my father didn't have a clear understanding of the situation, and seems to have thought I'd become a navvy who was going to be sent around the country digging wells. So he wrote and said if that was the best I could do I might as well come back to Niigata. And in fact, I didn't really know what I was doing there, either, so after I got paid in December I quit. I went to Grandpa's niece's place in Nakano to collect my things, and headed back to Niigata."

New Year 1949 was greeted at his father's home in Niigata without particular celebration. Kenji still had to find work, so in January he began reading the want ads in the local paper, answering one from a company called Imanari Ham in the city of Niigata that made ham, wieners, and frankfurters for nearby US Occupation forces. Kenji became the company bookkeeper.

It was too far to commute from Warino to Niigata, so he got in touch with his half-sister (Yūji's daughter by his first wife), who lived in the city with her husband and four children in company housing supplied by Nippon Light Metal, Ltd. The small apartment consisted of only two 4.5-mat rooms and a 3-mat room, but they let Kenji use the 3-mat room, which had been occupied by their nineteen-year-old daughter.

Imanari Ham, like many postwar startups, was a rather strange affair. It was small, only twenty or so employees, seven of whom were in sales and administration and the remainder in the meat-processing factory. The president lived in Muika-machi, about a hundred kilometers away, so the day-to-day operations were overseen by an old army buddy of his, a former colonel.

Although Kenji did not learn the story until much later, this president, a man named Imanari Takuzō, was a former young right-winger who had risen to some prominence during the war. After the war he became involved in plots by young officers of the former Imperial Japanese Army. He also helped conceal Ba Maw, the former prime minister of a pro-Japanese regime in Burma created with the support of the Japanese military. Ba Maw had fled to Japan in a Japanese army airplane at the time of the surrender in August 1945. The foreign ministry bureaucrats who welcomed Ba Maw to Japan in cooperation with former army personnel asked Imanari to provide the former prime minister with a safe haven in Niigata. But in January 1946, both Ba Maw and Imanari were arrested by Occupation forces. Imanari was released after six months, and Ba Maw was released in July 1946 and returned to Burma.* As Kenji recalls it, "Every so often President Imanari would drop by the office to talk with the former colonel who was in charge. He had big ideas about making ham for the export market and so on. But we were still under the Occupation at the time and exports were restricted, so I sure couldn't see how he was going to do the things he was talking about."

The administrative department Kenji worked in was housed in a two-story shop the company was renting on one of the main streets in Niigata. The first floor was a retail outlet for the company's meat products; the second floor was the office. The office workers, mostly middle-aged or elderly, included evacuees from Manchuria and former bank employees.

As mentioned previously, after Japan's defeat about 3.3 million military personnel and an equivalent number of colonists returned to the home islands from overseas. Among them were the army officers, civilian bureaucrats, and bankers and businessmen who had made up the ruling elite of Manchuria under Japanese domination. Without a firm foothold in Japan, these returnees depended on their ties to former colleagues from colonial days. In addition, the Allied Occupation

---

* Tsurumi Shunsuke, *Atarashii kaikoku*, in vol. 1 of *Tsurumi Shunsuke shū*, second series (Chikuma Shobō, 2001), pp. 93–97. See also Yomiuri Shimbunsha, ed., *Shōwa shi no tennō*, vol. 8 (Yomiuri Shimbunsha, 1969).

had dismantled the Japanese military and purged a number of former military officers and civilian bureaucrats, as well as individuals connected with the government of Manchukuo, from official positions in postwar public life. Imanari Takuzō seems to have been the type who liked to help his friends, and so the office at Imanari Ham was largely staffed with such former military men and bank employees who had used connections from their days in Manchuria to land this job. They did not appear to be terribly busy, and spent a fair part of their time drinking tea and gossiping. "Mostly they reminisced about the difficulties they'd had evacuating from Manchuria and complained about postwar life. One time I went on company business to the house of a bookkeeper who had evacuated from Manchuria. He was living in one rented room on the second floor of a run-down two-story house with a wife and three children. He told me they used to live in Fengtian, but now they appeared to be pretty poor. For people like him who had been well off before the war, it must have been really difficult to adjust to postwar life.

"At that point, everybody was just scraping by, and no one talked much about the war. The thirtysomething factory manager had been a sailor on the heavy cruiser *Nachi*, and I remember one time he spoke briefly about his war experience when we were chatting at the factory. After the air battle off Taiwan had been falsely reported as a major Japanese victory, *Nachi* was ordered to lead a squadron to 'attack enemy stragglers' in the area. The situation was actually the opposite, and *Nachi* narrowly escaped unharmed. But even he did not want to talk about the times things grew truly dire, such as when *Nachi* later fought in the Battle of Leyte Gulf or sank in an Allied air raid off Manila [in November 1944]. Everyone's memories were still raw, and they wanted to avoid dark tales; it was a period when the only war stories you could tell were funny ones.

"Even my father had a very close call just before the surrender. He'd been on a boat to Hakodate on one of his trips to buy medicinal herbs when it was strafed by an American fighter plane. But he only told me that story because it happened to come up while we were talking. I scarcely said anything about what I'd experienced in Siberia, either. Besides, I realized pretty soon after I got back that no matter how I explained it people didn't really understand."

Apart from its retail store and office in downtown Niigata, Imanari Ham had a small factory on about 900 square meters of land on the outskirts of the city. Since it was supplying the US forces, strict hygiene was maintained; the floor was concrete, and the facilities were modern. There was a smoking room for curing the ham, and the factory manager and workers wore white uniforms.

The factory workers, all local men and women, were kept quite busy. In prewar Japan, most people had never eaten ham, and even as Japan entered its postwar economic expansion, the only kind of sausage that enjoyed wide distribution initially was made from fish. So Imanari Ham was a pioneer in the domestic production of genuine ham—a venture predicated on US military demand and the changes that the postwar era was bringing in Japanese tastes and eating habits.

Occasionally the office workers were treated to free samples of the company's frankfurters. Kenji had never eaten anything like that, but tried them and thought they were tasty. This was a luxury item in those days, something Kenji could not have bought on his wages. But they were apparently selling well, and the factory was working at full capacity to meet demand.

In contrast to that of the bustling factory, the work of the administrative office was a bit sketchy. In Kenji's words, "My job was keeping two sets of books in order to evade taxes. The former bank employee in the office would show up for work about 10:30, go out, and then pop back in before going home for the evening. He spent the intervening time withdrawing funds from Bank A and depositing them with Bank B, then withdrawing other funds from Bank B and depositing them with Bank A. By pumping up the number of transactions in this way, the company was able to get better credit. But really it was running on loans, while putting up a front of successful management."

This setup of indolent white collar supported by diligent blue collar was a reflection of the prewar class system. In the Edo period, peasants worked from dawn to dusk (ten to thirteen hours, depending on the season), while the samurai in the government offices of feudal domains averaged about three hours a day. Even after the Meiji Restoration, the legacy of "samurai hours" continued. After the domains were abolished in favor of a centralized prefectural system in 1871, working hours in government offices were still only six hours a day; even when an eight-hour day was implemented in 1886, government workers had the afternoon off during the summer.*

Such customs made the short hours and high salaries of the bureaucratic elite the envy of ordinary people. The major corporations of the prewar period, which adopted the employment practices of the government ministries, not only differentiated white- and blue-collar workers by the terms and benefits of their employment; they often even had separate entrances to company facilities. As already noted in the description of Kenji's time at Fuji Telecommunications, one of the principal goals of the postwar labor movement was to eliminate such forms of discrimination.

That said, this period was one in which white-collar workers who had depended on the established order to give them a living despite their lack of productivity suddenly experienced a decline in status. Personal accounts of postwar declines in fortune come primarily from such members of the urban middle classes and their progeny.

Immediately after the surrender, Japan was confronted with a ruined industrial base, food shortages, and hyperinflation. The Japanese government pumped subsidies into critical industries to get them back on their feet, but this only fueled the inflationary spiral. In March 1949, the Occupation implemented a fiscal tightening known as the "Dodge Line" (after the American banker who proposed it), plunging Japan into a recession and leading firms that had employed large numbers of returning veterans to thin out their workforce.

This affected Kenji as well, for he received a letter from Fuji Telecommunications requesting his resignation. Kenji assented since he seemed to have been put out to pasture on indefinite home leave, and had no hope of ever returning to work with the company. He received a lump-sum severance payment, but since it was calculated on the basis of his prewar wage rate, it was not enough to meet even his immediate living expenses.

That April, Imanari Ham also reached an impasse, a result of managerial negligence that condoned an indolent office staff and slipshod accounting.

---

* Suzuki Jun, "Futatsu no jikoku, mittsu no rōdō jikan," in *Chikoku no tanjō*, ed. Hashimoto Takehiko and Kuriyama Shigehisa (Sangensha, 2001), pp. 109–10, 117–18.

"The factory was running at full capacity, and the ham was selling, but the company began to delay payment of wages. When I went round to the factory on my bicycle, the workers complained to me, saying, 'The products are selling like mad, and we are working our hearts out—so why are they delaying our wages?'"

Fed up with the sloppy management and poor future prospects of the company, compounded by the fact that it could no longer even pay decent wages, Kenji started to look for other work. In May 1949, the wife of a middle manager at the factory (another returnee from Manchuria) gave him an introduction to a brokerage firm in the city of Niigata, where he was hired as an office worker. However, this "brokerage firm" was really just a dolled-up version of the prewar stock speculators known as *kabuya*. Niigata had traditionally had a stock exchange dealing in rice futures, and a swarm of *kabuya* that worked it.

The company offices were in the home of the former *kabuya* who was the president. Now ill, he watched over the business from the house's main room, which was separated by a narrow veranda from an earthen-floored entrance space. There the employees, including an office manager, a floor trader, a messenger, and Kenji, serving as a clerk, had their desks. The office manager was the market strategist, giving instructions to the trader who went to the stock market to make the actual transactions. The woman who had told him about the job also worked in the office as a secretary.

Kenji left this company around August after an argument with the president. "I can't remember what it was about," he says. The so-called Japanese system of lifelong employment and seniority-based wages with a single company was at the time limited to employees of a handful of major corporations and government agencies. For workers at small and medium-sized companies where wages generally did not go up no matter how long one worked there, if something unpleasant happened on the job, it was quite natural to quit—and many of the companies were themselves not destined to last for long.

Kenji found his next job through the Imanari Ham factory as well. At this point, Kenji would eat breakfast at his half-sister's house and then, fortified with a box lunch she prepared, walk about the city looking for work. He had become friendly with the workers at the ham factory, and even after he had quit the company, he would drop by and visit. The constant stream of suppliers and purchasing agents in and out of the place made it a valuable information exchange.

Having made friends with a livestock broker who supplied pork to the factory, Kenji began to learn the trade from him. The broker would buy cattle and pigs from farmers, take them to the slaughterhouse, and then deliver the meat to vendors and factories. Kenji went round to the farms and slaughterhouse with the broker, who would smear cow dung on the weights of the scale when the farmers were not looking in order to underweigh the cattle and beat the price down. Kenji also helped to wash the intestines of the butchered animals in a pond in front of the slaughterhouse. This quick preliminary washing was necessary because at Imanari Ham the workers would use the intestines as casings for ham and sausage after turning them out and washing them again.

As the two made the rounds of the farm villages dealing in livestock, they also assisted black marketeers in transporting and selling contraband rice. Other commodities had been restored to the free market, but the government continued to control rice distribution.

"You could call it black market, but really all it amounted to was buying rice direct from farmers in the villages around Ogikawa and selling it at the Imanari Ham factory. Inspectors on the platform at Niigata Station were on the lookout for such activity, so we carried our rucksacks to look as though they weren't as heavy as they really were. But the police never bothered themselves much with such small quantities of contraband rice anyway. Nobody could actually live solely on the rice ration, and I think they realized how the people were suffering."

In the fall of 1949, the broker arranged for Kenji to work as a "pig rider," which involved minding around two dozen pigs being shipped in a freight car on a night train bound for Tokyo. The job was so called because the car had a second tier running along one side, above the animals, where the minder could ride and keep an eye on them.

"I was handed a knife and told that if any of the pigs became ill and looked as if it might die, I was to sever its carotid artery and drain it of blood. If the pig died without such bloodletting, the internal organs would rot and the meat would become worthless. So that was my chief responsibility. Siberia had gotten me used to riding in freight cars, but the stench of the pigs and their grunting and bellowing kept me from getting much sleep."

The train reached Tokyo about dawn. Having finally dozed off, Kenji was startled awake by the clatter of the cars being recoupled. After the car was shunted onto a siding at Shibaura, the pigs were unloaded and handed over to a Tokyo broker and his men for transport to a slaughterhouse there.

"I was able to rest up at the broker's house in Shibaura. They let me have a bath, fed me breakfast, and gave me a receipt for the pigs. The house was near the slaughterhouse, but I was surprised at how grand it was, including the bath. I'd known nothing but poverty both before and after the war, so I thought, 'I guess some people really are loaded.' In any case, I went back to Niigata, handed the receipt to the broker there, and that was the end of one run."

Food shortages and a controlled economy had created business opportunities for enterprising individuals, some of whom had elevated themselves from black-marketeers to postwar nouveaux riches. But Kenji had little involvement with this world. "I worked a few more times as a pig rider, but this was just an occasional job I did for the livestock broker, and it eventually dried up."

During this period, Kenji had all he could do simply to get by. "I wore whatever came to hand, work jackets, whatever. I don't really remember. I didn't own a suit. I don't remember ever wearing one, since I wasn't getting the kind of jobs that required a formal interview. Things were so tight psychologically and financially that I hardly even went to the movies, which I had loved. I have absolutely no recollection of what I did on my days off."

So Kenji lived from day to day, struggling to survive, until he went home for the New Year's holiday in 1950 and learned that his father had found work for him. "I guess he didn't like the idea of me working forever as a livestock broker's assistant." Up to now Kenji's employment had come through his own contacts or by chance; this was the first time his father had stepped in.

The job was an apprenticeship in a confectionery run by a nephew of Yūji's in Kameda, a small town southeast of the city of Niigata. "My father never went beyond elementary school, and had no conception of using your academic record to seek employment. Before the war people used to say that folks who sell food never go hungry. I'd heard that from Grandpa too when I was growing up, so I decided to go with it."

Three nephews and a niece of Yūji's, children of his younger sister, lived in Kameda. Originally there had been four sons, but the eldest had died in the war, and the second, already married, was the one running the sweets shop. The third son had married his eldest brother's widow upon returning from the war and inherited the headship of the family; he now ran a bicycle shop. The youngest son, still not out on his own, and the daughter, the youngest child, lived with the third son and his family.

At the time Kenji's younger sister Hideko, too, was boarding with the third son, after graduating in March 1949 from a normal school in Shibata and being hired as a middle-school teacher in Kameda under the newly reorganized postwar educational system. Kenji ended up living there as well and commuting to the sweets shop run by the second son.

"Living at the third son's were he and his wife and their two children, his younger brother, his sister, and Hideko and I. It was an old house with a lot of rooms, but that made eight of us altogether. The third son had married his brother's widow to maintain the continuity of the family, a practice common in the past."

The sweets shop made *an* (sweet bean filling). At the time sugar was quite expensive, so it was cut with artificial sweeteners such as dulcin. The proportions and technique of blending that the second son had hit upon were so popular that other local shops were placing orders for his *an*. This was why he had been looking for a hand at the shop, occasioning Kenji's employment. "But 'employment' is a bit too high-class a word for it. At the age of twenty-four I found myself a pastry cook's apprentice," says Kenji.

Kenji spent about six months at the shop learning to make the *an* filling and knead and roll out the dough for steamed buns and other sweets. But this job was not destined to last long, either.

"This cousin of mine was a daily drunk. The amount he drank gradually increased, and in the end he was getting drunk from noon onward. When he was really pickled, he'd sleep for an entire day. Then once he'd sweated out the alcohol and sobered up a bit, he'd start the whole process all over again. Before long he really couldn't handle the work anymore, and finally he developed a delusion that I was fooling around with his wife. At that point my father came over from Warino and chewed him out. In those days, elders carried a lot of authority, and my cousin apologized profusely. But by then I was fed up with it all, and in May I quit, with my father's blessing."

This time, Kenji went to a government-run employment office and found work with a photoengraving shop. The publishing industry was enjoying a major recovery at the time, and printers were doing a brisk business. This was another very small enterprise: three platemakers, the company president, and Kenji, hired as the general office clerk. Kenji moved into the second floor of the shop. Since the platemaking process involved chemicals and heat, the shop was equipped with water, a gas stovetop, and a sink, which Kenji used to cook for himself.

"My household possessions amounted to a futon, some clothing, a cookpot, and a few dishes, which I kept in an orange crate in the corner. You could say I cooked for myself, though about all I ever made was miso soup."

Yet here as well, Kenji was unable to concentrate on office work. The company president was expanding into the fuel business, and was more interested in having Kenji help with that. So Kenji made deliveries and canvassed for new orders. He got a motorcycle license and rode a small motorbike to deliver charcoal one or two bushels at a time.

In the types of small companies that Kenji had been working in—thirty employees or fewer—there was not enough office work to justify hiring someone to do accounting and bookkeeping alone, nor could the businesses have afforded it. The only places where people were employed to do administrative work all day long were the big corporations.

Nor would Kenji have ever shown up as "unemployed" in the government statistics covering the period after his return from Siberia. In Japan, unemployment statistics account only for those individuals who have actively sought work through the government-managed employment offices. Kenji, however, had moved from job to job virtually without a break, and the only time he ever used an employment office was in 1950 when he found the job with the photoengraving shop.

At the war's end, Japan's total population stood at 77 million, of which the general labor force numbered some 33 million and about 4 million more were in the military. The surrender caused a sudden flood of as many as 10 million demobilized military personnel and auxiliaries, civilian returnees from overseas, and workers dismissed from factories supplying the armed forces—yet there was no corresponding surge of unemployed. Statistics tell us that in April 1946 only 1.59 million people had been completely unemployed for more than a month.

It is said that one reason Japan's unemployment rate has been lower than that of other industrialized nations is that sectors such as the self-employed, small firms, and domestic help have been large enough to absorb surplus labor. From another perspective, though, this structure might be characterized as one in which a large segment of the population, because it is not covered by unemployment insurance or other safety nets, finds it necessary to put together a string of temporary jobs and/or depend on their families for support in order to survive.

The economists Tōbata Seiichi and Nomura Masami have argued that this should be distinguished from "full employment" in the other industrialized nations and should instead be called "total employment."* The official unemployment rate in Japan in 1948 and 1949, as Kenji struggled to make a living, was less than 1 percent.

3

Kenji and the people he knew were too busy trying to make ends meet to spend much time discussing politics. But even so Kenji was not entirely divorced from the political situation in postwar Japan.

In February 1949, while Kenji was still working at Imanari Ham, he received a summons from the Occupation forces. When he and the other returnees from Siberia had landed at the port of Maizuru, they had been interrogated by US military intelligence concerning Soviet army facilities in the vicinity of Chita, and it now appeared the Americans wanted to reinterview returnees who had reliable memories and might prove informative. There was also evidence that even after returning to Japan his mail was being examined by the Occupation forces.

---

* Nomura Masami, *Koyō fuan* (Iwanami Shoten, 1998), pp. 35–39.

The summons was accompanied by a transit pass issued by the Occupation. Shortages immediately after the war meant that trains were often filled to capacity with people going out to buy food in the countryside, and simply getting a ticket was an ordeal. But many of the trains had special passenger cars reserved for Occupation use, which were largely empty. Kenji's pass was only the equivalent of a regular third-class ticket, but it still meant a free ride all the way to Tokyo.

In Tokyo, he presented himself as directed at the Yūsen Building in Marunouchi, a large office building constructed during the post–World War I boom by the shipping company Nippon Yūsen and now commandeered by the Occupation. He was taken to a room for interrogation by a Japanese-American officer, who showed him aerial photographs of Chita along with illustrations of Soviet army uniforms and asked which types of uniforms he had seen on the men going in and out of various buildings. The interrogator's tone was mild and Kenji did not feel particularly intimidated. Others were there for interrogation, from a number of different camps. Kenji ran into someone who had been with him in Chita, and they talked for a bit.

Kenji also used this trip to Tokyo to visit a friend from his Waseda Jitsugyō days who had entered Fuji Telecommunications at the same time he did, but was now doing some sort of work connected with the Occupation forces. Later on, from the 1960s, when Japan had grown wealthier and more stable, his choice of leaving a safe position at a large company like Fuji Telecommunications would seem downright foolhardy to most Japanese. This was not necessarily the case in those days, however; indeed, given the terrible inflation, people said that even the black market was a better bet than white-collar work.

His friend was the same age as Kenji, but already married and with a little girl, which reminded Kenji of how fast the years had flown. They parted without speaking very deeply about anything, and thanks to the Railway Transport Office established by the Occupation at major train stations, Kenji was able to get a seat all the way back to Niigata.

After returning to Japan, Kenji would occasionally glance at a newspaper. Yūji's household subscribed to the major daily *Yomiuri shimbun*, but Kenji wasn't there that often, and read whatever he happened to come across at work. After moving to Niigata and then to

Kameda he still didn't have the wherewithal to buy newspapers himself, and read them at the workplace or elsewhere.

Even so, in those days Kenji had little time or energy for following the news. High-profile current events such as the 1949 Shimoyama and Matsukawa incidents (a murder and a sabotaged train wreck, respectively, that were said to be connected to labor disputes at the National Railways) aroused his interest somewhat, but that was about it. "I'd been interested in the international news since secondary school, so I read more about that than about domestic issues. Compared with before the war the press was much freer and there were more foreign wire reports, which I thought was good."

Kenji doesn't remember how he voted in the elections during this period. "I probably voted Communist or Socialist. It wasn't that I didn't care about politics, I just didn't have the time. Changes in cabinets and such seemed to take place on a completely different plane that had nothing to do with my daily life."

He voted in the Niigata First District, but has almost no recollection of campaigning by either the ruling conservative party, somewhat confusingly named the Liberal Party, or the opposition, which included the Socialists (JSP) and the Communists (JCP). Once during an election he came across his younger sister Hideko out campaigning in Kameda for the Socialists along with other schoolteachers who had been mobilized by their union, but he didn't think much about it one way or the other.

While Kenji may have voted for the Socialists or the Communists, his intention was purely "to trip up the conservative parties." He recalls, "I had absolutely no illusions about socialism or communism. I'd been in the Soviet Union and seen the reality of communist society. I preferred the US over the USSR. But I was even more fed up with the militarism of prewar Japan, so the conservative forces, which would not take responsibility for the war, were out of the question as far as I was concerned. It didn't matter much to me whether I voted Socialist or Communist as long as I wasn't voting for the conservatives. I figured whoever I voted for wasn't going to be forming a government anyway. In the January 1949 general elections the Communists had their 'great leap' and took thirty-five seats in the House of Representatives [out of a total of 466], and I knew that if that was the best they could do, it was not going to fundamentally change things."

In 1946, under the guidance of General Headquarters (GHQ) of the Occupation forces, the prewar Japanese constitution, which had vested sovereignty in the emperor, was replaced by a new constitution that vested sovereignty in the will of the people and renounced war and the maintenance of armed forces. But Kenji was not particularly interested in this new postwar constitution, either. "Maybe it's because I wasn't in the country when it was promulgated, but it didn't make an impression on me. I didn't read it, and I don't remember much about it. I never talked about it with anyone I knew. It was like, So what? It wasn't going to put food on the table, was it?"

In fact, this seemed to be the prevailing reaction at the time. In the "Food May Day" demonstrations led by the Communist Party in 1946, one of the most prominent slogans carried by demonstrators proclaimed, "Food before a Constitution!"

Initially, no political camp in Japan strongly supported the Constitution. The conservatives in truth wanted to restore the prewar constitution, though they could not admit as much to the Occupation forces. The JCP opposed the Constitution since it preserved the emperor as the symbol of the unity of the Japanese people and accepted capitalism. And many of the JSP representatives believed that it should be revised because its social welfare provisions were inadequate. Only after the Occupation ended in 1952 and conservative forces began to move toward revising the Constitution would the progressive camp (led by the JSP and JCP) raise the banner of "defending the Constitution," or garner broad support for such a position.*

What attracted Kenji's attention at this time was issues more directly related to the war that he had just experienced. "I wasn't much interested in domestic politics or the current scandals, but I read a lot in the papers about the Tokyo Trials." The trials, formally known as the International Military Tribunal for the Far East, delivered their verdicts in November 1948. Seven of the Japanese leaders designated as Class A war criminals were sentenced to death and sixteen to life imprisonment. Of the seven who were executed, six were military men, including Tōjō Hideki, who had been prime minister when war against the Allies was declared; the sole civilian was Hirota Kōki, who had been prime minister when the Second Sino-Japanese

---

* Oguma Eiji, *"Minshu" to "aikoku"* (Shin'yōsha, 2002), chapters 11 and 13.

War began in 1937. The Occupation decided not to pursue indictment of the emperor, deeming that putting him on trial would arouse public antipathy and make it difficult to maintain order.

"The Class A war criminals deserved what they got, it seemed to me. I was not going to forgive the guys who started that war and ruined the lives of my father and my grandparents. The fact that Hirota Kōki was a civilian official, unlike the others, wasn't an important distinction as far as I was concerned. But the failure of the emperor to be indicted did not sit well with me."

Preoccupied with trying to make a living, Kenji did not have much opportunity to speak with anyone about his war experience, but he maintained a continuing interest in learning the facts of that war. The first book he bought and read after his return from Siberia was a Japanese translation of *The Japanese at Leyte Gulf* by the American naval historian James A. Field.[*]

"Life was pretty hard, and I didn't buy things like books. But I really wanted to know the truth about this war that had caused me and my grandparents and my father such suffering—especially since we'd been lied to throughout it and were unable to know what was really going on. The Battle of Leyte Gulf had happened just before I got called up, and was the most vivid in my memory; at the time we'd been led to believe we'd won, to the point of parading with lanterns in the streets. I wanted nothing to do with heroic tales written by Japanese. I wanted to read an objectively written account of the facts, which was why I bought Field's book. And after that I read others, even if it was just while browsing in the bookstores."

About this time Kenji also read Yoshida Mitsuru's *Senkan Yamato no saigo*, a personal account of the final sortie of the battleship *Yamato* by a young lieutenant who had survived its sinking.[†] Despite being the world's largest battleship in its day, *Yamato* had proven to be useless in the Pacific War, in which air power dominated. Sent forth to bombard the US forces that had landed on the island of Okinawa, it was sunk by US aircraft before it could reach its destination in April

---

[*] James A. Field, *The Japanese at Leyte Gulf: The Shō Operation* (Princeton: Princeton University Press, 1947). Translated by Nakano Gorō as *Reite-wan no Nihon kantai* (Nihon Kōhōsha, 1949).
[†] Translated by Richard Minear as *Requiem for Battleship Yamato* (Seattle: University of Washington Press, 1985).

1945, four months before the Japanese surrender. Yoshida's book gave a firsthand account of the frustration felt by young naval officers at the senselessness of their mission, and of the terrible air attack that sank the Japanese flagship, killing all but a few hundred of the more than three thousand men on board.

The work had initially been slated to appear in 1946 in the journal *Sōgen*, but Occupation censors stopped its publication. That particular text was published in book form by Sōgensha in 1952, after the Occupation ended. What Kenji read was a revised version, with portions deleted that might run afoul of the censors, which ran in June 1949 in another magazine, *Saron*. This was one of the so-called *kasutori* magazines that sprang up right after the war: poorly printed on cheap paper, and with content tending toward the vulgar. (*Kasutori* was the name for the cheap homebrew liquor that made the rounds of the black market in those days and that symbolized the chaotic situation following Japan's defeat.)

"I was in secondary school when we started hearing rumors about the two great Japanese battleships *Yamato* and *Musashi*. But even their existence was secret, and I had no idea of where or how they were sunk. So I read the story of the last days of the *Yamato*. I was surprised to see such a memoir running in a lowbrow rag like that.

"I thought the account was valuable because the author gave an unvarnished depiction of his own views at the time while also presenting a more objective postwar perspective. There was a passage describing how, before *Yamato* completely sank, the engine room was deliberately flooded to correct the listing of the ship without ordering the personnel there to evacuate, drowning them. The author was later taken to task for not expressing any remorse for this act, but it would have seemed natural to any officer on the bridge. The military is like that."

Although Kenji was still interested in the Soviet Union and Siberia, he had little time to think about such things. But when the Chinese civil war ended in the victory of the Communist Party over the Nationalists and the establishment of the People's Republic of China in October 1949, he felt that the inevitable had happened. A cartoon he had seen in the propaganda newspaper *Nihon shimbun* in Siberia stuck in his mind: in it, a figure representing the Nationalist regime greedily devoured US aid dollars but was unable to digest them because the bills simply fell out of its body from where it was missing below the waist.

Immediately after the war, the Japanese Communist Party abandoned its advocacy of violent revolution, proclaiming instead a strategy of "peaceful revolution" to be achieved with the support of the masses through parliamentary means. The "great leap" in 1949 that Kenji noted earlier, in which the JCP won thirty-five seats in the House of Representatives, was a result of this shift in policy. But in January 1950, five months before the outbreak of the Korean War, the Cominform issued a scathing critique of the JCP line. The party went underground to engage in armed struggle with US forces in Japan, which had become a staging area for the Korean War, and consequently lost all of its seats in the Diet.

"I was interested in stories having to do with the Soviet Union, so I read the Cominform critique at the time. I thought it was appalling— it singled out Nosaka Sanzō [leader of the JCP] by name and used language to criticize him that shouldn't have been used against anyone. It brought back unpleasant memories for me of the so-called democratic movement in Siberia."

In June 1950 the Korean War broke out. "A disaster, I thought. In July or thereabouts a wire dispatch in the paper by an American correspondent reported that advance elements of US forces had attempted to use bazookas against North Korean T-34 tanks, to little effect. When I read this, I recalled the T-34s I had seen in Siberia."

In September, US forces landed at Incheon as full-scale American intervention in the war commenced. The North Korean army collapsed, and it looked as though the conflict would soon be over, but in October the Chinese army crossed the Yalu River. In Niigata, rumors flew that the United States would be forced to withdraw from Japan. Much was being made of an economic upturn due to military procurement for the war in Korea, but according to Kenji, "There was absolutely nothing to make me think the economy had improved."

In order to fill the void left by the dispatch of Occupation forces to Korea, in August 1950 GHQ issued a directive for the creation of a National Police Reserve (later renamed the Self-Defense Forces). The directive effectively ordered Japan's rearmament, in spite of the 1946 Constitution renouncing war and the maintenance of armed forces or "other war potential." Many Japanese did not welcome this development.

"The National Police Reserve was an army, no matter how you looked at it. I was against its creation, seeing as we'd had a terrible time as a result of the army and the war, and I was happy we didn't have one."

Many men in straitened circumstances signed up for the Reserve. Kenji was also having a hard time making a living, but it never occurred to him to join. "Going off to war again was totally out of the question. No, thank you!"

With the outbreak of the Korean War, Occupation policy appeared to shift decisively. Up to 1949, militarists and the prewar elite had been the objects of a bloodless Occupation purge removing many legislators, bureaucrats, and businessmen from public life. But from 1950 onward a "Red Purge" drove Communist Party members and sympathizers from public office, mass media, and the labor unions. The JCP protested, but Kenji says, "When I thought of my time in Siberia, it seemed to me that the very existence of the JCP showed that America was a tolerant, democratic country. It was unfortunate that the US had ordered the Red Purge, but if that was what the Occupation wanted then there was no going against it."

It was then, in the autumn of 1950, that Kenji met and became friends with a Communist Party member in the city of Niigata. "I don't recall how I met him, but I think he was a labor union activist or something of the sort. About the only companies in the city big enough to have unions were the Niigata Steelworks or Nippon Light Metal, so he might have been an activist there.

"He was four or five years older than me, about thirty, a nice guy, like an older brother. When I told him I had read an overview of imperialism when I was in Siberia, he said he had a book on the subject at home that he would loan to me. I went by to pick it up, but he was out, and his wife seemed a bit suspicious of this stranger dropping in. I borrowed and read it, but it was difficult and I didn't understand much of it.

"I got on well with him, but he didn't really try to recruit me into the movement. Nor did I want to get involved; the 'democratic movement' in Siberia had made me sick of political activism. I had no interest in taking any more orders from above."

Given Kenji's dislike of the Soviet Union and communist society, it might follow that the realities of the Cold War and the Chinese army's intervention in Korea would make him see Japan's rearmament as inevitable, but this was not the case.

"I suppose someone who thinks about everything purely in his head might reach that conclusion. But issues in the real world are not so cut-and-dried. That sort of thinking is far removed from the realities of human society."

Kenji was no fan of communism, but he was also completely opposed to war and rearmament. And in this his views likely coincided with those of a majority of the Japanese people at the time.

In 1951, a turning point came for the twenty-five-year-old Kenji. He was still going on with his rounds for the photoengraving company, but beginning in the winter of 1950 he caught cold repeatedly, with intermittent fevers. When his condition failed to improve, he took time off from work in January 1951 to see a local doctor, who referred him to Niigata University Hospital. There, Kenji was diagnosed with tuberculosis.

"When I heard the news it was a shock. A shadow passed before my eyes. My elder brother and sister had both died of TB so I thought, 'Well, my turn has come now too.' I figured it was because I'd been working so hard with such a poor diet."

He went on leave from the photoengraving shop in Niigata and returned to his father's home in Warino, where he convalesced for about three months before entering the national tuberculosis sanatorium in the township of Uchino (incorporated into the city of Niigata in 1960). Kenji would be there until 1956, a period of nearly five years.

Kenji playing guitar in the sanatorium.
On the wall are photos of popular singers and movie actresses.

Chapter 6

The Tuberculosis Sanatorium

In January 1951, Kenji was diagnosed with tuberculosis. While it is likely that he had an innate susceptibility, years of malnourishment and overwork, both during and after the war, were no doubt major contributing factors. After receiving this diagnosis—"the most depressing news of my life"—at the age of twenty-five, Kenji would spend the next five years, until he turned thirty, in a tuberculosis sanatorium.

1

On learning of his illness, Kenji took leave from the photoengraver's shop and returned to his father's home in Warino. There he convalesced for three months while applying for admittance to a national tuberculosis sanatorium.

"Back in the day folks were taciturn and stoic. When I told my father the news, all he said was, 'I see,' nothing more."

Kenji wrote to his grandparents Ishichi and Kochiyo in Okayama. He later heard that they had shown the letter to their relatives in the main house and asked them what to make of it.

"Nearly all the grandchildren they had taken care of had died of illness, and now the last one, who had finally returned from the war, was sick with tuberculosis. I think they just didn't know how to deal with it."

In Warino, Kenji went to a local doctor once every two weeks for artificial pneumothorax treatment, which involved inserting a hollow needle into the chest and pumping air into the space between the diseased lung and the pleura, collapsing the pulmonary alveoli that were the loci of the tubercular infection. In the era before effective drug treatments for TB became common, such surgical methods were among the few therapies available for those like Kenji other than rest, better nutrition, or a move to a better climate.

When his condition would allow it, Kenji took walks in the neighborhood for exercise. But at the time, particularly in the countryside,

TB was feared as a fatal disease. Afraid of contagion, the local farmers kept their distance from Kenji. Still, he needed to get out, so he would walk along the river embankment near his house.

"One time I happened to pass a group of locals while I was out walking on the embankment, and later my father warned me not to go by there again. He mentioned one of the women had said to him, 'Kenji looks so pale that it's scary.'"

In June 1951, Kenji was admitted to the national tuberculosis sanatorium in Uchino. In addition to private sanatoriums, mostly Christian, Niigata Prefecture had two national sanatoriums, in Uchino and Kashiwazaki.

The one in Kashiwazaki had been established in 1939 as the Niigata Sanatorium for Disabled Veterans before being transferred to the management of the Ministry of Health and Welfare and converted for tuberculosis patients in December 1945. The Uchino facility was established in 1941 as the Niigata Prefectural Tuberculosis Sanatorium and transferred to the Ministry of Health and Welfare in 1947. Thus it was that medical facilities created during the era of wartime mobilization served as the basis for postwar tuberculosis sanatoriums.

Neither Uchino nor Kashiwazaki ever had much by way of local industry. Later on, Kashiwazaki, like Shimokita Peninsula in Aomori Prefecture, would actively bid to attract nuclear power plants and Self-Defense Force installations.

"Tuberculosis sanatoriums were regarded as undesirable and so were built in out-of-the-way places. The Uchino sanatorium was near the Sea of Japan on the outskirts of a farming village, overlooking a sandy beach and tulip fields. The local farmers wouldn't come anywhere near it. Sometimes fishermen would come to sell fish, but they didn't want anyone to see them and they would be all but holding their breath, just barely forcing themselves to bring their catch around to the TB patients for the sake of the money. The patients would hold pots outside the windows for them to put the fish in."

When Kenji entered the sanatorium, his father accompanied him on the train and walked the ten minutes or so from Uchino Station with him. Once they arrived, Kenji said, "Be seeing you," and Yūji simply replied, "All right, then."

Kenji says he doesn't recall how his medical fees were covered during his time at the sanatorium, but the revision of the Livelihood

Protection Law in May 1950 and of the Tuberculosis Prevention Law in March 1951 would have affected his situation. The Tuberculosis Prevention Law, originally enacted in 1919, was revised in 1951 to prevent the spread of the disease by giving prefectural governors the power to prohibit stricken individuals from working and to order them into treatment at specified sanatoriums. After patients entered a sanatorium, they could not leave it until a doctor had certified complete recovery. On the other hand, all fees for medical examination and treatment would be covered by the prefectural government if the patient's guardians so requested.

The basic concept was to isolate patients but provide them with care and support, much as with the Leprosy Prevention Law of 1953. Compared with before the war, when patients had been expected to pay their own medical fees, this was an improvement in terms of financial burden. By being isolated from society, however, the patients were being essentially put out to pasture; their indefinite and lengthy incarceration ran the risk of removing them from social life altogether. There were also human rights issues in the facilities to which they were confined. The Leprosy Prevention Law was repealed in 1996; the Tuberculosis Prevention Law in 2007.

Kenji remembers that he received welfare payments for his living expenses at the sanatorium. The 1950 revision of the Livelihood Protection Law specifically limited welfare payments to persons of Japanese nationality, but it dropped other restrictions (such as those having to do with the character or behavior of recipients), marking a decisive shift in the direction of broad-based public assistance. In 1950, the first year under the new system, public assistance claimed 46 percent of the Ministry of Health and Welfare's budget.

However, under the provisions of the law at that time Kenji was eligible to receive only ¥600 per month. Later, in a well-known 1957 case, Asahi Shigeru, a patient in a tuberculosis sanatorium in Okayama, would sue the ministry on the grounds that this restriction on monthly payments made them inadequate to ensure "the minimum standards of wholesome and cultured living" guaranteed by Article 25 of the postwar constitution.

According to the plaintiff, the ¥600 monthly allotment did not provide him with enough money even to purchase raw eggs to supplement his diet, or to obtain a pair of underpants each year and an undershirt every other year. The Asahi lawsuit was decided in Tokyo District Court in 1960 in favor of the plaintiff; the ministry appealed the verdict, and in 1963 Tokyo Superior Court overturned the first ruling. The case was then slated to go before the Supreme Court, but the plaintiff died in 1964, and the court decided in 1967 that the legal case had ended with his death.

Kenji recalls, "I first learned of the Asahi lawsuit from the newspapers after I had left the sanatorium in 1956. I thought he was right to sue. In the sanatorium I, too, had to guard every stitch of clothing." As for how he came to use public assistance, he says, "I don't remember how I found out about it. The doctors never said anything about that sort of thing, so it might have been the office at Niigata University Hospital, where I was first diagnosed with TB. Or it could have been someone in the local community, I suppose."

The sanatorium housed some four hundred patients. There were six wards numbered one through seven, skipping "four" because it is a homonym for death (shi) in Japanese. Wards 1 through 5 were older buildings; wards 6 and 7 had been newly constructed, probably to accommodate the influx of new patients from the mandatory isolation prescribed by the revised Tuberculosis Prevention Law. Kenji was housed in the new ward 6.

Before the war, Kenji had been to the tuberculosis clinic in Ekoda where his elder brother Teruichi had been sent. At the time, it had been common for patients to use their own funds to hire caregivers called tsukisoifu, usually middle-aged women, to help them with their daily needs. With the postwar change in the system, such privately employed caregivers were no longer allowed, and registered nurses made the rounds of the wards.

Kenji was put in an eight-person room with two teachers, two policemen, a labor standards inspector, and two others. Teachers and public-sector workers were also well represented in the other rooms in the new wards 6 and 7. The patients were mostly in their thirties and forties; there were few as young as twenty-five-year-old Kenji.

One likely reason there were so many teachers and public employees at the sanatorium was that such people were in a better position to be informed about the newly established system and how to access it. The Japanese welfare system is administered on an application basis: only individuals who have completed the proper application

procedure may utilize it. Today as well, poor people who have no connection to public institutions and are hard-pressed simply to make a
living often lack the necessary knowledge to take advantage of the
services that are in place to assist them.

For his first year or so in the sanatorium, Kenji was treated with
the new drugs PAS (para-aminosalacylic acid) and Tb1 (thioacetazone).
PAS tended to have negative side effects on the gastrointestinal system,
so its use would be suspended if such effects appeared and resumed
when they subsided.

Kenji's stay at the sanatorium corresponded to a period of trial
and error in the treatment of tuberculosis in Japan. A few years later,
in the mid-1950s, effective anti-tubercular medications such as the
bactericidal antibiotic streptomycin would come into widespread use,
but at the time of Kenji's illness weaker drugs such as PAS were the
only available forms of pharmacotherapy.

Antibiotics, led by penicillin, first came into full-scale use during
World War II. Like radar, they were a new technology of the Allied
forces, one that proved revolutionary in the treatment of wounded
soldiers. After the war, penicillin was employed in the civilian sector
as well, and streptomycin, first isolated in 1943, was likewise widely
adopted as a treatment for tuberculosis. But in 1951 Japan it was still a
precious imported medicine that, as Kenji says, "wasn't going to make
it round to some poor patient in the countryside like me."

After a year of pharmacotherapy, the progress of Kenji's disease
appeared to have been slowed, and in May 1952 he underwent a surgical operation known as thoracoplasty, predicated on the same principles
as the artificial pneumothorax treatment he had received earlier. Rather
than using streptomycin or other medication to kill the tuberculin bacteria, the idea was to surgically collapse portions of the lung invaded by
the disease.

"It was really just an extension of artificial pneumothorax, so
the idea had probably been around for a while. But it had taken the
advancement of surgical techniques during the war and the appearance of antibiotics capable of suppressing infection to make such
major surgery for TB possible."

Since portions of the lung were being collapsed, its total capacity would be decreased, and the body's overall strength diminished as
well. The surgery also entailed the removal or resectioning of various

ribs, which would only grow back in spindly lengths, like the twigs of a tree, in conformity with the shape of the collapsed lung—so not only did the operation leave major scarring on the back, it also distorted the shape of the thorax.

The result was that the patient would essentially be left with only one functioning lung. But he might also be cured of what was then a predominantly fatal disease.

"I knew what the consequences of the operation would be. But it was what the doctors recommended, and I agreed to it, deciding it was the only way forward. They did it with local anesthesia, cutting seven ribs and pretty much completely collapsing my right lung. When they were sawing through the ribs it hurt so much I couldn't stand it.

"For the doctors I think my surgery also offered something of an opportunity to experiment with a new technique. Since I was only under local anesthetic, I could hear what they were saying during the operation. A senior doctor was guiding a younger doctor, who was by turns operating and observing. At one point I heard the lead doctor say, 'Oh boy, that doesn't look good.' The whole point of the operation was to collapse the infected areas of the lung, which would be meaningless if the tuberculosis bacteria had already invaded the bronchi, so before the procedure the doctors took a look there by sticking a metal bronchoscope down my throat. This was also done by a clumsy young doctor being instructed by a senior physician. It hurt a lot and I couldn't breathe."

By the following year thoracoplasty was already being replaced by pulmonary lobectomy, which removed portions of the lung with fewer ribs needing to be cut. Later, with the advance of antibiotics, these surgeries all became more or less obsolete. They were therapeutic dead ends, conducted over a limited period of time on only a small number of patients. Among them was the actor Atsumi Kiyoshi, famous as the lead in the long-running movie series Otoko wa tsurai yo (It's Tough Being a Guy).

Kenji says, "After I got out of the sanatorium, I would know right away when I ran into someone who had had that operation. With one lung collapsed, the shoulder on that side would drop, and the one on the other side would be slightly elevated. At my sanatorium, they started streptomycin therapy the year after I had surgery. If it had been a year earlier, I wouldn't have had to have it."

Following the operation, Kenji patiently took courses of PAS. At the sanatorium, cultures were taken of the patients' sputum every month and tested for the presence of the tuberculosis bacteria. If no bacteria were detected for a year, the patient's release would be initiated, but under the system established by the revised Tuberculosis Prevention Law, individuals still showing evidence of infection could not be released, no matter how long they had been confined. Six months after his operation, Kenji's sputum tested positive for TB.

"When I tested positive for the bacteria even after they had collapsed the lung, it meant that the surgery had been pointless. The doctor said, 'Let's be patient.' But I was terribly depressed. After that, there was nothing to do but convalesce and take the medicine while waiting until no more bacteria were detected."

2

The nearly four years that followed, until his release in 1956, were "the hardest time of all" for Kenji. In part because of the monotony of daily life there, "I don't remember much of anything about my time in the sanatorium. It was the absolute lowest point of my life. Siberia was also tough, but there was always the hope of going home. In the sanatorium, I had no prospects for how I might live even after I was eventually cured. Even if they let me out, I had no skills and no physical stamina, so I felt like the best I could do would be to work as a clerk in some office.

"Also, in Siberia everybody was in the same boat, and there was a certain sense of solidarity among the prisoners. But in the sanatorium, everybody's state of illness was different. I didn't belong to the same social status as the teachers and public employees who had guarantees of lifetime employment, either, so there wasn't much fellowship among us. When I tested positive, I don't recall receiving any words of sympathy from the other patients. And I don't remember ever talking with them about how to reenter society after being released. Everyone's situation was different, and we didn't have much to say to each other. Everyone avoided serious conversation. I didn't have any particularly close friends there."

Life in the sanatorium was a numbing routine of waking, eating, quiet bed rest, minimal exercise. Since patients were not allowed to leave the premises, even walks around the neighborhood were out. The only events were occasional fireworks parties in the summer.

"There was plenty of free time, but about all the sanatorium library had in it was haiku and self-help books. I couldn't afford to buy my own books on ¥600 of public assistance. The only book I recall buying was Takasugi Ichirō's memoir of his Siberian internment, Kyokkō no kage ni [In the Shadow of the Northern Lights], which I'd seen in an ad for cheap remaindered books.

"Meals were taken in bed in your room. They were free, as part of treatment, and I suppose they must have been reasonably nutritious, but I don't remember much about them. They weren't particularly tasty, just a tad better than what I'd had at home in Warino. Patients who wanted something better would wait until after five, when the doctors and day nurses went home, and then grill fish in the court-yard while keeping an eye out for the night staff. I think they got the fish direct from fishermen with their own money. I believe there were also others from farm families who got fresh produce sent to them from home."

The eight roommates chipped in to subscribe to a general news-paper and a sports paper. "But I don't recall much of the news from that period, aside from the 1953 cease-fire in the Korean War."

In September 1951, before Kenji's operation, the San Francisco Peace Conference was convened and the US-Japan Security Treaty signed; nei-ther, however, left much of an impression on him. The peace treaty con-cluded at the conference ended the Occupation of Japan in April 1952. But the US military, from its experiences in the Korean War, wished to maintain Japan as a base for its Asian operations, and so the US-Japan Security Treaty was signed at the same time as the peace treaty to allow US forces to remain in Japan. Despite the name, the treaty was not really a mutual security pact between the two nations, merely one that provided bases for the American military on Japanese soil. The Japanese government saw the signing as a condition for ending the Occupation, and also hoped that the continued presence of US forces would discourage attacks on Japan by other countries. But because of the security treaty the Soviet Union and Eastern bloc nations refused to sign the San Francisco Peace Treaty; moreover, China and North and

South Korea had not even been invited to the conference. As a result, some in Japan opposed both treaties, arguing instead for a comprehensive peace that would include the Soviet bloc and China.

Kenji says, "I could really sympathize with the people who were calling for a comprehensive peace treaty, but when I read the reports of the results of the conference, I thought they were about as good as could be expected. Neither I nor the people around me probably really had a clear idea of what the security treaty was about, but I think most of us felt that with the Korean War threatening to develop into an all-out confrontation between the US and the Soviet Union, there was nothing a weak, minor power like Japan could do no matter how hard it might try."

While at the sanatorium Kenji bought a small crystal radio for personal use, equipped with an earphone so as not to bother the other patients. He mostly listened to the national broadcaster NHK, especially its rakugo programs. He had loved these traditional comic monologues since his youth in Nakano, when he had been taken to the Suehirotei theater in Shinjuku.

"I also listened to the program Tazunebito [Missing Persons; aired 1946–1962], which was for people trying to find relatives who had gone missing in the war. But I didn't want to think too seriously about anything, so most of the time I listened to entertainment shows like Hanashi no izumi [Fountain of Stories; based on the US quiz program Information Please] and Nijū no tobira [Twenty Gates; based on Twenty Questions].

"S-ban awā [Standard Disc Hour] played the first pop music I'd heard in a decade. For ten years, through the war and early postwar years, I'd been completely out of touch with popular entertainment and music, and this postwar American-influenced light music was new to me."

A surviving photo of Kenji playing the guitar in his room at the sanatorium is reproduced at the beginning of this chapter. He liked to play prewar hits like Koga Masao's "Kage o shitaite" (Longing for Your Presence).

There was a guitar in the sanatorium that I taught myself to play, and the other patients told me that when I got out I could make a living as a busker. Of course they weren't serious, but it gives you an idea of how limited the prospects were for any of us."

Once every two months or so, Yūji would come to visit Kenji, bringing eggs and other things to supplement Kenji's diet. "But we didn't speak very deeply about anything. We really didn't have much of anything good to talk about."

During this period, Yūji was having his own difficulties in life.

Right about the time I had my surgery, my younger sister Hideko quit her teaching job and went to Tokyo, where she basically vanished. About six months passed before my father said, 'I suppose I can tell you now . . .' I guess he'd held back from saying anything on account of my operation. It must have been hard on him, but he bore up somehow, just like he never complained about losing all his savings in the aftermath of the war, or about having his son finally return home, only to float around for two years and then come down with TB."

Midway through 1953, Kenji saw an article in the newspaper Niigata nippō about a Japanese émigré to Brazil who was back in Japan for a visit, which at last gave him the lead he needed to locate his aunt Midori. As mentioned in the preceding chapter, Midori was his maternal aunt, his mother's younger sister, who had emigrated with her husband and two children to Brazil before the war and with whom contact had been lost, despite repeated letters sent after the war.

"The émigré in the article said that he hadn't really been able to believe that Japan had lost the war until he came back here, and that there were people in Brazil who still didn't believe it. I wrote a letter care of the newspaper asking him to contact me if he had any information about my aunt, and he came to the sanatorium to see me."

At the time the Japanese community in Brazil was divided into two opposing camps—the "victorists" who refused to acknowledge Japan's defeat, and the "defeatists" who did accept it. This situation was partly the product of prewar education and its emphasis on Japan as a divine and invincible land, coupled with the limited access many emigrants had to information as a result of their inability to read Portuguese. The clash between the two camps had escalated into incidents of assault and even killing.

"That émigré told me that Aunt Midori's husband was a leader of the victorists and burned any letters coming from Japan without reading them, believing them to be part of an American plot. Even when they got delivered, the victorists refused to believe any letters from Japan saying the war was over.

"I finally understood why there had been no word from Aunt Midori. I asked the person to deliver a message, but even after that, there was no response. In a broad sense, this is yet another example of how the war tore people apart."

In March 1954, Ishichi died in Okayama of a stroke. One of the relatives he had been living with wrote Kenji to tell him the news.

"That visit soon after I returned from Siberia turned out to be our last goodbye. After that, I couldn't go see him, since I was too busy trying to make a living. But Grandpa was seventy-eight years old and had already been paralyzed by a stroke since before the war, so it seemed like his appointed time. Still, he must have found it hard to go without having been able to reestablish contact with his daughter, Aunt Midori."

One other development that made an impression on Kenji during his years at the Uchino sanatorium was a movement among the patients to improve their living conditions that took place under the guidance of a national organization, the Nihon Kanja Dōmei (Japan Patients' Alliance, or JPA). The JPA, which was formed in 1949 as a consortium of existing patient advocacy groups, supported the Asahi lawsuit mentioned earlier.

The leader of the movement at Uchino was a young patient in ward 7 named Satō Katsumi. Born in Niigata Prefecture in 1929, Satō had been a Communist Party–affiliated labor activist during his time at the shipping company Kawasaki Kisen. After leaving the sanatorium, he campaigned to eliminate discrimination against Korean residents of Japan in the prefecture and also became involved in the movement for the en masse repatriation of ethnic Koreans to North Korea, whose economy was rapidly expanding at that time.* The movement began in 1959 and continued until 1984, but for many of the roughly 93,000 people who did relocate, the realities of life in the North betrayed their expectations. Disillusioned, Satō resigned from

---

* Ethnic Koreans first migrated in large numbers to Japan after Korea became part of the Japanese empire in 1910. By 1935 there were about 600,000 Koreans living in Japan, a number that swelled to nearly 2 million as a result of wartime forced labor drafts implemented beginning in 1944. Following Japan's defeat in 1945, the majority of the wartime laborers repatriated to the Korean peninsula, and after 1947 the population of Korean residents in Japan fluctuated between 500,000 and 700,000.

the Japanese Communist Party and shifted his attention to anti-communist and anti–North Korean activism.

At the sanatorium Satō was active in the Niigata branch of the JPA. At first he kept a low profile, but his unique style and eloquence soon won him the presidency of the sanatorium patients' association. "I remember Satō giving speeches on a microphone and playing the popular song 'Kaeribune' [The Boat Home] by Tabata Yoshio on the guitar," says Kenji. Satō and his followers issued a newsletter and organized patients' meetings.

One effect of this movement on Kenji was that he secured a physical disability certificate from the Japanese government. A considerable number of patients, including Kenji, had suffered lasting physical consequences from their surgeries, for which the patients' association encouraged them to gain disability certification. Kenji applied and was certified class 5 (out of six classes in descending order of severity of disability).

However, Kenji did not participate in the movement itself. One reason was that he felt making agitprop speeches in the confines of the sanatorium was a little too reminiscent of the democracy movement at the camp in Siberia.

Aside from the occasional visits by Yūji, no one came to see Kenji in the sanatorium. A friend from his Waseda Jitsugyō days who worked in the Tokyo metropolitan government sent him a letter once, but otherwise he cannot recall receiving any mail. He was not involved in the patients' movement, and he had no real friends in the sanatorium. Given this isolation and lack of prospects for the future, did he ever contemplate suicide? Kenji says,

"No, I didn't. No matter what the circumstances, people always find some hope. It was that way when I was in Siberia. I also thought that if I ever did anything like that, it would be really unfair to my father."

So life at the sanatorium continued for Kenji. For three years after the operation his sputum was tested monthly for the TB bacteria—with sometimes positive and sometimes negative results. In 1955, the results stabilized as negative, and he began to have hope that the doctors would release him. He finally left in May 1956. He didn't know what he was going to do with himself once he got out, "but I was happy to be leaving."

When a patient walked through the gate of the sanatorium there was a little ceremony, similar to that of a prisoner's release from a penitentiary, in which the other patients, the doctors, and the nurses assembled to see him off and say, "We hope we won't see you here again." It was also the custom to have a commemorative photo taken, in one's best clothes. No one came to meet Kenji, so he set out alone for his father's house.

He was already thirty years old. He had spent the decade of his twenties at war, in Siberia, and in a tuberculosis sanatorium.

3

As the time for his release drew nearer, Kenji was permitted to leave the grounds and go into the city of Niigata to look for a place to live and make other preparations for life after the sanatorium. But for the thirty-year-old Kenji, with only one lung, no particular skills, and even youth no longer on his side, it was difficult to see how he was going to make a living. A fair number of tuberculosis patients were released, only to suffer a relapse and head right back into the sanatorium due to poverty, poor nutrition, overwork, and weakened constitutions. Others, in their hopelessness and poverty, succumbed to alcohol and other bad habits that likewise brought on a reemergence of their illness.

The actor Atsumi Kiyoshi, who as mentioned earlier had undergone the same operation as Kenji, is said to have been very careful about his health upon returning to normal life, swearing off alcohol, tobacco, and coffee. Kenji, too, felt that above all else he needed to take care not to have a relapse.

"If I did, that would be the end. So after I got out, I paid attention to my health as I worked. Even so, there were lots of times when I had to push myself harder than I should have. My lung capacity was barely 2,000 ml [as compared with 4,000 ml for a typical Japanese male], and even a little hard physical labor would leave me out of breath."

He had his government disability certificate, but since he was classified as only mildly disabled, "I got a 50 percent discount on train fares exceeding a certain distance, and that was about the only advantage to having it." In reality Kenji's classification also made him eligible for reduced taxes on purchasing and maintaining an automobile, but he failed to learn this until 2009, and derived no benefit from the exemption up to that point, since he had not applied for it. As mentioned previously, Japanese social welfare programs are not widely publicized by the agencies administering them, even though potential recipients need to apply to utilize them.

After leaving the sanatorium, Kenji set out to pay a visit to his grandmother Kochiyo, reuniting with relatives and acquaintances in Tokyo and Shizuoka on the way. His first stop was Tokyo, where he saw his younger sister Hideko, who had gotten back in touch with their father and was now working on the administrative staff at Tokyo Gakugei University.

For the members of the Oguma family, who had lived a vagabond life moving back and forth between Hokkaido and Niigata and Tokyo, there really was no ancestral home anymore. Warino was where the main branch of the family lived, and thus their officially registered domicile, but none of them felt much of an attachment to it. There weren't many good jobs in Niigata, so the prospects for being able to care for Yūji in his old age were poor. Kenji discussed a plan with his sister in which they would both live and work in Tokyo until they could see a way to being able to care for Yūji and their stepmother, and then they would all live together.

Visiting Tokyo for the first time in seven years, Kenji found that most of the destruction caused by the war had disappeared. In 1956, the year of his visit, people were saying "It's no longer the postwar era," and Japan had already launched into its period of startlingly high economic growth. The taiyōzoku, or "sun tribe" of hedonistic and semidelinquent youth that took its name from Ishihara Shintarō's popular novel Taiyō no kisetsu (Season of the Sun), was attracting public attention, and there was a rush of commercial construction, including the Seibu and Mitsukoshi department stores in the Ikebukuro section of Tokyo.

"I hadn't seen the outside world for more than five years, so I felt like Urashima Tarō [a Japanese Rip van Winkle]. Compared with the prosperity of Tokyo, I felt left behind and broke."

While in Tokyo, Kenji stayed a couple of nights with the old friend from Waseda Jitsugyō who had written him in the sanatorium.

"During my five years in the sanatorium I guess I must have lost my social skills, because I turned up at his place without any sort of food or other present, which was bad. He'd also been drafted, but he got off with digging trenches on the seacoast near Tokyo in preparation for the final invasion of Japan. He was demobilized soon after the war ended and got a job with the Tokyo metropolitan government. In contrast, I'd spent practically all my time confined in one institution or another—three years in a Siberian prison camp and five in the sanatorium."

After Tokyo, he stopped in Shizuoka, where he visited the half-sister with a husband at Nippon Light Metal who had taken care of him while he was working at Imanari Ham in Niigata. Her family had since moved to Shimizu in Shizuoka Prefecture, where Nippon Light Metal had opened a new factory in 1952. After a few days there, Kenji headed for Okayama and his grandmother Kochiyo.

"Grandma still lived in the storehouse out back, and I spent about two months with her there. She was sweet, still called me Ken. My other relatives there were really busy with their own lives, but they knew I'd had TB, so none of them gave me a hard time for suddenly showing up after neglecting Grandma for so long."

His grandmother may have been living in the backyard, but the main house was still the one she had grown up in, and her younger sister lived there now. Unlike right after the war, life had gotten a bit more settled, and Kochiyo, now more than eighty years old, was getting on well with her sister.

"She was doing fine there, and there seemed no point in trying to move her anywhere else at her age. I was relieved to see how she was and decided to worry about my own life and how to take care of my father instead."

Returning to Niigata, Kenji began to work again at the photoengraving company he had been at before entering the sanatorium. He had stopped by there when making preparations for his release, and they had been happy to have him back. The company had given up on fuel sales and was doing quite well with printing alone. But Kenji's job only lasted about two months.

"They took me back on as an office worker and let me live over the shop again. But the owner was a drunk and a spendthrift, and he'd show up there in the middle of the night, completely plastered. So I quit. I don't like drinkers. I'm not physically able to drink myself."

Having quit the job, he also found himself without a place to live, and he rented an apartment on the second floor of a building that had formerly been an aquarium. He had no furniture, so moving in was simple: he loaded his futon onto a handcart and pulled it there himself.

At the time in Japan, the owners of apartments frequently lived in the same building, and renters might take meals with them, prepared by the landlord's wife or daughter. If money for food was taken out of the rent, the groceries could be bought in bulk and food costs for the owner's family reduced as well. "At that apartment, the landlord provided breakfast and dinner. The room was large—ten mats or so—but the building was full of a bunch of questionable characters from the streets of Niigata. Then again, I guess I must have seemed pretty questionable myself. One of the other residents was a schoolteacher, and he was the best of the lot."

Around November 1956, Kenji ran into an acquaintance from the sanatorium on a streetcorner in Niigata: Hara Ken'ichirō, a young man with aspirations to be a writer. This man helped Kenji get his next job.

Hara's father had been a secondary-school English teacher before the war, but had been in the atomic bombing of Hiroshima and died of its aftereffects when Hara was in the first year of high school. Hara was taken in by his father's younger brother, a doctor, who supported him with the expectation that in time Hara, too, would become a doctor. But Hara, who entertained literary ambitions, entered Kyoto University in the faculty of literature. Unable to get by financially, he dropped out and joined his mother in Niigata, where he fell ill with TB. At the sanatorium, he wrote for the newsletters published by the patients' movement led by Satō Katsumi.

When Kenji reencountered him, Hara was working for a small publishing company he had been introduced to by a former student of his father who was a reporter for the Niigata nippō newspaper—though "publishing company" was perhaps a bit too grand a name for it, since basically it was staying afloat by doing twenty- or thirty-page pamphlets of puff pieces on local notables in the political and financial circles of Niigata.

"If a skillful enough job was done flattering them, they would buy lots of copies and also pay for advertising. Hara was writing all the articles himself."

When Hara saw what a large room Kenji lived in, he asked if he could live there, too. Kenji agreed, Hara brought over his futon, and they began their life as roommates.

"Hara had gotten chased out of his apartment and didn't have any-place to live. I, on the other hand, had an apartment but no job. So I let Hara stay with me, and he got me work at the publishing company."

The company conducted its operations out of the owner's two-story residence in the city of Niigata. The first floor was rented out to a retail store. On the second floor, one room served as the editorial office, while another was home to the owner, his daughters, and his elder sister. The owner, in his fifties, lived off rents and editorial work. He also had literary aspirations and seemed to want to break into serious publishing.

"I wrote some, too, like a story on the taxi industry. But I wasn't as good at it as Hara was; I didn't think I was cut out for it. My business card was printed with a pseudonym—a pen name I guess you would say. One time when Hara and I went to a company to collect some advertising fees, they asked for my business card, and when I gave it to them they said suspiciously, 'Isn't that a different name from the one you gave over the phone?' So I just took the money and got out of there as quick as I could.

"There were some pretty shifty characters going in and out of our office. There was one guy who made the rounds of the various candidates' offices at election time cadging free meals, who told a lot of interesting stories about what went on behind the scenes. But none of these people dropping in were yakuza, and in fact I never met any. This was still before the big economic boom really got underway, and I don't think the yakuza had gotten their fingers into as many pies as they would later on."

This period was a rare one in Kenji's life, in that he actually indulged himself a bit in popular amusements. "Since Hara and I worked and lived together, we'd go out and have some fun in the city before going home to the apartment.

"We'd go to the movies. One time I won on a long shot at the horse races, and blew the money treating us both to a fine meal. We also went to a Suntory whiskey bar in the entertainment district of Niigata. I didn't really drink, but I still kept him company."

The economic boom was beginning to reach Niigata. The department stores were now equipped with escalators. But Kenji remained poor.

"I would go to the department stores, but about all I ever bought was a coat, which I got in late autumn because the Niigata winters are so cold. As far as clothing went, I had one decent suit, but aside from that I can't remember what I usually wore. Nothing special, I'm sure. I did my laundry by hand and didn't change my underwear that often. I couldn't just let my hair grow like I did when I was in the sanatorium, so I did get regular haircuts, but that was about it."

At the time, television sets were expensive and far from common. Broadcast networks needed viewers to attract sponsors, and electronics manufacturers wanted to get the public to know about TV, so "streetcorner televisions" were set up in many cities and towns for free viewing. People were delighted, and large crowds might gather, especially for live sports broadcasts. There was streetcorner television in downtown Niigata, too, but the reception seemed to be bad and the picture quality was poor. Kenji doesn't recall being very excited about watching it, even for the big sports events.

Nor was he particularly interested in the restoration of Japan's diplomatic relations with the Soviet Union, which took place in October 1956. The establishment of the Liberal Democratic Party (LDP; to this day Japan's ruling conservative party) and the unification of the right and left factions of the Japan Socialist Party (JSP), both in 1955, and the creation of the Hatoyama and Ishibashi cabinets all seemed to be happening someplace far away in his view. But as a "Siberian returnee," he did find himself drawn to newspaper coverage of the 1956 Hungarian Revolution.

"While I thought the Soviet suppression of it was terrible, I also couldn't believe people were actually spontaneously rising up against the Soviet system, given my own experience of it."

His response to this event notwithstanding, Kenji continued to vote for the Socialist or Communist candidate. He disliked communism, but he disliked Japanese militarism and conservatism even more.

"Of the Niigata politicians of that period I remember Inomata Kōzō, who was the JSP representative from Niigata Fourth District. He was a fine man, a civil rights and anti-corruption crusader, who in 1970 founded the Japanese branch of Amnesty International. In contrast, the LDP representative from the same district, Tanaka Shōji, was accused of extortion and fraud in various deals involving the sale of public land and the flipping of properties. I had heard of [Niigata-based future prime minister] Tanaka Kakuei, but at the time he was not such a major figure."

Amnesty International, founded in 1961 in Britain, is known for its efforts to free "prisoners of conscience" who have been unjustly incarcerated. During the Cold War, these included the prisoners in the Soviet gulags. In the 1980s, when Kenji's life had stabilized, he would join the organization and busily send the preprinted postcards in support of these prisoners that came attached to its newsletter, but that is a much later part of our story.

In February 1957, Kishi Nobusuke—who had been minister of trade and commerce at the beginning of the Pacific War before being imprisoned by Occupation forces as a war criminal—became prime minister. Kenji, who had his hands full just trying to make a living, remembers that "I was disgusted, and felt that reactionary forces were making a big comeback, but as an ordinary person I also felt powerless to do anything about it."

Meanwhile, after Kenji had been working there for four or five months, the publishing company began to have cash-flow problems. "The work we were doing was mediocre and the business community in Niigata was small, so it's not surprising it didn't last long." Bankruptcies and job changes were simply par for the course in the lives of workers for small businesses.

Around April 1957 Kenji quit, and through the government employment office found work as an office clerk for a tool company. Small factories and machine shops had sprung up in large numbers with the economic boom, especially parts makers for the auto industry. Kenji's company made sales calls on these small manufacturers, taking orders for wrenches and other tools.

The company consisted of the owner, Kenji, and four salesmen, and it, too, had cash-flow issues. It was located in a building of its own, with a warehouse on the first floor and the office above. Kenji continued to live with Hara while working at this new job. But he left it in December 1957 after he was discovered stealing.

"I pilfered a little bit of the company cash while working in the office. I think I am a pretty honest guy, but I surrendered to temptation. It wasn't much—I swiped about 100 yen when I thought nobody was looking. But somehow the owner seemed to know, and from that point on his attitude toward me changed. He never directly confronted me, but it became difficult to stay there, and I quit."

This became a turning point for Kenji, and he decided to go to Tokyo. In addition, his stepmother in Warino was failing from old age and was not expected to live much longer.

"There just didn't seem to be much point in staying in Niigata anymore. I felt that if I wanted to be able to live under the same roof with my father again, I would first have to go to Tokyo. My sister Hideko was already there and had a steady job. If she and I could combine our incomes, we might be able to establish a home base there and invite our father to join us."

Kenji had no leads on a job in Tokyo. He wrote Hideko and asked if he could stay with her for a while, so that housing, at the very least, was covered for the time being. Until he left the sanatorium in May 1956 he had been surviving on public assistance, so his savings were zero. "I'd worked for about a year from the time I left the sanatorium until I went to Tokyo, but I had very little to show for it."

His decision to go to Tokyo ended his life with Hara, who simply said, "Well, I guess this is goodbye, then," when he heard the news. There was not much to move; Kenji took a bag with him and asked Hara to ship his futon.

Soon after quitting the tool company, on a weeknight in the middle of December, Kenji boarded the night train for Tokyo at Niigata Station. Yūji was already getting old; he didn't have the energy to come to the station. A few of his colleagues from the tool company went out for a drink after work and then stopped by to see him off. Kenji was already thirty-two.

Chapter 7

The Postwar Economic Boom

In December 1957, Kenji headed to Tokyo from Niigata with only one small bag of belongings. Already thirty-two years old, he was without skills or much of a résumé, and had almost nothing in the bank. Since his surgery for TB had essentially left him only one lung, he could not engage in manual labor. The previous year people had been saying that the immediate postwar era was now over, but Kenji says it didn't really feel that way to him.

"I knew that movies were now in color and TVs were selling, but my life was still really unsettled, so what difference did that make? I'd heard about the 'sun tribe' [of hedonistic postwar youth] but it didn't have anything to do with me."

Arriving without fanfare at Ueno Station, he made his way to the western suburbs of Tokyo for Musashi Koganei Station and the campus of Tokyo Gakugei University, where his sister Hideko worked as an administrative assistant.

October 1962. From left: Hiroko (33), Gōichi (5), and Kenji (36)
at an elementary school field day.

1

Tokyo Gakugei University had been formed in 1949 as a consolidation of six existing normal schools in the Tokyo area. Hideko, who had graduated from the normal school in Niigata, had been working on the staff since arriving in Tokyo five years previously.

After meeting Hideko on the Gakugei campus, Kenji moved into her apartment nearby, on the Itsukaichi Kaidō highway in the city of Kodaira. From there, he intended to look for work.

"The apartment was in a two-story building on land owned by a farmer. The upper floor had a hall running down the middle, with a total of ten or so tiny three-mat rooms on either side, including Hideko's. Most of the other rooms were empty, except for one or two. On the first floor there was a small, dirty toilet and storage, nothing more. Across the way was the main house, where the farmer lived and where Hideko paid the rent. I think she checked it out with the landlord before agreeing to let me live there."

In those days there was still a lot of farmland in Kodaira, but urbanization was gathering speed. This was the takeoff period for Japan's "economic miracle," and Kenji was already hearing rumors about how land prices in the area were shooting up.

Kenji and Hideko shared her three-mat room. Aside from a kerosene burner near the window and a small low table, there was no furniture. Nor was there water or gas. Water had to be drawn from a well near the main house and stored in a large earthenware urn in the room. Cooking was done on the kerosene stove. Wastewater from cooking and cleanup was tossed out the window.

The room was so small that they could lay out only a single futon. When one of them was laying it out the other would have to leave the room; they slept in it together.

"It's true we were family, but for four months or so, there we were: people in their thirties back to sharing a bed. The only difference from prewar life was that the cookstove used kerosene instead of charcoal. Hideko did most of the cooking, but I don't remember anything fancy. In the morning we were in a hurry and didn't have time for a hot meal, so we ate bread.

"We didn't produce much garbage aside from vegetable scraps. We didn't take any newspapers, and most everyday goods weren't packaged in those days. So we'd toss the garbage out the window or drop it off at a collection point when we went out.

"In April of that year our stepmother died, and Hideko went to the funeral in Niigata. I'd barely even known her, but she had raised Hideko. One of the folks at the funeral said to Hideko, 'You're living in Tokyo, and yet you don't even have running water or gas?' Even from the perspective of country people, we were living a miserably poor existence."

At this time, the rental market in Japan was at a low point. During the war, the Land and House Rent Control Ordinance and revisions of the Land Lease Law and House Lease Law had imposed rent restrictions in order to help secure housing for the workers flooding into industrial areas to support the war effort. But when the war was over and inflation sent land prices climbing, those restrictions kept rents from rising correspondingly, and the housing sector faltered. As limits implemented immediately after the war on the influx of population into the cities were removed and the period of high economic growth commenced, people poured into Tokyo, creating overpopulation and insufficient and substandard housing. The supply of private rental housing did grow as the economic boom progressed, but according to a 1965 survey, 36 percent of the working population of Tokyo still lived in accommodations with three mats or less of area per person, and 50 percent of workers aged seventeen to twenty-four had no lodgings of their own, but boarded with their employer.[*]

While it can thus be allowed that Kenji arrived in Tokyo during the worst possible period for rental housing, still, Kenji and Hideko's situation was abysmal.

"Our apartment had apparently been built by our landlord immediately after the war when the housing situation was incredibly bad. It had no gas or running water or even a communal kitchen, and by the time we were there, very few people were willing to live in such conditions, which is why most of the rooms were vacant."

As a way of making ends meet, Kenji took a two-week clerical job at Gakugei punching stacks of documents and binding them together

---

* Yūki Seigo, *Kamitsu, kaso* (San'ichi Shobō, 1970), p. 73.

with twine threaded through the holes. "It was bureaucratic work, without any quotas, so it was pretty undemanding."

This was the first time Kenji had set foot on a university campus. Prior to the postwar economic boom, most accounts of campus life written by non-university graduates portrayed professors and students as a privileged leisure class, inspiring a sense of inferiority toward these lucky few. But Kenji says, "I didn't feel anything of the sort, because it was a completely different world. I was the lowest of the low, so it never even occurred to me to compare myself with them."

For Kenji, who had lost a career with a major corporation as a result of the war and Siberian internment and had lost his youth to tuberculosis, it was impossible to imagine how he could rise out of the "lowest of the low." His frank impression of Japanese society at the time was that "once you ran off the rails there was no chance of ever getting back on track." But in the end, Japan's postwar economic boom proved positive for Kenji as well. As Japanese society as a whole lifted off, Kenji managed to seize upon a new business opportunity that would determine the second half of his life.

2

Kenji's major break came in January 1958 when he joined a start-up company called Tachikawa Store, Inc., after meeting the head of the sporting goods department, a man named Takahashi, who was frequently on the Gakugei campus.

At this time at the dawn of Japan's era of high economic growth, hiking, mountaineering, and skiing were beginning to become popular. Prior to that, sports and outdoor recreation had been pursuits of the wealthy, or at least the well-off, and sports equipment had thus been beyond the reach of most Japanese. But as the economy began to take off, people with a certain amount of income began to adopt the lifestyles of the prewar bourgeoisie. Since before the war, even ordinary workers had been introduced to an idealized version of the lives of the urban middle classes through children's magazines such as *Shōnen kurabu* (Boys' Club), mentioned in chapter 1. Illustrations showed parlors furnished with pianos and chandeliers and sofas, bookshelves stuffed with encyclopedias, and people playing golf and skiing.

Without other models for a modern lifestyle, workers whose incomes improved in the economic boom began to purchase such goods.

Takahashi, who hired Kenji, was the head of leisure and sports equipment sales for Tachikawa Store. His job was to mount exhibitions of ski equipment on university campuses, targeting faculty members with disposable income. Hideko, who had learned how to ski while growing up in Saroma, got to know Takahashi and told him about Kenji.

"Takahashi-san was a graduate of Hosei University about forty years old at the time. In his younger days he had been a tennis player. College kids were about the only people who played tennis before the war. I heard that right after the war he ran a sports equipment shop, but went bankrupt and had to sneak off and hide out somewhere for a couple of years. After things had cooled down, he reemerged and began working for Tachikawa Store as head of the sports department. Back in those days, if you could just disappear for a couple of years, your bad credit with wholesalers and other vendors often would just sort of go away."

The headquarters of Tachikawa Store was in a prime location a few minutes' walk from the south exit of Tachikawa Station, out a little farther west from Gakugei on the Chūō Line connecting it to Tokyo. The upper floor of the two-story building was home to the owner and his family, while the ground floor held the shop with some ten employees; the core of the business was stationery and office supplies. Five women, including the owner's wife and eldest daughter, worked as shop clerks and office staff. The male employees meanwhile went out canvassing for direct sales.

"The boss, Watase Banri, was a self-made man in his mid-fifties from merchant origins in the Kōshū region of Yamanashi Prefecture. Most of the employees were from there, too, and were like his apprentices; he was seen back home as a successful businessman and so had given jobs to many local relatives and acquaintances. But he wasn't involved with any prefectural associations or anything. He had apparently been a member of the Communist Party in Japan right after the war, and he claimed to have been quite radical."

In those days people migrating to Tokyo from the countryside often formed clubs or associations with others from their home prefectures. These groups provided a base of support mostly for the conservative political parties, and a number of powerful politicians got their start there, but Watase apparently had no such ambitions.

Tachikawa Store had risen to success based on its innovative approach of selling merchandise directly to clients. Retailers of stationery and office supplies were common enough, but almost all of them depended on customers coming to their shops. Watase instead sent his sales force to do the rounds of places where there was likely to be demand—city offices, schools, large businesses—and offer significant discounts on group orders. It was a kind of extension of the age-old Japanese tradition of small tradesmen visiting their regular clients for orders, but at the time it was quite new, making his company something of a pioneer in the stationery market.

Noticing that where there was a demand for stationery and office supplies, there was also a demand for sporting goods, Watase next created a sports department to pursue this new market and hired Takahashi to spearhead it. Takahashi in turn made the decision to hire Kenji, which was approved by Watase. This was a bit different from the procedure in large Japanese corporations, where the human resources department determines hiring, but it was not and still is not uncommon in small and mid-sized businesses.

In European- or American-managed firms, too, people are usually hired for specialized positions such as lathe operator or bookkeeper; often a factory foreman might decide a lathe operator is needed and human resources simply goes along with this judgment. In this sense, it is the practice of large Japanese corporations—in which the personnel department hires each new crop of graduates and then rotates them among the various divisions of the company—that is more uncommon.

When Kenji first visited the Tachikawa Store, he saw skis and baseball gloves on display in the retail shop, but principally the company marketed its sporting goods through direct sales. Kenji was the second hire in the rapidly expanding sports department. His monthly salary was ¥12,000, a bit higher than the normal starting salary for a college graduate in those days.*

However, Kenji had no sales experience. He wasn't a former athlete, and had no special interest in or knowledge of sports. Why was he hired?

"I think it was because they wanted a person whose background they could be sure about to some degree, since he would be handling

---

* From 1949 to 1961, the exchange rate was fixed at ¥360 to a dollar.

substantial amounts of money from customers. Still, later on the boss said to me, 'With your résumé, I didn't think you'd last very long.' And in fact a lot of other people who got hired after me in direct sales didn't stick with it."

But Kenji worked like mad. Given his age and circumstances, it seemed as though it might be his last chance.

The customer base for Tachikawa Store's stationery and office supplies was mainly educational institutions and municipal government offices. Marketing for sporting goods was initially targeted at schools, which had physical education classes and an official budget for sports equipment. From the beginning of Japan's modernization in the late nineteenth century, the government had made physical education a compulsory part of the school curriculum; in addition, during the postwar economic boom sports clubs were formed in many schools, large corporations, and government offices.

Takahashi made the rounds of universities in the Tama region, including Hitotsubashi University and Gakugei. Kenji was tasked with developing the middle-school and high-school market. His turf was the western satellite cities of Tokyo: Tachikawa, Kunitachi, Kokubunji, Kodaira, Akishima, and so on.

So Kenji set out on a motorcycle, armed with a sporting-goods catalogue and a list of schools copied out of the telephone book. At first he had a Yamaha 125 cc two-wheeler, but it had almost no cargo space, so he later switched to a Fuji Heavy Industries scooter called the Rabbit; around 1961 he upgraded to a light-van version of the Subaru Sambar, also made by Fuji.

"I had a hard time getting used to direct sales at first. I'd begin by calling on gym teachers and chatting with them. But I wasn't interested in sports, so making small talk was hard—I'd open with something like 'Nice weather, isn't it?' or maybe comment on a plant they had in their office. Somehow I'd manage to keep the conversation going, but I imagine it was as awkward for them as it was for me. A lot of them just showed me the door, of course. Many of the teachers were younger than me, but I deferred to them without letting that bother me.

"I had no interest in sports and made no effort to learn about the equipment I was selling. Just to have something to talk about, I'd look a little at the sports results in the newspaper, but that was about it. I was working with the stuff purely to put food on the table. Baseball equipment and volleyballs sold well. The gym teachers, once you got to know them, would order what they needed for their classes—'OK, give me five volleyballs.' I'd report that to the school office and make the delivery, and then every once in a while I'd go round with an invoice.

"After a while the wholesalers began to give rebates to stores that hit certain sales targets. For example, if we placed annual orders of ¥10 million or more, they would take 3 or 4 percent off the wholesale price and give it back to us. Based on that, we would offer our own discounts on large orders. The manufacturers and wholesalers set their price, and then it was up to us retailers what sort of margin we would try to take. Once we had our orders together we'd cut prices accordingly."

Inexperience led to lots of mistakes. "Once when I was just starting out, the chief administrator of a school stopped me after I'd entered the building and said, 'The normal thing to do when you are coming and going is to introduce yourself to the administrative staff, isn't it?' and I had to apologize. I suppose from the point of view of the school authorities I just looked to be some random stranger." Another time, Kenji made a deal with the captain of the baseball team at a private high school to take ongoing orders from him and the other students—some of whom never paid up. Even so, direct sales proved to be a success, in part because it was still an unusual marketing technique. "At that point no other business had begun direct sales in the area. They just sat around waiting for orders to come from schools and such, I guess. Most of the people I talked to at the schools said I was the first sales representative to come there."

A second reason was Kenji's perceptiveness. As the narrative so far has shown, Kenji had a capacity for calmly and objectively observing the social relations of a local community, or a prison camp, and analyzing what lay behind them. This was not something he had learned in any schoolroom, but it did prove quite useful in direct sales.

"In the schools, the purchase of athletic equipment was decided either by the physical education teacher or the administrative staff. It differed from place to place, so it was quite important to figure out who had the authority in each school. If it was the phys ed teacher, you'd make friends with him. If it was the staff, since there wasn't really any reason for a sales rep to be calling on them, you'd still make friends with the phys ed teacher, and get him to talk to the staff. Then you would go round to the staff and persuade them to make the final decision by telling them that was what the phys ed teacher wanted. Schools being bureaucratic organizations, it was not good business to get on anyone's bad side."

Such strategies, of course, might seem fairly basic. But understanding the principles is one thing; it still takes individual ability to successfully apply and adapt them to different situations.

Direct sales was also work that suited Kenji's state of health. He only had about half normal lung capacity, and would get short of breath quickly, but sales let him pace himself as long as he met his quotas. Later, he would even manage to take naps on his rounds, which became part of his routine for maintaining his health.

"After I started to drive, I would eat the lunch I'd brought from home, drink some tea from a thermos, and take a snooze in the car. Manual laborers couldn't do that, nor most store clerks or office staff. Taking a nap after lunch had been part of my regimen at the sanatorium, so this was sort of a continuation of that."

As sales got on track, the company began to go after corporate clients in addition to schools. The Musashi factory of Hitachi, Ltd., in Kodaira, which made transistors, had a large workforce. Also in Kodaira was a Bridgestone Tire factory, and the Prince Motor Company had a factory in Murayama.*

Prince was an offshoot of Nakajima Aircraft and Tachikawa Aircraft, both of which had had factories in Tachikawa before the war. Like Hitachi, they had once been dependent upon military demand; now, the shift of these and other manufacturing industries to the civilian market was driving Japan's high economic growth, and new factories were being built one after the other. Such factories typically had gymnasiums on their grounds to encourage employees to reduce stress and improve their health through sports.

"In the case of the corporations, I'd go with salespeople from Tachikawa Store's office-supplies department who had already established a relationship with them. Companies like these had baseball and volleyball teams that would buy equipment and uniforms

---

* Prince merged into Nissan Motors in 1966, and the factory closed in 2004.

with club dues, supplemented by money from the company. I'd have the team captains talk to personnel, which would place the orders. Sometimes I would also get to know the people in corporate health and welfare and get them to order sports equipment.

"In those days, human relations in companies were a lot more relaxed than they are now. Generally speaking, people didn't work so hard and so late into the night. From my experience visiting clients, I'd say that it was from the late 1970s that working hours started getting longer at major Japanese corporations. I myself would leave home about 8:30 in the morning, drive about twenty minutes in the company car to work, and be home by 6:30 or 7."

The factories were supported by low-wage female workers hired locally. Both Hitachi's Musashi plant and the Nissan-Prince Murayama factory would become known for serious labor disputes in the 1960s; in that sense, encouragement of sports was both a program for employee health and a part of labor management.

"From time to time I would exhibit and sell skiing and other sporting equipment in the dormitories for male employees, which stood separate from the factory grounds. College grads, who were candidates for the top management track, lived in separate dorms from the high-school grads slated for middle management. Most of the workers in the auto factory were male, but the transistor factory had many locally hired women who commuted from their homes in the surrounding rural areas.

"The women in the factory were not called 'operatives' (kōin) as in the prewar years, but 'employees' (shain) like the white-collar staff. But a distinction was still made between administrative staff on the white-collar management track and the shop-floor workers down in the factory.

"Since some of the women workers were married with children, the Hitachi Musashi plant had a company-run childcare center right next door, staffed by single women in their late twenties."

Volleyball was very popular among the women workers, and the team from the Hitachi Musashi plant was a powerhouse in the corporate volleyball leagues. In fact, the team that won Japan the gold medal in women's volleyball in the 1964 Tokyo Olympics—nicknamed the "Witches of the Orient"—was made up of workers in similar factories. This was precisely the period when Kenji was selling sports equipment to those places.

3

In May 1958, when Kenji had been working at the Tachikawa Store for about four months, he and Hideko moved out of their unsatisfactory housing after a conversation he had with the chief administrator of a private high school in Tachikawa during a sales call.

"When I told him what our situation was like, he asked me if we'd like to live rent-free in a house located between Tachikawa and Kunitachi stations."

This house stood on an open lot cut across by a spur single-track freight line that connected the Chūō Line with what had once been the Imperial Japanese Army air base at Tachikawa. After the war the base had been commandeered by the US military, and the line was now being used to carry supplies by the US forces and Tachikawa Aircraft.*

The freight on this line was mainly tank cars full of jet fuel for US planes. Later on, in January 1964, one of these tank cars caused a fire at Tachikawa Station, and in August 1967, as the Vietnam War intensified, another such incident took place at Shinjuku Station. As a result, these fuel tankers would become the object of antiwar protests.

"At the time [I was offered the house in 1958] there was a movement to try to get a new station built between Tachikawa and Kunitachi. The house was on land that would sell for a substantial price if the deal went through, which I suppose is why they'd left it unoccupied. The owner wasn't interested in making money off of rent; he just wanted someone to live there and keep the place from falling apart in the meantime."

We might note that all through these years Kenji never used a real-estate agent to help him find housing. He always either lived with relatives, on the second floor of a business he worked for, or in some other arrangement he'd simply fallen into by chance. This was not uncommon among the lower classes of Japanese society in the era before the postwar boom. "When we went to take a look at the place

---

* Later renamed Tachihi Kigyō and restructured as a real-estate company.

it turned out to be a four-family row house that had probably been built during the war. It was in pretty bad shape. The doors had locks, but it looked like it would be easy enough to break in. The third and fourth houses in the row were decrepit and half fallen down; the roofs leaked and they were not habitable.

"The first house in the row was occupied by the administrator's son, who worked at a trading company, and his daughter, who was a college student. They lived there because their father's home in Ōme was too long a commute into the center of Tokyo. But they weren't around during the day and thought it might be good to have someone there in case of an emergency, so they were looking for someone else to move in next door.

"Those days—between the Korean and Vietnam wars—were the quietest period for the Tachikawa Air Base. Even so, there was frequent noise from planes taking off and landing; you definitely knew you were living next to an air base. What was especially annoying was that the aircraft manufacturers subcontracting to the Americans would run engine tests even in the middle of the night."

Still, it was far better than the siblings continuing to live together in a single three-mat room, and it was free. Their stepmother's death in April had left their father, Yūji, alone in Niigata, so from the point of view of bringing him to Tokyo it was also convenient.

"The offer was a godsend, so we moved right away. Hideko thought it was a good idea, too. Of course Hideko and I would be off at work in the daytime, but my dad would still be there to fulfill our responsibility of looking after things while everyone else was out."

In October of that year Yūji joined them from Niigata. "Dad sold off his house and land, but it was out in the sticks so I doubt he got much for it. I didn't even ask. I was just happy that the three of us could finally all live together as a family. We now had a single electric bulb with a shade, though still no gas or running water. As before, we drew water from a well outside the house and cooked on a kerosene stove. But the place was bigger, and we saw it as a step up."

Around the same time, Kenji's former roommate Hara Ken'ichirō arrived in Tokyo from Niigata. Like Kenji, he had found the prospects for employment in Niigata to be meager and had decided to come to Tokyo to try to catch the wave of economic growth. "He didn't have a place to live, so he wound up with us. We put him up for about a week. You never know, one of these days you might end up needing a little help yourself."

Meanwhile, the sports department of the Tachikawa Store was growing rapidly. According to Kenji, President Watase was "a real go-getter"—an entrepreneurial type who believed in throwing up a quick framework of ideas for others to flesh out. And he had lots of ideas for expanding the business. In April 1958, the sports department added a third member, named Ōki, to the team of Takahashi and Kenji. He was assigned to take charge of the region just beyond Kenji's, cities like Fuchū and Chōfu.

"Ōki was about ten years younger than me, the eldest of three sons. He had lost his father after the war while he was still young, and to help his mother out he had gone to work for a wholesaler of general merchandise. He had been going around selling goods out of a hand-drawn cart along the Ōme Kaidō highway when he got to know Takahashi. At the time Takahashi had just folded his sporting goods business and gone into hiding, but meanwhile he had gotten his wife to open a small general store, and she happened to be one of Ōki's customers."

Ōki had been going to school while working; when he started at the Tachikawa Store he was enrolled in the economics department of a university offering night classes. Unlike Kenji, who remained indifferent to sports, Ōki was an avid hiker, and friends had taught him how to ski. Between them, Kenji and Ōki covered the Tama area of western Tokyo.

From around 1959, however, they started to encounter competition from other vendors. As Kenji and company expanded into the regions beyond Tachikawa, they encroached on the turf of established local stores that had previously simply waited for orders to come in from the schools and other clients. Realizing that the Tachikawa Store was stealing business, they too began direct sales. As more local stores followed suit, it became more difficult for the Tachikawa Store team to advance into new market areas.

Kenji and his colleagues were forced to increase the frequency of their rounds and engage in a price war to keep orders coming in. Takahashi and President Watase aggressively countered the competition by expanding operations and hiring new salesmen for the sports department.

"The other sales staff hired after Ōki were assigned to areas even farther out. There was some division of labor as well: for instance, there was one guy who specialized in selling tennis equipment. All this was after Takahashi and I had already gone in and exploited the market, though, so sales didn't take off. Competition with other stores got fierce, and our numbers didn't improve that much."

As usual for small and medium-sized businesses, there were no automatic annual raises like those common in larger corporations. Instead, Tachikawa Store employees received a bonus on their monthly salary according to sales performance—a wage system that generally favored experience. It was a form of meritocracy, but one also subject to the discretion of the boss. "You wouldn't be fired for poor results, but if you didn't perform well, you didn't have much hope of doing better financially, so a lot of guys just quit."

Through his sales rounds, Kenji gained an intimate knowledge of the roads of western Tokyo. Around this time, the main streets and arterial routes of Tachikawa were being finished with asphalt. Meanwhile, the Itsukaichi Kaidō highway and National Route No. 16, which connected the air bases at Yokota and Tachikawa, had been given priority treatment for use by the US military after the conclusion of the Japan-US Security Treaty, and these "administrative roads" (as they were commonly known) were especially well paved.

In the autumn of 1959, Kenji was in a traffic accident on the Kōshū Kaidō. "I was on my motorcycle, waiting to make a turn at an intersection, when I got rear-ended. I wasn't wearing a helmet—nobody did in those days. I hit my head on the ground and was rushed unconscious to Tachikawa Hospital. While I was lying on the ground, I thought I heard another me calling from a distance, 'Hey, what are you doing down there?' I've heard such things happen quite a bit to people who come close to dying in a major accident."

A "near-death experience"—and if there had been serious complications, Kenji would likely have been plunged back down to the bottom of the ladder again.

Luckily, the hospital tests showed no major problems. The person who hit Kenji did not report the accident to the police, but did carry him to the hospital and pay for his treatment. "I think he sent some sort of get-well gift afterward. It was clearly his fault, so he probably was worried what would happen if I made it an issue. In those days most people did not have accident insurance, and accidents got resolved in a rather slipshod manner."

Around this time skiing was growing popular, and now and then people began coming into the store to buy skis. They were almost always male salarymen working stable jobs in major corporations or government offices: the time had not yet arrived that people bought skis and other sports equipment as a family affair. The sports department would have to continue to rely on the direct sales approach.

As competition intensified, Kenji and his colleagues began to organize ski tours by bus to promote sales. At the time, almost all vacation travel was done in large groups, typically of office colleagues and the like, who stayed overnight at hot-spring resorts such as Hakone and Atami primarily to enjoy parties with geisha. Sightseeing trips to Kyoto and Nara were still rare, and group ski tours even rarer.

In fact, there were still only a few travel agents putting together package tours. Established agencies of the time included the Nippon Travel Agency, founded in 1905 to organize group pilgrimages to religious sites such as Mount Kōya and the Ise Grand Shrine, and the Japan Travel Bureau (now JTB), created in 1912 to serve foreign visitors to Japan. Group package tours organized by these and other companies, however, did not become commonplace until the late 1960s.

Kenji himself had never in his life gone on a vacation trip, save for an overnight excursion to Hakone around 1959 with other employees of the Tachikawa Store who all chipped in to pay expenses. They of course had not gone through a travel agency, and had used company vehicles to save money.

Although no companies were yet organizing ski trips, the number of skiers was increasing, and the building of new ski lodges was beginning to be a money-making venture for local entrepreneurs. So the facilities were there, and the potential guests; what had not yet developed was the business of linking the two. The idea for the Tachikawa Store to do just that came when members of the skiing league in Tachikawa told Ōki they wished someone would put together a ski trip. Taking the hint, Kenji and his fellows negotiated directly with a bus company and an inn to arrange group rates.

Their first tour, in January 1960, was led by Kenji and another Tachikawa Store employee, with about forty participants. "Since a complete setup with ski boots and all would run ¥20,000 to ¥30,000 each, our sales were very good. Most of the participants were small groups of office colleagues." In the 1960s, a typical starting salary for a white-collar university graduate was about ¥13,000 per month.

In those days there was no Internet, and no catalogues of inns and hotels. Neither Kenji nor the other staff had the time or money to check out prospective lodgings in advance, and since all arrangements were made over the phone, people frequently arrived to find something very different from what they had anticipated.

"For business reasons we wanted there to be a tour in December, at the beginning of the ski season. But this was in the middle of the ski lodge construction boom, and one time when we got to ours, which was supposed to have been completed that month, we found that the building was still not weathertight and snow was getting in. On top of that, the young guy who came with me from the store broke his leg on the slopes, and I had a hard time getting him down to the hospital in the foothills.

"Although Tachikawa Store was small, we were enrolled in the government-managed health insurance program, which paid for his treatment. President Watase had been a Communist Party member, so he took care of things like that. Still, when I got back to the inn, the guests were all complaining about the snow coming into their rooms, and I recall feeling overwhelmed by it all, though I managed somehow.

"Back then, customers weren't so demanding and didn't complain a lot. I don't really remember what the food was like. Probably nothing worth mentioning. I didn't feel that lucky at being able to travel, either. I wasn't particularly interested in skiing, so for the most part I didn't."

Japan's health insurance system began with the formation of insurance cooperatives among employees in economically powerful sectors—the large corporations and government offices—before being expanded during the era of wartime mobilization. While small and medium-sized businesses were eligible to enroll in the government-managed health insurance program, many did not. In 1958, the National Health Insurance Law was overhauled to provide health care to those not covered by employer-based systems, but it was not until 1961 that universal coverage was realized.

The Tachikawa Store stopped doing ski tours after two years, when due to the economic boom people started buying ski equipment without the added inducement of the tours. "The tours were a lot of trouble, and we quit after doing five or six of them. More individual customers had begun to come to the store, but sales exhibitions at offices and factories still worked the best."

The ski craze was followed by the golf craze. "We'd go around the companies taking orders for golf equipment. If we could talk a section chief into buying stuff, frequently the other members of his staff would join in. Somebody just starting off with golf needed some clubs, a caddie bag, shoes, and so on, so it was a pretty good business."

Both skiing and golf required expensive equipment that most people would use only a few times a year. "Now you could sell stuff like that. I didn't balk at the extravagance of it. I welcomed the fact that people were living better, plus we made a lot of money. But I didn't buy any of it myself, or play any of the sports."

In those days, Tachikawa was shifting from its early postwar identity as a US base town into the commercial and business center of the rapidly growing Tama region of western Tokyo. There were still bars with English signs out front, catering exclusively to US military personnel, and you would see both American soldiers and the so-called "women of the streets." But Kenji had no contact with either.

"I didn't go to the entertainment districts at night. If I saw those women, I just thought, oh, so there they are. And since sporting goods were not something the yakuza were into, I never ran into them, either. It never occurred to me that US military personnel might be potential customers, or that the base might be someplace to go. To begin with, the equipment we were selling was all sized for Japanese. Maybe every once in a while we'd get a military family coming in to buy a kid's baseball glove or something like that. One time only, I had an American come in to order about thirty baseball caps made for use at the height of the summer, with shields both back and front to keep out the sun. I thought, 'Americans sure are practical.'"

By this time the Sunagawa area, where Tachikawa Air Base was located, was about the only part of the vicinity with any farmland left. During Kenji's career at the Tachikawa Store, the "Sunagawa Struggle" by students and locals against the expansion of the base to handle jet bombers had forced the US military to abandon its plans, and the movement itself (at its harshest from 1955 to 1957) had quieted down for the time being. Kenji accordingly has little memory of the protests. "The noise of the planes was annoying, but I took it as a matter of course and didn't think much about it." With the American withdrawal from Vietnam it was decided in 1973 to return the Tachikawa base to Japan, which was done in 1977.

4

In September 1959, Kenji moved again after winning the lottery for an apartment in a Class 2 low-income public housing development in the city of Akishima. With this, he was finally liberated from his housing woes.

In Japan, housing policy was under the jurisdiction of the Ministry of Construction (since 2001, the Ministry of Land, Infrastructure, Transport and Tourism), not the Ministry of Health and Welfare. It accordingly tended to aim more at stimulating the economy than at providing for social welfare, and gave greater weight to commercial rather than public housing. But in the 1950s the private sector was still weak, and so the Ministry of Construction ended up also promoting public housing to fulfill quotas for new housing starts unmet by private-sector construction alone. While it was not the ministry's primary intent, this did contribute to alleviating housing shortages brought on by the economic boom, and also dovetailed with the general trend toward more comprehensive social welfare policies exemplified by the implementation of the nationwide health insurance system in 1961.

In short, the late 1950s, when Kenji moved into public housing, were a time of temporary expansion in such units. As Japan's period of high economic growth got well underway in the 1960s, policies encouraging new private housing starts would be prioritized, and public housing would begin to contract.

At the time, public housing was classed according to income, and Kenji applied for Class 2, intended for low-income families. That he managed to get into this program at all was a fortunate consequence of the overall expansion of public housing taking place during this period. Timing likewise contributed to Kenji's success with direct sales of sporting goods, which had only been possible because in the late 1950s it was still new. If Kenji had arrived in Tokyo five years earlier or five years later, he might have missed these opportunities to improve his position in society.

The nature of Kenji's work also helped him find a place in public housing. "I was making sales calls to government offices all the time, and I found out about the housing applications there by chance, while just chatting with people. Then, when I looked closely at the newspaper, I saw that the results of the housing lotteries were being published there."

As mentioned in the previous chapter, Japanese welfare programs operate on an application basis—individuals must first gather information about specific programs and apply for them if they are to utilize the system. Many underprivileged people, overwhelmed by the pressures of their lives and with little free time, fail to learn about available programs and therefore never apply. In Kenji's case, his frequenting of government offices as part of his sales routine worked to his advantage.

Kenji applied unsuccessfully twice before getting selected on his third try, in March 1959. As the building he had won a place in was still under construction, he had to wait until September to move in. "I went to see the place around May while it was still being built. It was on an overgrown piece of former farmland, and there were still fields all around. I remember noting how it was being built of concrete block rather than wood."

As it happened, in March his landlord suddenly died. "I figured this meant his widow and youngest daughter in Ōme would be moving to Tachikawa to be with the son and elder daughter, and we'd be asked to move out. I went to the funeral and told the family that we'd qualified for public housing and would look for another place to tide us over until we could get into it, if they would just give us a little time to make arrangements."

So around May Kenji and his family moved to the second floor of an apartment building along one of the main streets in front of Kunitachi Station. It was an eight-mat room without any conveniences; there was a communal kitchen with a sink and two gas burners, and a toilet also shared with the other tenants. The move was accomplished using a three-wheeled motorcycle provided by one of Kenji's subordinates. Kenji, Hideko, and Yūji would live there for a bit more than three months.

This was Kenji's ninth move since returning from Siberia. Aside from the five years in the sanatorium, he had never spent more than nine months on average in any one place. Depending on how you counted it, he had changed jobs more than ten times, averaging about six months in each position.

In September 1959 the family at last moved into Metropolitan Housing No. 6 in Akishima. "The younger guys at the Tachikawa Store helped us with the move. New employees had been hired one after the other, and after three years I was already an old-timer."

In May 1960, Prime Minister Kishi Nobusuke, formerly imprisoned by the Allied Occupation as a Class A war crime suspect, had opposition party members ejected from the House of Representatives by armed police in order to ram the revised Japan-US Security Treaty through the Diet. This inspired enormous public outrage and protests, and in June some 300,000 demonstrators surrounded the Diet building in central Tokyo. From April to June of 1960, the newspapers were filled with articles about the movement against the revision of the treaty. Kenji was sympathetic to the protestors, but to him it all seemed to be happening someplace far away.

"I figured demonstrations were for union activists and college students. I was too swamped to take time off from work, and it never occurred to me to go all the way in from Tachikawa to protest at the Diet building. But I hated Kishi Nobusuke, and no matter how you looked at it, the security treaty was contrary to pacifism. If I'd run into a demonstration on the street, I'd have probably joined in."

Ironically, Metropolitan Housing No. 6 was adjacent to Yokota Air Base—the home of the US Fifth Air Force, stationed in Japan by virtue of the treaty—right under the flight path of the planes as they took off and landed. In addition, the National Railways Ōme Line ran along another side of the complex, so the noise was awful. Apparently there had been no better site available for Class 2 housing.

Similar to council housing for the British working class, the complex was made up of about two hundred standardized single-family units arranged into blocks of four along a street grid surrounded mostly by farmland. Kenji's neighbors in his four-unit block were the families of a Self-Defense Forces member, a policeman, and a bus driver. The other residents, too, generally appeared to be lower-level civil servants or those with similarly stable livelihoods. "The other residents seemed like honest and conscientious folks. The bus driver was married to a woman who'd worked as a bus tour guide. The neighbor down at the end was mildly retarded, but he was a good guy—when it snowed he would shovel the entire sidewalk for us."

Until about 1960, most private homes aside from those of the well-to-do did not have a telephone, and ordinary people relied on face-to-face communications or, in an emergency, an express letter or telegram. At Kenji's housing complex, three residents who worked for the Tokyo metropolitan government had phones in their units that the others were also allowed to use. These three were assigned to different parts of the complex, and their families would go get their neighbors if an urgent call happened to come in for them.

"I think these people had been selected by the metropolitan government to serve as caretakers and were probably given some sort of stipend. They helped organize a residents' association to convey messages and information from the government, and also put together events like the Bon festival dance in the summer. I was too busy to do that kind of community work. Since it had been sort of hastily established, I doubt this association had much to do with things like organizing voting in the elections."*

The apartment consisted only of one 4.5-mat room and one 6-mat room, but the kitchen had running water, a sink, and a counter, as well as a stovetop fired by a propane gas tank. Each household was also equipped with a non-flush toilet and, later, a bath heatable with firewood or coal; outside was a small yard. It was modest housing aimed at the lower classes, but Kenji was delighted at the stability of lifestyle it gave them.

"I felt at long last that I had found a home. Although it was a rental, it was the first time I'd ever lived in a place where I couldn't just be tossed out at the whim of the landlord. The building was tenement-style, but you were separated from your neighbors by concrete block walls that did not carry sound the way the old wooden tenements did. And you had a bit of space of your own both out front and in back, so it felt a bit more like a proper house.

"The three of us were able to live together as a family, and we finally had gas and running water. My father was happy, too. We'd

---

* Many similar associations and older working-class areas did organize voting for elections, mainly on behalf of conservative party candidates.

managed to rise from the lowest of the low to somewhere in the middle of the low. The noise was annoying, given we were right next to the air base and the train tracks, but I felt like we couldn't ask for a lot more."

Before the war, Kenji had lived in a house (albeit a rented one) with gas and water. For him, the postwar recovery at last reached a significant milestone when, in 1959, he had these conveniences once more. Meals improved as well: in their new home the family began to eat ham and sausage—though they were made from fish, not meat. Kenji parked a company light van in a vacant lot by the complex and drove to work at the Tachikawa Store, twenty minutes away.

"At the time the area was full of abandoned farmland and whatnot, and I didn't even think of renting a parking space. I don't think anyone in the complex even owned a car. The one I had belonged to the company. There might have been a couple of other people who also had use of company vehicles, but I don't recall ever seeing any there."

Not long after moving in, Kenji bought a black-and-white television set, soon followed by a simple washing machine and an electric rice cooker. "I bought them with cash at an appliance store near the Tachikawa Store. I wouldn't buy anything on an installment plan."

Other furnishings consisted of little more than a dresser, a low dining table, and a small wooden bookshelf. "In Akishima, we finally had some furniture that felt like real furniture, limited as it was. Up to that point I'd moved around so much that I'd always kept myself ready to pack up and leave at any moment, with no more than a bag and a futon to my name."

Rent was ¥2,500 a month, out of a monthly salary that had risen to ¥18,000 by the time of the move. In front of Akishima Station on the Ōme Line was a long-established market where Hideko did most of the shopping. They subscribed to a newspaper—the *Mainichi shimbun*, the successor to the paper Kenji had read before the war, the *Tōkyō nichinichi shimbun*.

Power outages were infrequent, but if food was left out uncovered, flies would gather. In part this was because of insufficient garbage collection and lack of sewer service. The population of Tokyo was growing so rapidly at this time that waste removal and processing could not keep up, and the majority of it was being dumped in a landfill in Tokyo Bay. At Metropolitan Housing No. 6, each unit had a concrete garbage collection bin, but there was no sorting of trash and collection tended to be delayed. With no sewer hookup, the toilets had to be emptied periodically by a vacuum truck. "But no one had a refrigerator, so you ate everything up, and there was almost no packaging. As a result we really didn't produce a lot of garbage and didn't find any of this too inconvenient."

5

After life had settled down in this way, the next issue to be faced was Hideko's marriage. "Hideko was over thirty and still single, and she did the cooking for us, but she really wanted to be out on her own as soon as possible." Since that would leave the Oguma household without a caretaker, the best solution seemed to be for Kenji to find himself a wife as well, and a go-between had arranged two interviews with prospective mates beginning in 1958. In Japan on the eve of the economic boom, it was still the norm for family members or others from local communities to introduce prospective marriage partners and arrange matches.

But the results were not encouraging. "One of them I just didn't get on with, and I broke things off. The other was advised by a relative who was a doctor to have a look at my chest X-rays, and after I sent them, I was rejected. That was a shock. It was a stark reminder of the handicaps that I faced."

However, a chance turn of events brought Kenji a marriage partner. In the spring of 1961, Hideko brought home a friend—Kumaoka Hiroko, a classmate from her elementary-school days back in Saroma. At the time, Kenji was thirty-seven and Hiroko was thirty-two. The daughter of the elementary-school principal in Saroma, she was divorced and had a five-year-old son named Gōichi. Her parents had moved to Hiroshima Prefecture after the war, and Gōichi was living there while she was working and living on her own in Tokyo. But her father's sudden death in October 1960 had changed things.

"Hiroko's mother gave her strict orders to find a marriage partner before Gōichi entered elementary school. I was also looking for a mate, and Hideko wanted to get out of the house. So things worked out well for all three of us."

Kenji was not exactly prime marriage material. He was living in public housing with an elderly father, and had a sketchy résumé. He effectively had only one lung, which left the state of his health in doubt as well. "But her relatives agreed to our marriage knowing how eager her mother was to get her settled."

Even so, when soon after their marriage Hiroko had her first look at the operation scars on Kenji's back while he was getting out of the bath, she was horrified. "I'd told her about it, but I guess it was a lot worse than she'd imagined. If she'd actually seen it before we got married, I don't know if we would have."

Kenji and Hiroko were married in November 1961. The same month, Hideko moved out, and she herself married in June 1962. Her husband was a colleague on the staff of Tokyo Gakugei University, and Hideko continued to work there after their marriage.

Kenji and Hiroko's wedding was held at Shinjuku Seikatsukan, a wedding hall run by the Tokyo metropolitan government offering simple and inexpensive ceremonies. Kenji found out about it through an inspector he knew from his sales rounds to the Tachikawa External Labor Management Office, an agency created by the Tokyo Metropolitan Labor Bureau for the Japanese workers on the US air base at Tachikawa.

"I made sales calls just about everywhere that there were a lot of people coming and going, including this office, where someone mentioned to me that Shinjuku Seikatsukan was a good place for a wedding if you wanted to do it cheaply. President Watase served as our official go-between, and I invited some friends from my Waseda Jitsugyō days, a few relatives like my half-sister in Shizuoka, and my father and Hideko. Hiroko's family and relatives all seemed a bit higher class than us. Since we had fewer guests on our side, I also invited my friend from Niigata, Hara Ken'ichirō."

The ceremony was non-religious. The two read written vows to one another, and then the director of the wedding hall spoke a few words of felicitation. During a certain period after the war, such non-religious ceremonies in public wedding halls were quite popular. Historically, weddings in Japan were a convening of the two families, not a religious service; the Shinto religious wedding ceremony standard today was actually invented in 1900 for the marriage of the crown prince (later the Taishō emperor). As the purchasing power of the masses increased during the postwar economic boom, wedding halls offering Shinto and Christian services came to the fore, and non-religious ceremonies in public venues like Kenji's fell out of favor.

The honeymoon was a three-night trip to the Izu peninsula. Kenji had traveled from Hokkaido to Tokyo, Manchuria, Siberia, and Niigata and then back to Tokyo, but aside from his company holiday with other employees of the Tachikawa Store, this was his first private pleasure excursion. "When we got back from our trip, Hideko had already left, so it was like a changing of the guard."

In May 1962, Gōichi's grandmother brought him up from Hiroshima, and Hiroko went to meet them at Haneda Airport. Six-year-old Gōichi was a clever child and, perhaps because he'd been apart from his mother for so long, seemed quite mature for his age.

Everything seemed like smooth sailing, but as Kenji says, "Nothing in this world goes quite the way you want it to." Hiroko became pregnant not long after they were married, but also grew moody and a bit unstable. Part of it was the cramped living quarters, so they decided that Yūji should go live with Kenji's half-sister in Shizuoka. This sister had previously lived in Nippon Light Metal company housing in Niigata, where she and her husband had let Kenji board with them for a time. After that, she and the other four members of her family had moved to company housing near a new plant opened by Nippon Light Metal in the city of Shimizu in Shizuoka Prefecture.

The half-sister agreed to take care of Yūji, but first needed to find a house to rent as her own place was too small. In the meantime, another half-sister in Yamagata agreed to take Yūji temporarily. This sister had been given up for adoption soon after her birth, but in those days the ties of obligation that bound children to their parents were much stronger.

In July 1962, Yūji left for Yamagata, accompanied by Hideko. In October, he returned briefly to Akishima for about three nights, accompanied by the half-sister's eldest son, and then headed to Shizuoka. Since the preceding year Yūji had suffered from stress-induced high blood pressure and could not travel alone.

The half-sister in Shizuoka took care of Yūji in a small rented house. In May 1964 he died of a stroke at the age of seventy-nine. "I had known he was still having trouble with high blood pressure, but suddenly there was a phone call from my sister in Shizuoka saying that he was in bad shape and I should come at once. By the time I got there he was already dead. In any case, it was a shock." The Tokyo Olympics were the big news at the time, but Kenji says that he remembers absolutely nothing about them.

Once relieved of Yūji's care, Hiroko's mental state improved. In September 1962, Kenji's only child, a boy, was born. This younger son was named Eiji. The following summer Kenji took Eiji to Okayama to visit his grandmother Kochiyo, who was delighted to see Ken's little boy.

As the daughter of an elementary-school principal, Hiroko was keen on education, buying Gōichi and Eiji picture books and subscriptions to children's magazines like *Shōgaku ichinensei* (First Year in Elementary School). Before her marriage, Hiroko had received a letter from her mother urging her to start setting aside money for her children's university education. This type of family culture was alien to Kenji. Like Ishichi and Yūji before him, he left the children's education to his wife.

Gōichi was enrolled in an elementary school in Akishima, where he did quite well. Eiji was sent to one of the private kindergartens that had just begun to appear in the neighborhood. There were still no day care centers close by, and so Hiroko concentrated on housework and raising the children. Kenji would occasionally look after Eiji and take him along on sales rounds, but only when Hiroko had other business to take care of.

Around 1965 they began to celebrate the children's birthdays with cake and candles. For Kenji this was an unfamiliar custom. "Before the war, ordinary people went by the traditional method of age counting, in which everyone grew a year older at New Year's. Only the intelligentsia and upper classes celebrated individual birthdays. But Hiroko came from an intellectual family, and I guess they had that custom."

Kenji was busy with work and simply turned his salary over to Hiroko, not interfering in any way with how she spent it. It was Hiroko who did the family bookkeeping and saved money to buy a house so they could get out of public housing. According to the family account book Hiroko kept, in 1962 Kenji's monthly wages were a bit more than ¥30,000, though the amount was not fixed and payment was frequently delayed by as much as a week. When this happened, sometimes there would be virtually no cash left on hand. "Whenever the company developed even a bit of breathing room, President Watase would do something to expand operations. And every time, this meant everybody's pay would be delayed. When Eiji was born I had to borrow ¥40,000 from the company."

In 1962, a day's worth of food for the Oguma family ran ¥300 to ¥400. A trip to the barber cost ¥130. A month's rent was ¥2,500. The electric bill ranged between ¥500 and ¥800 a month, and milk (including delivery) was ¥1,480. The biggest expenses of the year were a vacuum cleaner at ¥11,200, a fan at ¥10,000, a ¥6,000 camera, educational materials and school supplies for Gōichi at ¥23,713, and expenses for Eiji's birth at ¥21,800. Even so, that year the family was able to put ¥52,185 into a postal savings account and ¥10,000 into life insurance.

Income for the Oguma family in 1962 included ¥408,477 from Kenji's wages, ¥40,000 in bonuses on large orders, ¥5,061 in stock dividend payments, and so on for a grand total of ¥506,757. Household expenditures were ¥432,416 and purchases of stock amounted to ¥11,100.

"When we put together a really big deal, the wholesalers gave us rebates. After the Tachikawa Store secured its profit, the rest was given as a bonus to the person who made the sale. The stock purchases were made by Hiroko under the influence of her younger brother, who worked in a securities company."

As the overall economy took off, life gradually became easier. In 1961, a "leisure boom" was being touted by the mass media, though Kenji says, "About all I recall doing by way of 'leisure' was the year after Eiji was born when I drove all four of us out to see the fireworks along the riverbank at Hamura. The year after that we went cherry-blossom viewing at the botanical gardens in Jindai. In other words, a few excursions that didn't cost anything."

Even with the advent of the postwar economic boom, the lives of ordinary people remained modest. In 1968 a survey of leisure activities and entertainment experienced within the preceding three months found reading books to be in first place, followed by a trip lasting at least overnight (mostly to a domestic destination) at number two. Third place (high among women only) was sewing and handicrafts, fourth was having a drink at home, and in fifth place was going to see a movie or theatrical performance (in both cases, mainly in popular rather than highbrow genres).*

The character of the new postwar generation would be the center of much attention in the 1960s, but the mainstream of society was still formed by the prewar generation Kenji represented. The continuing dominance of this generation is clearly indicated in the terminology adopted by the mass media of the time, which labeled the major peaks of the high-growth era with names like the "Jinmu Boom," "Iwato Boom," and "Izanagi Boom" taken from ancient Japanese mythology (a prominent part of prewar but not postwar public education). Similarly, the three major consumer durables most sought after in the boom years—refrigerators, washing machines, and black-and-white TVs—were dubbed the "Three Sacred Treasures," a reference to the Imperial Regalia.

In 1968, Kenji's grandmother Kochiyo died in Okayama at the age of ninety-one. Kenji had seen her for the last time in 1965, when he had taken Eiji with him on a sleeper train from Tokyo. By this time, the centenary of the 1868 Meiji Restoration, the generations of Kenji's parents and grandparents had largely joined the ancestors. For Kenji, Kochiyo, with whom he had spent the formative years of his life from six to nineteen, was his real mother. In keeping with local custom, the funeral was a burial, rather than a cremation as is more common in Japan today. Years later, Kochiyo's body was exhumed and cremated along with Ishichi's for transfer to the plot in Tama Reien cemetery in Tokyo that Ishichi had purchased before the war. By that time, their remains had already almost completely returned to earth; only Kochiyo's burial attire, made of synthetic materials, remained bright and completely unfaded.

6

While Kenji's life was becoming increasingly stable, the fortunes of the Tachikawa Store had begun to decline. Intensified competition from other stores, the end to the effectiveness of growth through

---

* November 1968 survey by Video Research Ltd., cited in Uemura Tadashi, *Henbō suru shakai* (Seibundō Shinkōsha, 1969), p. 174.

direct sales, and President Watase's tendency to overreach were all factors.

One harbinger of the crisis in the company's management came in 1961. For a long time Isetan had been the only department store with a branch in Tachikawa, but that year the rival Takashimaya chain teamed up with local retailers to build a five-story shopping center named Takashimaya Tokyo Store. Watase eagerly purchased the rights to open two outlets in this new building to sell sporting goods and accessories. His wife was put in charge of the accessories business.

This expansion led to cash-flow problems, and, as evidenced by the Oguma family account book, payment of wages began to be delayed.

"With direct sales, you have a pretty clear idea of how much you are actually going to sell and bring only what you need into inventory, so in a month or two you make your margin and have cash in hand. But with in-store retail, even if you put money into stocking the shelves, you can't recover your investment until the stuff sells. So I knew right away that opening new stores was going to make things tough. But the boss was just a real go-getter."

In the midst of all this, Takahashi, who had headed the sports department, left the Tachikawa Store and opened his own business. In the world of small and medium-sized businesses, where annual raises were rare, there wasn't much point in continuing to work at a company for too long. Once you had acquired the necessary skills, it was quite sensible to strike out on your own.

"Takahashi-san had a strong personality and a lot of pride. I think he felt that he was really the one responsible for the success of the sports department at the Tachikawa Store. He'd gradually been getting out of sync with President Watase, and when our wages started getting delayed in 1961 he got into an argument with the boss and quit. Both of them liked to drink, and from what I heard they started shouting at each other at some bar.

"Takahashi-san came to me and Ōki to say that he was setting up shop on his own and wanted us to join him. He seems to have thought we'd just naturally follow him. But I felt that if I did, I would always be playing second fiddle to him. So I asked Ōki, 'What do you think? Seems to me that this isn't the time to go independent.' Ōki nodded, 'I was thinking the same thing.' So at that point, we both decided to stay.

"Takahashi-san ran a sporting goods store in Koganei for about three years, but in the end it failed. He had a wife and two kids, and I don't know what happened after that. But he knew a lot of people, so I imagine he did OK."

The crisis at the Tachikawa Store subsided as the newly opened outlets got on track. But in 1965, Yamaichi Securities, one of Japan's "Big Four" securities companies, ran into severe financial difficulties, triggering the "securities recession." In December of that year, Tachikawa Store went bankrupt.

The immediate cause of the bankruptcy was President Watase's decision, in the fall of 1963, to put up a three-story reinforced concrete building near the existing building at the south exit of Tachikawa Station. The first and second floors were used as warehouse and office space, while the third floor served as the boss's residence. This construction project immediately threw the company into cash-flow trouble, and once again, payment of wages began to be delayed.

"I figured the boss had done the math before deciding to put up the new building, but one of our wholesale suppliers asked me if I thought everything was OK. At the time there were a number of cases of small businesses that had done relatively well in the economic boom running into cash-flow issues and going under as soon as they got themselves a fancy new building or something. I imagine the wholesaler was aware of this pattern.

"The fundamental reason for the bankruptcy was the boss's management strategy, which, as in the case of the new building, was geared completely to expansion. As soon as direct sales of stationery took off, he went into sporting goods, then office equipment, then musical instruments, all following the same formula. When he ran into increasing competition in a particular field, and the effectiveness of his business began to decline, he'd expand into a different field, and then another, over and over. He was actually pretty good at predicting what would hit it big next, like musical instruments, for example, but he wasn't so good at keeping his feet on the ground."

The aggressive style of start-up businesses can result in big hits, but also equally large misses. A large corporation can cover a loss in one division with profits from the others. But for a small business it often only takes one big mistake to fail.

"Since the company was always borrowing money to keep expanding, there was never actually any cash on hand. On top of this came the new building. By around the time of the Tokyo Olympics [in the summer of 1964], our pay often began to be delayed by as much as a month. The number of employees had gone from about ten when I joined the company to about thirty in the end, so there were a lot more personnel expenses. The bankruptcy happened to coincide with the recession, but I think we would have run aground before long anyway."

By this time just before the bankruptcy, Kenji was the number-two man at the Tachikawa Store. In addition to becoming head of the sports department after Takahashi's departure, he had wound up managing the company's finances due to his accounting and bookkeeping background.

"The accounting clerk who had been hired around 1960 was fired in 1965 when the boss found out he'd received a kickback from the construction company that put up the new building. After that the boss and his eldest daughter handled the accounting, but during the final six months or so I got involved because I just couldn't bear to watch what they were doing."

In order to keep the company from insolvency, Kenji made the rounds of its principal wholesalers and other creditors asking for a "jump," which meant holding back from cashing a check until the next settlement period.

"One month, on the settlement date, I went around making this request of several of the wholesalers I thought most likely to say yes. 'We've done business together a long time,' I would say, and managed to get some of them to listen. But others refused. Then, the next month, I went to different companies with the same request. I did this only twice, but it was hell. The man at one of the wholesalers I talked to, a real veteran, advised me that if things were really this bad I should just let the company default on its payments rather than drawing out the pain."

Meanwhile, the employees also began to get fed up with the lateness of their wages. One of them went to the council of unions in Tachikawa to complain, and in the summer of 1965, a local union organizer showed up at one of President Watase's morning assemblies to open negotiations. (In Japanese schools it is customary for the principal to deliver a brief speech to the students each morning, and similar morning assemblies are common at many companies, to this day.)

"At these morning assemblies, President Watase would report on management and give pep talks. When the local labor organizer proposed the formation of a union at the Tachikawa Store he agreed, seeing as he'd been a Communist Party activist and was sympathetic to the labor movement. But by that time, even with a union to negotiate for the workers, the company no longer had anything it could give them." Finally, in December 1965, Kenji filed the company's bankruptcy.

"The banks were all saying they couldn't wait any longer on loan payments, and the wholesalers couldn't wait any longer to be paid either, so that was it. In the end our main bank and the biggest wholesaler took control of matters. They'd already repossessed the company land in front of Tachikawa Station. Other creditors called in smaller assets that had been put up as security, and the rest were out of luck. At the final creditors' meeting, the major creditors had already agreed on the plan to be followed.

"Wholesalers from central Tokyo couldn't really be bothered to come all the way out to Tachikawa to collect on small debts. In those days, when a small or mid-sized business went bankrupt, a month or so later people would simply say, 'Gee, that was too bad,' and then forget about it and turn to other more productive matters.

"In terms of the priority of paying off obligations, employee salaries and wages came first, then taxes, followed by the banks. This was apparently standard procedure. The banks wrapped themselves in the flag of social responsibility, arguing they should come after tax debts were settled since they had been entrusted with the savings of the nation's citizens. The banks didn't lose anything, and the other creditors were mollified one way or another, so one of the bank representatives told me, 'That was a very clean bankruptcy.'"

In the bankruptcy negotiations, Kenji managed to keep the rights to the retail outlets in the Takashimaya Tokyo Store concealed from the creditors so he could pass them on to President Watase and his family. At least one of the wholesalers knew about it, but since it did not amount to much of an asset for seizure they apparently turned a blind eye.

"As far as I was concerned, I thought the best thing would be for the boss to run these shops as a family business. That way he wouldn't

216

have to make payroll. Almost all the employees, including the people from Watase's old home in Kōshū, had been terminated except for two or three of the women, so it was as though the boss and his family had been put into a space capsule at the head of a rocket while the rest had been jettisoned."

Watase invited Kenji to stay on and work at the stores. But Kenji declined, deciding to team up with Ōki and go independent. In January 1966, Kenji founded Tachikawa Sports, Inc.

"Both the Tachikawa Store and Tachikawa Sports were incorporated, but mostly in name only. The only shareholders in Tachikawa Sports were Ōki and myself; the 'Inc.' at the end was something I added just for show. I'd done a solid, responsible job of seeing the Tachikawa Store through the bankruptcy, so the banks and the wholesalers trusted me and there were no obstacles to doing business.

"By the early 1960s social conditions had stabilized, and in contrast to the immediate postwar period, credentials mattered. In other words, you now introduced yourself with your business card. The first business card I'd ever had was the one I'd made with a pseudonym when I was working at that publishing company in Niigata, but later when I started at the Tachikawa Store I had a proper one made with my real name. The use of 'Inc.' was part of this kind of thinking. 'Oguma Store' just didn't have the right ring, and wouldn't inspire trust."

Kenji and Ōki opened up shop in a small rented building on the edge of the town center with about twenty-five square meters of floor space. It was primarily intended not as a retail outlet, but as an office for receiving direct sales orders by telephone. The two of them retained their contacts from the direct sales operations at the Tachikawa Store. In effect it was as though they had broken off from their old company with their clients in tow.

"Our new store for Tachikawa Sports was about half a kilometer from the department store where President Watase had his shops. I thought we'd picked a place far enough away, though I recall that after we opened, he came by and complained. But I'm not bothered by what other people think of me. Making a living comes first."

In the beginning, Kenji and Ōki were the only employees of Tachikawa Sports. A little later, they hired one of the Kōshū women from the Tachikawa Store to do office work and answer the phone. Kenji was in charge of accounting, and Hiroko helped with keeping the books. The woman working in the office would later marry Ōki. In short, it became a two-family operation, though both women were put on payroll.

The two men were able to work their sales routes without having to share their revenue with other employees, which cut some of the dead weight of the Tachikawa Store days. Naturally, this made for better business. Immediately before the Tachikawa Store closed, Kenji was making about ¥40,000 a month; by the end of 1966 this had risen to nearly ¥100,000.

"After about a year, when it looked like we were going to be a success, we decided to legally incorporate. I picked a good time to start a new business. A bit later, and we would have missed the boom. Or if I'd stayed with the Tachikawa Store, I would have ended up just taking care of President Watase and his family, and would have never gotten anywhere."

Around this time, even in Kenji's public housing complex, a gap was beginning to emerge between the people able to ride the wave of the economic boom and those who had missed it. Kenji's household got its own telephone in 1967, and a color television in 1968—the latter provoking considerable excitement among the neighborhood children.

"At the time, even if you applied to the telephone company to have a phone installed, it took a long time to go through, maybe because they were getting so many orders for new service. In any event, you couldn't even apply without buying a fixed bond. Since Hiroko was helping with the company bookkeeping from home, we applied for a business account as the Akishima branch of Tachikawa Sports. I think we were probably the first people in our complex to put in a private phone line. They even installed a telephone pole just for us."

On the other hand, there were housewives in their neighborhood who apparently could not afford washing machines and still did their laundry outdoors in washtubs under the eaves of the building. Gōichi, who was always rather mature for his age, referred to the complex in English as a "slum."

The Vietnam War was reaching its peak in those years. Huge American military transport planes were constantly flying at low altitude in and out of Yokota Air Base just next door. Each takeoff or landing was so loud that it was impossible to carry on a conversation;

they also interfered with TV reception. When Hiroko's younger sister came for a visit her five-year-old son was so startled by the noise that he began crying. "Though Eiji was only a year different, he'd been used to it since he was born, so it didn't faze him. But for people coming from outside it must have seemed quite loud."

The year 1968 also brought the student movement. For Kenji, the universities were another world entirely. "I thought the demands of Akita Akehiro and his student group at Nihon University for the investigation of shady accounting practices were quite reasonable. As for the University of Tokyo, I was able to follow that things had begun with protests by interns in the medical school over their treatment, but after that I had a hard time understanding what all the ruckus was about. Later on it seemed like the radical New Left groups got involved in both places, and things went completely crazy."

One other event of the period that made a lasting impression on Kenji was the Cultural Revolution in China. "I'd experienced the so-called democratic movement of reeducation in the Soviet labor camps, so I knew what it was like to be surrounded by a mob of people and accused in that way. When I saw the reports, it brought back the past and sickened me."

Kenji in 1966, visiting Gifu Prefecture at the invitation of a sports equipment manufacturer.

In January 1969, Kenji and his family left Metropolitan Housing No. 6 to move into a house they had built in Murayama township (from 1970, the city of Musashi Murayama) in Kitatama-gun, Tokyo. The house stood in a new development, Mitsufuji Homes, that had been created by the Tokyo Metropolitan Housing Supply Corporation. Hiroko had decided the family should move there after seeing a brochure about it that had been circulated in their complex, which was also managed by the Tokyo government.

As noted earlier, by this period public rental housing was beginning to contract, and home ownership was being promoted, in part to help stimulate the economy. Since Kenji had built up trust with the banks through his management of the Tachikawa Store bankruptcy, he was able to get financing to cover building a new home.

"Our neighbors, the families of the Self-Defense Forces soldier and the bus driver, remained in Metropolitan Housing No. 6. The Self-Defense Forces guy had three kids, and his life did not look easy. The bus driver's family lost their little daughter when she fell into a ditch along the road. Nowadays it would make the news, but back then such accidents were fairly common.

"Even if you were working hard, it was not that simple to save enough money to build a home and get out of public housing. I was lucky—I caught the wave. When it came time to leave, we took care not to show how happy we really were. I think we were the first people we knew to make it out of public housing."

The new home in Murayama, built of reinforced concrete, was designed to meet Hiroko's dreams. Kenji was already forty-three years old, and he felt like he'd finally reached the goal in his game of life. Little did he know that in only three years, they would have to let go of this house.

Chapter 8

Memories of the War

In January of 1969, Kenji and his family left public housing to move into their newly built home—a modern two-story reinforced concrete house with central heating, air conditioning, and rooftop access.

The layout was what is described in Japan as a 4LDK: four rooms in addition to an open-plan living/dining/kitchen area. The living room was spacious. One of the additional rooms was in Japanese style, with tatami mats; there was also a master bedroom, and each of the two boys got his own room. The plans had been drawn up by a designer at a construction company who was the brother of a Tokyo metropolitan government employee Kenji had gotten to know through work. The house had been designed as much as possible to Hiroko's wishes, with furnishings including a chandelier and a sofa, and she was delighted with it.

Tachikawa Sports, Inc.—founded by Kenji in 1966.

1

The family's new home was in the township of Murayama (from 1970, the city of Musashi Murayama) in western Tokyo. It stood in a housing development, Mitsufuji Homes, recently created by the Tokyo Metropolitan Housing Supply Corporation on farmland that had been subdivided into individual privately owned lots.

Also in the same township was the Nissan-Prince Murayama automobile factory, opened in 1961. The area surrounding the housing development, however, was still largely rural, with fields of vegetables and mulberry groves for raising silkworms.

"Mitsufuji was a new place-name made by combining the names of two farm hamlets in the area [Mitsuki and Nakafuji]. There was no railway serving Musashi Murayama, so transportation was a bit inconvenient, but that was what you got with a public development. I was going to be driving to Tachikawa anyway, so the lack of a train didn't strike me as a problem. Gōichi was entering middle school and Eiji starting elementary school that same year, so Hiroko went to both their entrance ceremonies, one in the morning and the other in the afternoon."

Their home was custom-built in what was, at the time, a fairly innovative design. Kenji recalls the construction costs as having been in excess of ¥10 million, at a time when starting monthly salaries for college graduates were usually no more than ¥30,000. However, because Kenji was not working for a big corporation—indeed, he had only just started a small business—he could not put together a standard housing loan.

"I paid cash for the land. Then I arranged financing to build the house itself through Japan Mutual Bank,* which Tachikawa Sports did business with. I was able to borrow from them because of the trust I'd already established as a client."

In time with the move, he traded his company light van for a standard passenger sedan, a Nissan Skyline. "I was at the Nissan-Prince factory in Musashi Murayama all the time on business, so it

---

* Later merged into Taiyō Bank and then the Mitsui Sumitomo Banking Corporation.

had to be a Nissan. If I'd been driving anything else, security wouldn't have let me through the gate."

Hiroko was delighted with the new house built to her speci-fications, Kenji less so. "It was too fancy, and it somehow made me uncomfortable. To be quite honest, I wasn't as happy about moving in there as I had been about moving into Metropolitan Housing No. 6. It was big, though, and I thought how nice it would have been if I'd been able to have my father or grandmother come to live with us."

Mitsufuji Homes was laid out on a grid, as Metropolitan Housing No. 6 had been, with several hundred families living in newly built houses.

"Our neighbors on either side were a schoolteacher and the owner of a greengrocer's in central Tokyo. Across the way was a woman who appeared to be the mistress of someone in the entertainment industry, and a guy who was middle management in some company. There was also a painter nearby. Overall the people were higher class than at Metropolitan Housing No. 6. Since the transportation was so inconvenient, I don't think any of them were commuting into central Tokyo."

At this point, Tachikawa Sports was doing well. The economic boom had inspired a series of sports fads—skiing, golf, bowling—and the related equipment was selling briskly.

"With the exception of bowling, they were all sports of the prewar bourgeoisie that ordinary people had dreamed about. When the bowling boom started, lots of people wanted their own ball. We'd use model balls in the store to measure where the holes should be to match each person's grip and send the specs to the manufacturer, who would drill the holes and send back the completed ball. I would never buy anything like that myself, but there seemed to be a lot more people with money at that point."

Tachikawa Sports's mainstay continued to be direct sales. In 1969 a third salesman, Takenaka, was added to the original team of Kenji and Ōki. "He was a young guy, just a few years older than the baby-boomers, whose family ran a shop making and installing interior fittings. He'd only completed middle school, but since he was from a tradesman's family that had probably been considered enough. He loved the mountains and often went rock climbing." After him, more staff were added, reaching a peak of around ten.

In the 1960s the children of the baby boom were advancing beyond primary education, and new middle schools, high schools, and universities were being built in rapid succession. Among the initial customers of Tachikawa Sports were Tachikawa High School (founded 1901), Kunitachi High School (founded 1940), and Kitatama High School (founded 1948). Afterward there was a rush of new school openings—including Hino High School (1966), Kokubunji High School (1969), and Haijima High School (1978)—and Kenji targeted them all.

"With the high schools and middle schools, you wanted to get in right when they were setting up. A new school had a substantial budget for equipment, out of which it bought most of what it needed from the big vendors in central Tokyo. After that, the local small and mid-sized vendors would come scrabbling for orders to supplement or replenish what had already been purchased. None of them had any help from the big boys; it was all an open race. At the time the schools looked at competitive bids as a waste of time and just picked whichever seemed the most convenient.

"At the beginning of April, when the school terms would start, I would go straight to the gym teachers and drop off my business card and a catalogue. Then I would make the rounds of the schools in turn, popping into each place about once every week or ten days. I didn't want to annoy them by coming right on the first day of school on April 1, or by calling on them too often; I would give it some space, and then drop by again. I didn't really do anything in terms of entertaining clients. The real key to getting orders was to avoid doing anything that would upset people or give you a bad reputation."

During the final years of the Tachikawa Store, Kenji and his colleagues had been acting as middlemen who took orders from schools and other institutions and placed them with sports equipment wholesalers and installers of gym equipment, while taking a cut for the store on each transaction.

"At Tachikawa Sports, like at Tachikawa Store, we supplied goods based on what the budgets of the Tokyo metropolitan government and the various city governments made available. From the early 1970s, we also began to take orders for the installation and maintenance of equipment like horizontal bars and basketball hoops. We didn't do the installation or maintenance ourselves, of course; that would be contracted to the equipment vendors. We served as the middlemen. However, things like painting outdoor equipment, which was easy enough, we would take care of ourselves.

"With school sports facilities, I think the projects big enough to involve construction companies required a lot of political clout to get. Smaller companies simply didn't have that kind of power, and a swarm of us were always competing with one another. For the metropolitan high schools, the really big orders at any new school would be doled out beforehand to the big vendors by the metropolitan government; the smaller businesses had to make do with what was left. At the level of the municipal middle schools and such, project allocations were determined by the finance department of Tachikawa City Hall, for example, so that was where we went to negotiate. Once you'd targeted a potential client and developed some connections, it was surprising how long the relationship could last."

By this time in the 1970s, the situation had shifted somewhat from the relatively open competition among newly established businesses that had characterized the 1960s. Back when Kenji and his associates had first started out, direct sales had primarily involved organizing displays and demonstrations in places with many potential customers, or going around to schools and company offices to attract large orders. But at some point, their work slid into cultivating relationships with schools and other public-sector clients to get contracts on a regular basis.

The times were changing. In the era of ruined cities and the black market immediately after the war, farmers, who had direct access to foodstuffs, and shady marketeers and distributors had cut larger figures than white-collar workers. Into the 1950s, the general mood favored practical ability over credentials and titles. But by the time Kenji and his fellows opened Tachikawa Sports in 1966 and sought to spruce up their image by adding "Inc.," the company name inscribed on one's business card had become much more important. The shift of the core of their business to steady orders from public institutions paralleled this overall social trend.

"From the early 1950s onward, everyone gradually turned into 'salarymen' and the number of dyed-in-the-wool 'merchants' declined. By 'merchant' I mean someone who starts from nothing, with nothing, and makes something out of it with his own talents and smarts. Ōki-san was like that—a merchant and self-made man.

"I on the other hand thought of myself as a salaryman, basically because I'd started out at Fuji Telecommunications. Even at the Tachikawa Store, the feeling was that if you were collecting a monthly wage, then you were a salaryman. After we started Tachikawa Sports, I was on the side telling people what to do, and so I was called 'President.'"

Kenji's trajectory through life does not even come close to the image of lifetime employment at a major Japanese corporation that is usually summoned up by the word "salaryman." In that sense, it seems odd that Kenji would have conceived of himself in such terms.

Yet it is also true that our self-images are frequently distorted by the assumptions of the society in which we live. In fact, the "salaryman" employment characteristic of large corporations has never accounted for even 20 percent of the Japanese labor force. Far more than the actual numbers, though, it defined the image in Japanese society of an "average person" or a "secure lifestyle" during that era. The fact that a person like Kenji saw himself as a salaryman underscores the point.

One contributing factor was that the educated stratum of people working in the mass media, thinking themselves and their classmates to be representative of the rest of society, popularized the image of their own salaryman lifestyle. Lacking other models, working-class households that achieved a certain level of income defaulted to copying this lifestyle, albeit superficially. No doubt other factors were involved as well, but in any case it was during this period that the image of Japanese society as equal and uniform—a nation that was "entirely middle class" and "ethnically homogenous," as the common catchphrases went—became firmly established.

In a survey published by the Prime Minister's Office in 1969, the year that Kenji and his family left public housing, 90 percent of respondents placed themselves in the "middie" of Japanese society. Of course, since the survey was of self-reported evaluations chosen from the categories of "upper," "upper-middle," "middle-middle," "lower-middle," and "lower," responses naturally tended to skew in the direction of "middle," broadly defined. In fact, an international comparative survey using the same categories found that even in the

United States, India, Singapore, and the Philippines, more than 90 percent of respondents also placed themselves in the "middle." Kenji says, "If you'd asked me at the time, I'd probably have said 'middle,' too."[*]

At any rate, this emerging social configuration did prove beneficial in terms of bringing stability. One of the biggest effects in this regard for Kenji was the participation of Tachikawa Sports in the Employees' Pension Insurance program.

The pension system established by the Japanese government in 1958 was divided into two basic components: Employees' Pension Insurance (kōsei nenkin) for salaried or wage-earning private-sector workers whose employers provide employee pension plans, and the National Pension Fund (kokumin nenkin) for the self-employed, unemployed, or employees of very small firms without pension plans. Employees' Pension Insurance, modeled on the system established earlier for public-sector workers, is organized into industry-based pension associations that are funded by deductions from employee wages and matching contributions from employers. In contrast, the National Pension Fund is administered by regional pension associations and funded only by contributions from those enrolled, so that the benefits paid by this program are only half to one-third that of the Employees' Pension. Therefore, everyone in Japan is guaranteed a pension of some kind, there are great discrepancies in the amounts that individuals receive, and in the twenty-first century the number of elderly people living in poverty has been on the rise.

"Because Employees' Pension Insurance requires contributions from the employer, many individual business owners prefer to avoid the extra burden and let the National Pension take care of such matters. That was what we did for the first two years or so as well, but then once the business got on track we shifted to the Employees' Pension. It wasn't for any profound reason; we sort of felt it gave the company some class, like attaching 'Inc.' to our name.

"At the time, I was still operating on the prewar idea that you should set aside enough money on your own while you could still work to make it through your old age. I never had any thought of living on a pension. But because of the decision we made then, I'm able to receive Employees' Pension benefits now. For people enrolled

---

[*] Hashimoto Kenji, *"Kakusa" no sengoshi* (Kawade Shobō Shinsha, 2009), p. 139.

only in the National Pension, full benefits don't amount to any more than ¥60,000 a month [about $550 at present exchange rates]. I used to exchange New Year's cards with a man who also owned a small sporting goods company but hadn't incorporated [leaving him ineligible for the Employees' Pension], and I remember him writing about how tough old age had been on him financially.

"I didn't even realize it until I began receiving benefits, but Tachikawa Store had been enrolled in Employees' Pension Insurance as well. Maybe because the boss had been a member of the Communist Party, he took employee health and welfare seriously. The pension I receive today was accumulated during the years I worked at Fuji Telecommunications, Tachikawa Store, and Tachikawa Sports. It's certainly helped me out, but it's only because I've been lucky. The Japanese bureaucracy seems unable to adapt institutions to the changing demands of the times, which I think is why so many people have been left out and why there is such a sense of unfairness and inequality."

2

Tragically, the Oguma family's peaceful life was abruptly interrupted in February 1972 when Gōichi, then a third-year middle school student, died in an accident.

"The company had organized an employee ski trip to Chino in Nagano Prefecture, and Hiroko and Eiji took advantage of the opportunity to come along too. Gōichi stayed at home alone to study for his high school entrance exams. When we got back from our trip, we found family and relatives gathered at our place, and they told us that Gōichi had died after falling from the roof of the house."

Knocked out by the fall, Gōichi had frozen to death in the midwinter cold. Gōichi's grades had been good and he had always been mature for his age; even as a middle school student he had been reading Chinese and Western literature. Hiroko became extremely depressed and distraught, and the entire household was plunged into deep gloom.

As it happened, an armed student radical group had just taken over the Asama Mountain Lodge in Nagano Prefecture and was holding hostages against a police siege.

"The TV was constantly streaming news of the shootout between police and the student radicals and the discovery of bodies in the mountains. The combination of all this with Gōichi's funeral made for a suffocatingly dark atmosphere."

The funeral was conducted in the living room of the family home, with Gōichi's body laid out before a Buddhist altar and mourners coming to pay their last respects. The offering book for the funeral listed 113 mourners who made the traditional *kōden* (monetary offering to the bereaved family) and an additional 68 who did not. Including still others such as Gōichi's classmates, that made for a total attendance of more than two hundred people. Only a few of them were Kenji's business contacts; the majority were relatives and neighbors. Compared with an average funeral today, this was a very large number of mourners.

Hiroko was so grief-stricken that she said she could no longer bear living in the house. So they decided to move from Musashi Murayama, where they had spent three years.

"I'd put a lot of money into that house, intending to live out my days there, but there was no other choice. We found buyers, but given the circumstances, I heard that after we moved out they tore the house down to build a place of their own. Since it was made of reinforced concrete, the demolition must have been quite a chore. We may have only gotten what the land was worth; I can't remember now. At the time profit or loss was the farthest thing from my mind."

The family bought a condominium in Tachikawa, where Kenji worked. It was on the tenth floor of a newly constructed twelve-story building, with only a 2DK floor plan—about a third of the floor space of their home in Musashi Murayama. Their unit looked down onto a metal scrapyard across the street where workers were busy breaking up and recycling used fuel tanks from American military jets apparently brought in from the Tachikawa Air Base. The unit across the hall was occupied by an employee of the Tokyo metropolitan government; the other tenants were mostly elderly or middle-aged, and in any case Kenji and his family had little contact with them.

This made the eleventh time that Kenji had moved since returning from Siberia. Kenji was forty-six, Hiroko forty-three. Their only child, Eiji, was still only nine, and it would be another decade before he would be ready to go out on his own. After losing Gōichi, Hiroko was depressed and sickly. Kenji occasionally took her and Eiji on family vacation trips by car, including one in 1974 to their shared hometown of Saroma in Hokkaido. But they did little else besides call on some of their distant relatives, and they never went back again.

Tachikawa Sports was still hiring new employees, but by this time the business had begun to lose momentum. The oil crisis of 1973 brought an end to the era of high economic growth in Japan. Academic credentials became ever more entrenched as a determinant of socioeconomic status; small and medium-sized businesses had an increasingly difficult time recruiting and retaining outstanding employees.

"In 1970, we had someone come to us from an administrative position at the Musashi factory of Hitachi. He was a mid-level guy with a high school education, but I heard that some sort of workplace accident had made him want to get out. I was at the plant regularly on sales calls, and he said he wanted to come work for me, so I hired him. I think part of it was that he had really gotten tired of the routine of a big company. He loved music and was into the guitar and audio equipment. He was a good guy, but his sales performance was not that great. His pay didn't go up, and I guess working for a tiny firm was not what he'd imagined it would be, so he quit.

"Another time we hired a professional bookkeeper at the recommendation of Takenaka-san. He was smart, knew what he was doing with the books, and understood things like the tax system better than I did. But he was one of the first to take off when the business began to run into difficulties in the late 1970s. There were various others we hired, too, none of whom stayed for long. Like me, they were all people who had sort of run off the rails. I don't think any of them even particularly liked sports. My generation worked like mad simply to live and to eat, but as the times grew more relaxed, people changed—though I don't want to preach."

In 1975, Tachikawa Sports opened a branch in Hachiōji, albeit as the result of a merger and acquisition rather than the creation of an entirely new store.

"We took over a sporting goods store that had originally been a two-man operation near the south exit of Hachiōji Station. They'd run into difficulties, and one night one of the owners skipped town to escape his debts. At the request of the remaining owner, we merged his business with ours, though without taking over responsibility for his outstanding loans. Our reason for the merger was that sales had slowed as a result of the oil crisis, and we hoped that by increasing in-store retail we might create a new direction for ourselves."

At the time, Kenji was fifty. He was still optimistic about his business. But the high-growth era was coming to a close and the social and economic order was growing more entrenched. In sporting goods, as in many areas, big-box stores had risen to prominence, and consumers were being drawn to their vast selections of goods and discount prices. Smaller stores rapidly felt the impact of this competition.

"The merger gave us a location close to Hachiōji Station, and the first five years or so went well, but then competition increased and sales didn't. We just didn't see the kind of sales growth we'd anticipated, only more and more red ink, and so in the 1980s we pulled out, leaving the business to the original owner."

After the misfire in Hachiōji, Kenji and his colleagues moved the Tachikawa store closer to the station and tried once again to increase their presence, but this, too, failed to meet expectations.

"The new shop was near the station, but not on a route to it that drew a lot of foot traffic, and the rent was high, so we were unsuccessful. We hadn't put that much of our energy into store retail in the past, so we didn't really anticipate the problems."

At this point, all they could do was hope to hold on to the loyalty of the customers and clients they had built up through direct sales. In this period, public institutions were increasingly tending to privilege the big vendors rather than conducting competitive bidding. With neither political clout nor the financial strength to give large discounts, smaller and weaker firms naturally fell into collusion and bid-rigging.

"Vendors talked a lot to one another. In the late 1970s, Takenaka-san went to an orientation meeting for bidding on contracts at city hall. While outside talking with some fellow vendors he apparently said something like, 'Look, I've got dibs on such-and-such a school, so let me have that piece of the action.' One or two of the vendors snitched on him to the municipal authorities, who called him in, accusing him of bid-rigging. I told him that in a situation like that all you can do is brazen it out and pretend nothing happened, and we managed to get out of it that way.

"Eventually what happened was that a kind of unspoken agreement over turf grew up among the vendors regarding which schools belonged to which company. Once we established a relationship with a school, we continued to supply it for many years, like the sets of gym clothes the students purchased in their first year."

While continuing in this stable but stagnating financial position, Kenji moved the family into a home in a new development in Hachiōji called Nan'yōdai ("Sunny Hills") that had been carved out of the Tama hills by Sumitomo Realty & Development, a unit of one of the four major business conglomerates in Japan. Financing for the house was again provided by the Japan Mutual Bank, on the basis of the long-standing business ties Kenji had with it. As before, he left the design completely in Hiroko's hands.

The house was a 6LDK layout built of wood by a highly skilled carpenter-contractor. When the family moved into it, Kenji was fifty-four. In the living room were a Persian carpet, a chandelier, and a piano they had purchased used from Tokyo Gakugei University through his sister Hideko. Kenji showed little interest either in the details of the loan or in the design of the house itself. In the end, he was able to pay off the loan in a little over ten years. Once more, he drove his car to work in Tachikawa.

Although Nan'yōdai was a new housing estate far out in the western hills, there was bus service to a rail station on the Keiō Line, so many people who lived there commuted to jobs in central Tokyo. The neighbor to their right was a union leader at Sumitomo Light Metal who later took a management position with the company. To the left was a man who worked for a construction company, and behind them, a Korean resident of Japan who was an attorney. "Since the development had been built by Sumitomo Realty, a lot of the residents had some kind of tie to Sumitomo." The majority were around forty years old; there were few small business owners in their fifties like Kenji.

Having just bought a new home, Kenji wanted to play it safe as he entered the 1980s. Around this time, Takenaka, third in command at Tachikawa Sports after Kenji and Ōki, proposed a new direction for the company: since both direct and store sales seemed to have stalled, he suggested that they should try to increase their customer appeal by offering uniforms and sports apparel customized with the logos or names of their clients. But Kenji did not go for this idea.

"To achieve Takenaka-san's plan, we would have had to invest in equipment like computer-controlled sewing machines and presses. I talked it over with Ōki-san, but he always went along with my opinions, so I couldn't really rely on him. In the end I decided that if we were going to have to borrow money to expand, it would be better not to do it at all. I suppose I was at least partly influenced by what I'd learned from the mistakes of the Tachikawa Store.

"Takenaka-san was just barely forty at that point. A short time after we rejected his idea, he went into business on his own. We talked before he left, and I felt it was an amicable parting. He ran the business out of his home, just his wife and himself, and I hear it was a modest success. For that sort of work, renting an office and taking on staff just don't make sense for the bottom line."

In 1985, Kenji turned sixty. By that time, Tachikawa Sports had devolved into a thoroughly routine operation, with Kenji and Ōki working to keep their small shop in Tachikawa afloat by getting the same orders to come in from the same roster of loyal clients and customers. The business model they had created around 1960 had already become obsolete by the end of the 1970s, leaving them entirely dependent on the relatively fixed demand of an established set of public institutions in the 1980s.

3

Although Kenji says that he does not recall ever discussing politics or the war when out on business or in other casual encounters, of course he did not forget the war. In fact, as his life acquired more stability, he began to have more leisure in which to look back upon that time.

In December 1957, Kenji read what is regarded as a classic of Japanese war literature, Gomikawa Junpei's Ningen no jōken (The Human Condition; 1956–58), the story of a soldier sent to Manchuria who fights oppression and injustice within the Imperial Japanese Army but eventually is captured by the Soviets and meets his death in the frozen wastes of Siberia. Kenji had come across the book in the library at Tokyo Gakugei University when he worked there part-time after the war.

According to him, "It was a long book, but readable and real, and I could identify with it." Even so, he was not all that moved by it. "If you'd actually rebelled that much against the army, they'd have left you half dead. Nobody could take that. It seemed like a superhero story to me."

Kenji picked up another classic of war literature, Noma Hiroshi's *Shinkū chitai* (Zone of Emptiness; 1952), not long after his release from the tuberculosis sanatorium. The novel compared the dehumanizing effects of the brutal treatment of first-year soldiers to a vacuum obliterating everything within. "It was over my head—I didn't really get it. It wasn't the kind of book you could just skim through, and I was too busy to be able to give it a serious read."

He also read *Kike wadatsumi no koe* (Listen to the Voices from the Sea; 1949), a famous collection of posthumous manuscripts by fallen young soldiers who had been drafted from Tokyo Imperial University and other schools, but remarks, "It didn't leave much of an impression on me, aside from making me think that smart guys sure had a lot of things that troubled them." Ōoka Shōhei's *Furyoki* (Record of a Prisoner of War; 1952), the story of the author's capture and imprisonment in the Philippines by US forces, had more of an impact: "I read it in the sanatorium because I was interested in the experiences of POWs."

From the mid-1950s onward, a flood of films depicting the war was in the theaters. Kenji however had little interest in most of them.

"I saw *Nijūshi no hitomi* [Twenty-Four Eyes; a popular 1954 film about the wartime experiences of twelve Japanese schoolchildren] on TV sometime in the '60s or early '70s, but I thought it was too sentimental. Hero-worshipping war films like *Rengō kantai shirei chōkan Yamamoto Isoroku* [Yamamoto Isoroku: Commander of the Combined Fleet; 1968] seemed stupid to me since they were so at odds with what I had experienced. Pro- or anti-war, fiction just can't cut it."

From around the time of their move to Musashi Murayama, Kenji had a little more disposable income to buy books. He did not splurge on a big set of encyclopedias just for show; instead, he bought works on the Pacific War by American authors because he wanted objective historical accounts, not hero stories.

"One of my friends from Waseda Jitsugyō was the son of a saké-shop owner named Kawada who was a big navy fan. He was the one who said in class that two Japanese carriers had actually been sunk at the Battle of Midway. Before the war he lived in Shinjuku, but afterwards he moved to Shin Ōkubo, where he ran a butcher shop. About the time we moved to Musashi Murayama, I finally went to a Waseda Jitsugyō class reunion, where I happened to hear about Kawada, and went to visit him at his shop. He gave me books like Robert Sherrod's *Taiheiyō sensō shi* [A Concise History of the Pacific War] and [the Japanese translations of] Samuel Eliot Morison's *A History of United States Naval Operations in World War II* and Hanson Baldwin's *Battles Lost and Won: Great Campaigns of World War II.**

"Kawada was a butcher and so he didn't go to class reunions—those were for the successful guys. I didn't go to one myself until my own business got on track. But one of the guys at the reunion told me where Kawada lived."

As for the Vietnam War, "Well, it was a war, so I was against it," says Kenji. "I was opposed to the Soviet Union expanding its sphere of influence, but I was also against using war as a means to prevent that."

In 1969, the massacre of Vietnamese civilians by US troops at My Lai the previous year came to light. Like many Japanese at the time, Kenji was reminded of the actions of the Imperial Japanese Army in China.

"I learned of the atrocities committed by US soldiers from the media, but they seemed almost child's play compared with what the Japanese army had done. When I was in secondary school, a classmate secretly showed us a photo that he'd been given by a soldier who'd just come back from the China front. It showed a Chinese prisoner right at the moment of being beheaded with an officer's sword. In Japan in those days, I think even secondary school students frequently could come into contact with such things.

"While I was in the camp in Siberia, the *Nihon shimbun* ran an article on the Nanjing Massacre. A guy in my work detail who'd been a reporter for the *Manshū nichinichi shimbun* newspaper in Fengtian said that though this news was suppressed in Japan, it was well known everywhere else in the world. Sergeant Takahashi, who was a veteran

---

* Robert Sherrod and *Nakano Gorō, Taiheiyō sensō shi*, 2 vols. (Kōbunsha, 1952); Samuel Eliot Morison, *A History of United States Naval Operations in World War II*, 15 vols. (Little, Brown and Company, 1947–62), first four volumes trans. *Taiheiyō sensō Amerika kaigun sakusen shi* (Kaizōsha, 1950–51); Hanson Baldwin, Battles Lost and Won: Great Campaigns of World War II (Harper & Row, 1966), trans. *Shōri to haiboku* (Asahi Shimbunsha, 1967).

of the China front, would often shift from dirty jokes to stories such as gang rapes of Chinese women and girls they found trying to hide from the fighting. From what I heard from other vets, I had a pretty good idea of what the Imperial Japanese Army had been up to.

"So when the arguments denying the Nanjing Massacre started to come out, I thought, 'Are there still people around who can say such things?' Maybe they can write like that because everything they know comes out of some book. The perpetrators of the atrocities had been complete animals on the battlefield, but after the war was over they came home and kept mum, living with that shut up inside them."

In 1970, the novelist Mishima Yukio, who had embraced Japanese ultranationalism and created his own right-wing militia group, led his followers in a takeover of the Self-Defense Forces headquarters in Ichigaya and called on the troops there to carry out a coup d'état. When they failed to respond to his exhortation, Mishima and a follower committed ritual suicide by seppuku. Kenji's impression: "I had absolutely no idea what he thought he was doing creating a group like that all dressed up in military-style uniforms, and I didn't care. His behavior at the time of his suicide simply seemed to prove that he was crazy."

In 1972, the former Japanese soldier Yokoi Shōichi was "discovered" on Guam. This sudden reappearance of a soldier who had concealed himself for twenty-seven years after the war caused a public sensation. "I was amazed at Yokoi-san. It was startling that he could have hidden out for so long and still kept himself alive. When I heard that he had spoken of the 'shame' of finally being caught and that he'd returned his rifle to the imperial palace, I thought to myself, there's someone whose thinking hasn't changed a bit. I felt so keenly what a harsh fate he'd been dealt."

Then, in 1974, former lieutenant Onoda Hiroo was brought back from the island of Lubang in the Philippines, where he and three of his subordinates had hidden out in the mountains to keep from having to surrender at the end of the war. Two of them were shot by Philippine police in 1954; the third, former private first-class Kozuka Kinshichi, was killed in another shootout with the police in 1972, leaving Onoda the sole survivor. Compared with Yokoi, Onoda cut a more proper figure as a former Imperial Japanese Army officer, giving a snappy salute upon his return to Japan and generally feeding the popular tendency to see him as a kind of hero. But Kenji had a harsher view of the man.

"Onoda was given a hero's welcome—but what about his responsibility for Kozuka-san's death? The war had ended long before, but Kozuka-san was caught up in Onoda's delusions and wound up dying when he didn't have to. Kozuka-san's relatives must have hated Onoda. It upset me that by treating Onoda like a hero, the mass media seemed to be lauding the militaristic spirit of the past.

"I'd first learned of the island of Lubang in 1954, while I was still in the sanatorium, from a newspaper report that a Japanese soldier had been shot by local police. I was preoccupied with my own issues at that point, but the story did make an impression on me."

In contrast with Kenji, Hiroko was genuinely moved by Onoda's return. Hiroko was politically conservative and a fan of right-wing politicians such as Ishihara Shintarō, Nakasone Yasuhiro, and Margaret Thatcher. Kenji continued as always to vote against the LDP. For the most part Kenji and Hiroko got along well with each other, but in this regard their opinions differed.

In the 1970s, Kenji bought all six volumes of the Japanese translation of Alexander Solzhenitsyn's *The Gulag Archipelago*.

"He depicted the extraordinary situation of the *lagerei* camps in a unique style. It was a long, densely printed work, and difficult to read, but I managed to get through the entire thing. In the translator's note to the final volume was a passage that has remained in my mind: 'Eventually (perhaps unexpectedly soon), the day will come when this book will be accepted in its entirety even in the Soviet Union. And that will be the day that true freedom comes to the Soviet Union, regardless of its social system.' Those sentences were written in September 1977, but at that time it was impossible to imagine that the Soviet system would ever come to an end."

Kenji became more interested in the nations under the domination of the Soviet system—Hungary, Czechoslovakia, Poland. "Later, in the 1980s, when the Solidarity movement for democratization arose in Poland, I followed the news of it with great interest."

Meanwhile, the Chita-kai (Chita Association), made up of former prisoners of Twenty-Fourth District Camp No. 2, became quite active. According to Kenji, the founding of the Chita-kai was as follows.

"In 1959, when I went to apply for public housing, I happened to run into a former campmate, Yasuda-san, for the first time in at least ten years. Later, in 1963, a man named Moriyama-san got a group of about ten of us together at a restaurant in Ueno for an evening reminiscing about our days in the camp. That was the beginning, and the next time we got together we named ourselves the Chita-kai. Moriyama-san had lived in Fengtian during the war and was drafted into the army during the final all-out mobilization."

So the Chita-kai was started with Moriyama as leader and sole administrator, though before too long Kenji and Yasuda began to help as well. Early on, they met about once every six months in Tokyo, but eventually they began to take excursions together to various regional resorts and sightseeing spots. In 1976 they began a newsletter, *Chita-kai*.

The Chita-kai was an organization of equals, with no ranks or titles. The Seventeenth Signal Regiment and Second Air Signal Regiment [to which Kenji had belonged] also probably had some sort of veterans' association, but I never heard from them. Generally speaking, groups of that kind were centered on people in the region where the unit had been headquartered, and they preserved the old system of ranks. So they wouldn't send invitations to a guy like me from Tokyo who had just happened to wind up in their unit, and I had no desire to join them anyway."

At their meetings the Chita-kai members for the most part simply talked about old times, without engaging in any sort of political activism. Regional veterans' organizations frequently served as vote aggregators for the conservative parties, but the Chita-kai never played such a role.

In the 1980s, the Chita-kai began to have meetings in western Japan as well, but after a while its activities declined as a result of the aging of its members and internal disputes.

"Some of the guys who joined later on and didn't know the history challenged Moriyama-san's leadership, thinking him too autocratic. At that point Moriyama-san kind of lost heart and stopped coming to the meetings. He had been very driven and had been doing all the work himself out of his own time and pocket, so not only was it a bit too much of a burden for him, but he was also easily misunderstood.

"As was true of veterans' associations everywhere, in the late 1980s as everybody got older, the number of participants began to fall off. We called it quits in the mid-1990s with a trip to Atami. The leader at the time consulted with me about it, and I advised him it was time to bring down the curtain."

Most regional veterans' associations got started during the postwar economic boom and declined or ceased activity altogether in the 1990s. The Chita-kai was unusual in not having preserved the traditional system of army ranks, but not so unusual in terms of the course it followed.

In the 1970s, as Kenji's personal and business life gained more stability, another preoccupation arose: memories of Kyōsaka, his friend who had died in Siberia in January 1946. "As my own life grew more secure and affluent, I began to feel a certain remorse about having come back alive. I began to want to do something for those who had died."

One day in 1979, taking a break from work, he called the Ministry of Health and Welfare to try to find out more about Kyōsaka. A woman in the archives there was able to provide him with a full name, Kyōsaka Kichiji, and a 1946 family address in Toyama in northwestern Japan.

"She said there was no record of the family's current address. When she asked me why I was looking him up after so many years, I just gave some sort of vague answer. I really couldn't explain why."

After several months of indecision, Kenji wrote a letter to Toyama City Hall. He asked whether any surviving members of Kyōsaka's family were still living at the 1946 address, and if they were, whether they might be given a message that Kenji had information about Kyōsaka's final days in Siberia.

"I got a reply, but it was a typical bureaucratic response—they enclosed a copy of the residence registry for that address and asked me to contact the family directly. His parents had passed away, but it seemed that an elder brother and his wife were still living there."

Two more years slipped by as Kenji dithered over whether or not to send a letter. Then, in the autumn of 1983, he made up his mind and wrote to Kyōsaka's brother. "Two or three days after I sent the letter I got a telephone call. And not long after, the brother came to Tokyo and we met at a coffee shop near Tachikawa Station."

Kyōsaka's brother was also an army veteran who had been taken prisoner in the Philippines.* At their meeting he showed Kenji a

---

* In the final stages of the fighting in the Philippines, some 336,000 Japanese soldiers died in combat with US forces or as a result of malnutrition and illness. Around 23,000 American soldiers and more than a million Filipinos also lost their lives in this conflict.

photo of his younger brother. Asked where it had come from, he said he had brought it from the Buddhist memorial altar at home.

The photo was a portrait in army uniform of the kind that all new soldiers, including Kenji himself, had been required to have taken during their first three months of basic training and to send to their families to show that they were safe and sound. On the back of Kyōsaka's photo were the signatures of the platoon leader and the military doctor who had confirmed his death.

"I'm just guessing, but Lieutenant Tashita, the platoon leader, must have found the photo among Kyōsaka's effects after his death and kept it hidden from the Soviet guards so he could bring it back to Japan with him. None of us had much of anything at the time, and the photo was probably the only possession of Kyōsaka's that mattered.

"Soviet control of intelligence was very strict, so you couldn't bring anything back with you that would have provided information about the situation in the camps. Bringing back a picture of a dead man would have required somehow smuggling it through a body search. I heard that Nishida-san, who was work team leader from 1947 onward, rolled up a slip of paper with the names of about thirty men who had died in the camp and concealed it in the string of his loincloth in order to take it with him to Japan.

"As soon as returnees boarded the repatriation ship from Siberia, they were told to write down the names of as many of the dead as they could remember. At that time, or maybe when the boat landed in Maizuru, Lieutenant Tashita probably handed over the photo, which must have made its way through official channels until it reached his parents in Toyama. And then it was placed in the drawer of the family altar."

Kenji told the brother the story of Kyōsaka's final days. "He took it calmly. We both had been through the war. I didn't have to say much for him to get the picture. He didn't weep or wail or show any strong emotion. We understood each other without needing to say anything. Weeping and wailing were for people who didn't know what it was all about.

"The brother had been captured in the Philippines, so he'd probably suffered a lot, like the characters in Ōoka Shōhei's writings. I didn't ask him where in the Philippines he'd been captured or anything like that. We didn't talk much about ourselves. He returned to Toyama the same day."

Afterward, Kenji sent Kyōsaka's brother a copy of "Aru waka-mono e no tsuioku" (Memories of a Youth), an essay about Kyōsaka's death he had written for the Chita-kai newsletter that was virtually the same as the account quoted in chapter 3. The brother sent Kenji a reply, along with a small gift. In the letter, he wrote,

I cried when I read "Memories of a Youth." You gave my brother much help and encouragement, but I suppose he was fated to live only so long.

In the Philippines there were many times when I thought, "This is the end," and I also thought of killing myself with a hand grenade, but in the end I was held as a POW for a year and a half and then repatriated to Japan.

Oguma-san, I hope you will healthily and happily live out the portion of life my brother could not.

I am sending you some of the fish cakes my brother loved to eat as a child. I hope you will enjoy them. Thank you so much for all that you have done.

Having conveyed the circumstances of Kyōsaka's death to his surviving family, Kenji felt as if an enormous burden had been lifted from his shoulders. He believed he had gained a measure of closure regarding his memories of the war. Yet about a decade later, Kenji would begin a correspondence with a fellow Siberian internee, a Korean veteran of the Imperial Japanese Army, that would draw him into a lawsuit demanding postwar compensation from the Japanese government.

Chapter 9

The Wartime Compensation Lawsuit

In 1987 Kenji turned sixty. His son, Eiji, had graduated from university and found work with a publishing company, and Kenji himself became eligible for a pension. Work at Tachikawa Sports now centered almost exclusively on making the rounds of established customers; Kenji gradually scaled down the business and left more and more of it to Ōki, reducing the number of days he went to work. His salary decreased as well, but he was done paying off his mortgage and had a stable livelihood.

Then, through a chain of coincidences, he became involved in a wartime compensation lawsuit against the Japanese government.

Revisiting Chita after forty-three years in July 1991,
Kenji stands near the site of his former camp.

1

Kenji had begun to involve himself in social activism in the 1980s, join-ing Amnesty International in 1982 after gaining a renewed interest in human rights issues in prison camps through reading Solzhenitsyn's *The Gulag Archipelago* in the 1970s and witnessing the rise of the Polish Solidarity movement from 1981 on. Kenji's involvement took two forms: local activism, and activities related to war and remembrance. The former was occasioned by a movement in his home community of Nan'yōdai in Hachiōji opposing the construction of a motor vehicle inspection facility.

As mentioned in the previous chapter, Nan'yōdai was a housing estate carved out the Tama hills, with a population of 3,363 residents as of the end of March 2013. When it first opened in 1972, the community retained the place-names and addresses of the rural area it had been, but from 1986 onward its subdivisions were renamed Districts 1, 2, and 3 in the order in which they had been constructed. Kenji's family lived in the earliest of the developments, District 1.

Nan'yōdai started out with brand-new houses, but its infrastruc-ture lagged behind. Initially there was no sewer system; the wastewater and other effluents from the houses were processed at a waste treatment facility in the development. So in the beginning the main area of activism among the residents had to do with improving their own living stand-ards, such as working through their residents' association to demand a sewer from the municipal government.

Then, in 1982, the environmental conservation movement came to Nan'yōdai when the Kantō District Transport Bureau announced plans for the construction of a motor vehicle inspection and registration office in the foothills across from the neighborhood. Since 1951 the Japanese government had instituted a motor vehicle registration system requir-ing regular inspections at specified facilities to make sure no improper modifications had been made and that vehicle taxes were paid up. The construction of such a facility in the area would mean not only the cut-ting of forested land to provide sufficient parking, but also an increase in local traffic from cars coming for inspection.

Nan'yōdai enjoyed a relatively unspoiled natural environment of hills and forest, traversed by a hiking course established in 1929 by the Keiō railway company with a local partner. In the 1950s the course had been popular as a recreational escape from central Tokyo, and had even been visited by Crown Prince (now Emperor) Akihito. Tama Zoological Park opened in the area in 1958, and the Inter-University Seminar House in 1965. Though gradually new roads were installed and housing estates added, still, when Nan'yōdai was built in the 1970s the surrounding Tama hills retained much of their natural beauty. The northern slopes above Nan'yōdai became Naganuma Metropolitan Nature Park in 1980; in the foothills to the south, meanwhile, were baseball fields belonging to Nakano Hachiōji High School, affiliated with Meiji University.

The proposed site for the new motor vehicle inspection office lay in the area including these ball fields. At the time the only motor vehicle inspection office in western Tokyo was in Kunitachi; hence the Ministry of Transport's decision to build another one here in Hachiōji. "It being an area of old farming villages, there were probably various local interests involved in the plan," Kenji notes.

Soon a movement against the facility arose among those living in Nan'yōdai and along the nearby main highway. According to Kenji, residents' reaction to the plan divided along generational lines. The protest movement was centered on the younger residents—mostly in their thirties and early forties—of the more recently developed Nan'yōdai Districts 2 and 3. Mainly members of the baby-boom generation, they had been educated entirely in the postwar period and were sensitive to environmental issues. "The real standard-bearers of the movement were full-time housewives who were in the neighborhood in the daytime. Because their kids all went to the same school, they already had a network and had no trouble communicating with one another."

On the other hand, the residents of District 1, the oldest of the developments, were mainly in their late forties and older. Born in the prewar period, they were not particularly interested in these kinds of issues and tended to cooperate with the government.

"The people in District 1 were older and, like me, not as environmentally conscious. Among the older folks from District 1 who served in the residents' association, the attitude was that maybe a motor vehicle office would liven things up. To convince people to accept the facility, the bureaucrats from the Hachiōji city government came with a lot of sweet talk about license plate numbers with a Hachiōji prefix and a new elementary school for Nan'yōdai. At least some of the older men running the residents' association seem to have seen the whole thing from the beginning as an opportunity to get as many concessions out of the city as they could."

At this time, the children of Nan'yōdai had to walk for about twenty minutes to get to an elementary school that had been built during the days when the area was still a farm village—thus the appeal of the proposal to build a new school.

Beginning in the 1970s, many areas of Japan saw the rise of citizens' movements protesting environmental pollution and unregulated development. Before that time, the key figures in such protests had been farmers and fishermen whose way of life and livelihood were being destroyed. But from the 1970s onward, a new generation of young city-dwellers came to the fore, equipped with postwar educations and a stronger consciousness of civil rights.

Particularly in the late 1970s and 1980s, the full-time housewives of the baby-boom generation became the motivating force for environmental protection, natural foods, and consumer cooperatives. These were women who, despite being well-educated, had been cut off from jobs and other avenues of societal participation by the expectation that once married, they should stay at home. The huge apartment complexes and housing estates developed from the 1960s onward became staging grounds for their many and varied social movements.*

The opposition to the motor vehicle inspection office at Nan'yōdai can be regarded as one such movement—and in view of the results, a successful one, as the facility was stopped. Factors in this success were the commitment of the residents and good strategic planning.

"The movement centered on young housewives, but a lawyer living in Nan'yōdai who served as their strategist advised them to put pressure on their city council representatives. The city was still at the stage of choosing potential sites, and officials were trying to win over the residents of Nan'yōdai. But if Nan'yōdai was voted down in the city council, that might put an end to the idea. So the strategy was

---

* For social movements in the housing developments of the 1960s, see Hara Takeshi, *Danchi no kūkan seijigaku* (NHK Shuppan, 2012).

to make a concerted appeal to the members of the middle-of-the-road Komeito,* since the votes of the Socialist and Communist Party representatives alone would not be enough to secure a majority.

"The young mothers of Nan'yōdai were so strongly united that when there was a meeting of the city's environmental affairs committee, they would charter a bus to attend. This sort of pressure rattled even some of the conservative council members, winning them over to the opposition, and the proposal was voted down in the committee. The older residents of District 1 were dumbfounded, not having imagined such a reversal possible. Even if we had bargained with the city and gotten the elementary school, by now it would have been shut down again given the decline in the school-age population in the area."

So the movement succeeded, and the environment around Nan'yōdai was preserved, although the motor vehicle office itself was simply relocated to another site in Hachiōji. "It was another new housing estate, but one built so recently that the residents had little solidarity, and construction had begun before a movement opposing it could be organized."

Kenji did not have much to do with the residents' association. In the first decade of the 2000s, he served as the head of the advisory committee when a hall for the association was built on the site of the wastewater treatment plant that had finally been superseded by the installation of a municipal sewerage system, but that was about it. "Even that was only because my neighbor, a former union leader at Sumitomo Light Metal, happened to be head of the residents' association at the time, and he asked me to do it. I really just served as a moderator."

Instead, Kenji was active in a local citizens' group called the Tama Hills Nature Conservancy (Tama Kyūryō no Shizen o Mamoru Kai), which grew out of the Nan'yōdai Nature Conservancy founded by participants in the movement against the motor vehicle inspection office after their victory. Although that project had been stopped, residential construction and other forms of development continued apace in the vicinity of Nan'yōdai, reaching its peak around 1991,

---

* The party that emerged during the postwar economic boom as the political arm of the Buddhist organization Soka Gakkai.

near the height of Japan's bubble economy, when Tokyo Metropolitan University moved its campus there.

The environmental destruction wrought by residential development of areas like the Tama hills was a major social issue of the time, as symbolized by the popular animated film *Heisei tanuki gassen ponpoko* (1994, directed by Takahata Isao; released abroad as *Pom Poko*), which depicted the struggle of *tanuki* raccoon dogs to protect their homes from human development. At the time, *tanuki* and wild rabbits still lived in the vicinity of Nan'yōdai, but more housing was being planned for the area; the Tama Hills Nature Conservancy was created to reduce its environmental impact.

Kenji began to participate in the association from around 1990, as he was reducing his workload at Tachikawa Sports. At the time the group had perhaps a dozen members, most of them women who had been active in the movement against the vehicle inspection office, but with a few older people like Kenji also joining in.

"The participants were mostly lovers of nature and animals. I hadn't been that interested in environmental issues and nature conservation until I got involved after my de facto retirement. I wasn't particularly interested in plants, and was bad at learning their names. You could tell me and I would forget them immediately. But I did like going out for walks in nature."

One regular activity of the association was patrolling the nearby Naganuma Metropolitan Nature Park. The Tokyo Metropolitan Parks Office worked to involve citizens in managing the parks, and the Tama Hills Nature Conservancy became one of the local groups participating in this effort. "A pair of us would walk the park every week on Tuesdays, Thursdays, and Saturdays, monitoring the state of the woods and checking for any damage. To help maintain the ecosystem, we would also weed and do some selective felling of trees." During the 1990s these activities received a small subsidy from the metropolitan government, but after the conservative politician Ishihara Shintarō was elected governor of Tokyo in 1999 the budget was cut.

The association also worked to protect the *ōtaka*, or northern goshawk. Not long after the motor vehicle office had been halted, the Housing and Urban Development Corporation raised another plan for a new housing estate south of Nan'yōdai. But then the members of the Tama Hills Nature Conservancy discovered active nests of goshawks in this area. The northern goshawk had been placed on the national list of endangered species in 1993, with limitations on new development in its nesting habitats, so the discovery of active nests was a favored tactic of the environmental protection movement, as environmental assessments had been included in the Basic Environment Law of 1993.

"We would take turns monitoring the goshawks' nests from a distance to determine their habitat, numbers, and so on. Pairs of us would observe their activity from 8 am to 5 pm from five or so stations near the nests. I personally didn't know the difference between a goshawk and a black kite, but they needed as many people as possible and I wanted to be helpful, so I joined in. Even so, I would sight a bird and point it out to someone who knew more about identification, and they'd tell me it was just a black kite.

"We worked with the company conducting the environmental impact assessment to analyze the bits the goshawks left behind after feeding on small birds and animals. People in the assessment company were also opposed to runaway development, so we built up a good relationship. But it took a lot of hard work to clamber down into ravines looking for spoor. With only one lung, I get out of breath easily, and I only did it once.

"We also protested to both the city and metropolitan governments about companies dumping industrial waste and construction debris in the ravines. And we worked to revive abandoned farmland next to the ravines in order to stop further development there. We talked to the owners of the unused paddy fields and got their permission to weed and rebuild the dikes between them. This was hard manual labor and men were needed; I helped with the weeding."

The waste companies ignored Hachiōji municipal orders, but a further appeal to the Tokyo metropolitan government put an end to the dumping. The restored fields eventually became a metropolitan nature preserve and then a metropolitan park.

Nonetheless, residential development of the surrounding hills continued. In many places, housing lots were created only to end up unsold once the bubble economy collapsed and the population went into decline. The empty lots stood abandoned and untended, the environmental damage already done. Thanks to local activism, though, development to the south of Nan'yōdai was minimized, and from

1987 to 2009 a number of ravines and wild plant habitats were success-fully designated by the Tokyo metropolitan government for protec-tion as green spaces.*

The key figures in the Tama Hills Nature Conservancy were the wife of a professor at the Tama campus of Chuo University and a piano teacher from Nan'yōdai. They had started out just as rank-and-file members in the movement against the motor vehicle office, but through determination and commitment they grew to take on central roles. I really respect them for quietly persisting with their cause even when, as with most movements, the results were not everything they might have hoped for in the beginning."

In the middle of the 1990s, another movement arose among the housewives of Nan'yōdai: a cooperative called Katakuri (Arrowroot) that cooked and delivered meals to seniors and others in need. The generation that had settled in Nan'yōdai and the other "new towns" of the western Tokyo suburbs in the 1970s was aging, and their sons and daughters had moved elsewhere, disliking the inconvenience of the long commute into central Tokyo. An increasing number of elderly inhabitants was having difficulty with everyday necessities such as shopping.

Katakuri sought to deliver meals to such needy senior households. It worked initially with organizations such as the Seikatsu Club con-sumer cooperatives,† and became a certified nonprofit organization after the enactment of the NPO Law in 1998. It also checked in on sen-iors when delivering the food, for which activity it began to receive a subsidy from the city of Hachiōji.

The founder of the NPO was a good friend of Kenji's wife, Hiroko, which led Kenji to become involved as well. In addition to becoming a formal paying member of the organization, he served as a delivery truck driver once or twice a week. He had done a lot of driving on his sales rounds and was good at it.

"As a formal member, I participated in the annual general assem-bly, but since I had no experience I didn't say much. Not many of the

---

* Tama Kyūryō no Shizen o Mamoru Kai, ed., *Mamotte ikitai Tama kyūryō no shizen* (Tama Kyūryō no Shizen o Mamoru Kai, 2014).

† A national organic food association founded in 1965 whose members also began to run for local political office starting in 1977.

members attended, but I decided to go, figuring even an old guy like myself could at least help liven it up a bit. If people don't show up for events like that, it kind of kills the spirit of the ones who are involved."

As mentioned earlier, during this era environmental protection and consumers' cooperative movements were taking place all over the country, and some were officially incorporating as NPOs. The demographic core of the activists was housewives of the postwar generation, but older people living on pensions and with more free time also participated. Kenji was part of this general trend.

Many older retirees possess a wealth of knowledge and skills built up during their working years: a driver's license, bookkeeping and office experience, legal knowledge. Experts have frequently pointed out how effective this human capital can be when put to use within the local community.

However, as is likewise often noted, many older men with such skills and experience also tend to be rather arrogant and look down upon women, which hampers their own participation in local groups. Kenji had spent long years in the lower strata of society; he didn't put on airs but acted like any other member. His native humility might be said to have smoothed his path into local activism after his retirement.

2

In April 1988, after Kenji had reduced his work at Tachikawa Sports to a few times a week, he had his first letter published in a newspaper. This text was in response to a letter to the editor from a nineteen-year-old student in the 26 March *Asahi shimbun*.

First, though, we should consider the context in which Kenji read that student's letter. Although Japan's postwar constitution, adopted in 1946, had renounced war, the country had begun to rearm at the order of the Occupation forces during the Korean War in the early 1950s, leading to the establishment of the Self-Defense Forces in 1954. Kenji and many others who had experienced war firsthand were critical of a rearmament not based in public consensus, and were strongly antipathetic toward the notion of a military itself. In the 1980s, as this older generation began to relinquish its central position in society, politicians in the right wing of the ruling Liberal Democratic Party began to argue for emergency legislation that would provide for significant restrictions on civil liberties during times of crisis, including war.

"The gist of the student's letter was that the emergency legislation was not in conflict with the constitution, since defending one's country is only natural, and he himself would willingly give his life fighting for Japan if it were attacked. In my response I basically wrote that I wished he had a better idea of the realities of war and that he should at least read the letters of students who had been killed in World War II. I had expected the paper would simply forward the letter to the student, but instead it was published."

About the same time, Kenji learned in the newspaper of the Veterans Against War (Fusen Heishi no Kai). Increasingly disturbed by the rise of popular opinion ignorant of the reality of war, he sent a copy of his published letter along with a cover letter to the address that had been listed in the newspaper article. He received a reply from one of the principal members, Kojima Kiyofumi, and began to participate in the organization's activities.

Born in 1919, Kojima had graduated from the Faculty of Economics at Keio University and completed the Imperial Japanese Navy reserve officers' training program with the rank of lieutenant. After serving as a signal officer aboard the battleship Yamato, he was transferred in December 1944 to a land-based air unit on the island of Luzon in the Philippines. When US forces landed in February 1945, he was suddenly ordered to lead his troops into the fighting on the ground.

Kojima and the other members of the air unit had no experience in or equipment for ground combat, but fought on. Driven into the hills by the attacking Americans, they fell close to starvation, until in April 1945 they decided to surrender. Such a surrender by a Japanese officer was quite unusual, but Kojima's father was a liberal and Kojima himself had studied about the United States in his university days, which may have contributed to his flexibility of attitude.

After the war, Kojima worked to launch a local newspaper in Shimane Prefecture. Much later, when he was sixty-six, he wrote about his war experiences in a 1987 article published in the *Asahi shimbun*. This article came to the notice of Takeoka Katsumi, former chief secretary of the Defense Agency, who before long met with Kojima and friends. Takeoka, born in 1923, was known as a pacifist amid the defense establishment, and was working to oppose the State Secrets Law that was then being considered. Other veterans were attracted to the group, and in December 1987 Veterans Against War was formed.

At this time, some forty years after the war, the "erosion" of wartime experience was being much discussed in the media. In addition, as those with direct experience of the war began to reach retirement age, they had a chance to look back over their lives, and also gained the time to engage in social activism. Kenji's letter to the newspaper fits squarely in such developments.

At Kojima's invitation, Kenji began attending the regular monthly meetings of Veterans Against War. The meetings were structured as lecture-discussions, with invited speakers including Utsunomiya Tokuma and Kujiraoka Hyōsuke, both pacifist members of the LDP; Ishibashi Masashi, chairman of the Japan Socialist Party; and Toyoda Toshiyuki, a physicist active in the movement against nuclear weapons.

When Kenji began participating, the association had about thirty members, which within a year increased to about one hundred. Membership was open to veterans, regardless of political persuasion, who were sympathetic to the organization's belief that passing on the lived experience of war would contribute to preventing it. About a third of the members were former student-soldiers like Kojima; there were no former career military men.[*] The chairman was Ōishi Tsuguo, the pastor of Himon'ya Church in Tokyo, who had been a naval combat engineer fighting in the Philippines. The vice chairmen were Kojima and a Waseda-educated former naval lieutenant who had been a reserve officer candidate in the Andaman Islands at the time of the surrender.

Looking at the membership rolls for August 1988, what strikes the eye is the number of members whose "war experience" was as lower-ranking officers and whose "present occupation" is listed as corporate executive, educator, doctor, or other professional. Out of roughly seventy members, only Kenji and one other were

---

[*] Chamoto Shigemasa, "Fusen Heishi no Kai," *Masukomi shimin* (July 1989), p. 41.

"self-employed." Even so, Kenji recalls that "there were people of all sorts, not just officers and university graduates." The average age was sixty-eight, and many were pensioners.

"Kojima-san was a member of the International House of Japan, so that was where we initially held our meetings. After a while we moved to the Aoyama Metro Kaikan, and then to the Labor Welfare Hall in Shibuya. Kojima-san and a number of other members also worked with local schoolteachers and such to relate their wartime experience to young people.

"Speakers at our meetings included [the political scientist and historian] Fujita Shōzō. We listened to talks on topics like Japan's war responsibility toward Asia, and the need [for the Japanese public] to move from a sense of victimhood in the war to accepting their own culpability. I don't usually think about things theoretically, and what was said could be difficult to follow, but it was interesting to get that perspective."

In September 1988, the health of Emperor Shōwa (Hirohito) took a turn for the worse, and he passed away in January 1989. Kenji describes his feelings on the emperor's death in the following words.

"I'd been a soldier myself, and the emperor had been commander-in-chief, so I felt he bore responsibility for the war. I didn't feel like making a big fuss about it, but still I thought he had been to blame for the deaths of an enormous number of people. He should have apologized while he was still alive and conscious, and I wished he had."

During the three months of Emperor Shōwa's final illness, public "self-restraint" became a watchword. The annual intercollegiate baseball tournament at Jingu Stadium in Tokyo was cancelled; variety shows were replaced with other programming; posters with the ad copy "The Joy of Living" were removed; and people were even urged not to have year-end or New Year parties and to refrain from sending out the usual New Year's greeting cards. Controversy arose in December when the conservative mayor of Nagasaki, who had been an officer trainee in the Imperial Japanese Army at the time of the surrender, made a reference in the municipal assembly to the emperor's war responsibility; for these comments, he was shot and gravely wounded by a member of a right-wing organization a year later, in January 1990.

Veterans Against War published a statement protesting the mood of self-restraint. In October 1989, the organization also subsidized a return trip to Japan by former women members of the Manchuria-Mongolia Colonial Youth Brigades who had remained in China after the war. This effort was occasioned by an NHK television documentary on the lives of these women, who as children had been left behind in their families' flight from Soviet forces once the Imperial Japanese Army had retreated without attempting to protect the Japanese civilians still in the region. With the restoration of Sino-Japanese diplomatic relations in 1972 and the end of the Cultural Revolution in 1977, some of these children, now middle-aged, had begun to come to Japan in the 1980s to find members of their birth families.

While Kenji was in sympathy with the intentions behind these actions by Veterans Against War, he was uncomfortable with how they were carried out.

"A lot of things were decided by a few key members, who then sought approval from the rest of us after the fact. Even at the regular meetings, pretty much only the same people ever spoke up. I participated because I didn't want what I had experienced in the war to be forgotten, but I was unhappy with the politicization and the pundits."

In January 1993, a heated debate broke out among members in the pages of the organization's newsletter, *Fusen* (Anti-War), when an essay by Kojima advocating "absolute pacifism" was criticized in the same issue by another member, a former POW captured on Saipan.

"The main point of the critique was that the struggle against fascism was a 'just war' and that pacifism alone is insufficient: one must be willing to fight to achieve a better society. I myself couldn't believe the Soviet Union was on the side of justice, and it seemed to me they were just squabbling over a bunch of stuff I didn't really understand.

"I'm not much of a writer, but I did send one letter to *Fusen* urging them to abandon this quarrel.* I even served once as chairman of the regular meeting in connection with this issue, but after that I more or less stopped going. I really can't stand people who are harsh and judgmental toward others."

---

* Oguma Kenji, "'Zettai heiwa shugi to heiwa undō' o yonde," *Fusen* 61 (April 1993), pp. 30–31.

So Kenji began to distance himself from the Veterans Against War. At the same time he became involved in another activity—a return visit to the Siberian POW camp in Chita.

3

In 1989, the year Emperor Shōwa passed away, the Berlin Wall fell and the countries of Eastern Europe were caught up in a wave of democratization. For Kenji, who had experienced the Soviet system firsthand, this evoked profound feelings.

"Given my experiences as a prisoner of war, I was sympathetic to the democratization movements in Eastern Europe and the Soviet Union, beginning with Solidarity in Poland. Still, I never imagined that the Berlin Wall would come tumbling down in my lifetime."

Kenji now had more leisure, and with the end of the Cold War he traveled to Poland in 1990, drawn there by his interest in the Polish democracy movement and his study of Polish history. This was his first time traveling abroad for pleasure; in 1969 Hiroko had gone by herself to Taiwan on a tour ticket that had been given them by a wholesaler Kenji dealt with, but that had been it. Kenji found Eastern Europe to his liking, and he made trips every couple of years throughout the '90s to various areas in the region, including the former Czechoslovakia and Yugoslavia.

Before restrictions on overseas travel from Japan were lifted in 1964, it had not been possible for Japanese to travel abroad without a clearly stated commercial or educational purpose. In 1964 the number of Japanese nationals leaving or reentering the country was 127,749; in 1969, the year Hiroko went to Taiwan, it was 492,880. But by 1990 this figure had spiked to more than 10 million, and in 1995 to over 15 million. Kenji's journeys abroad came during this period of internationalization.

The number of Japanese traveling overseas peaked around 1996. From then until 2014, it fluctuated between 15 and 18 million people annually, a stagnation that correlated more or less directly to the stalling out of the Japanese economy and of growth in wages during those two decades.

In April 1991, Soviet leader Mikhail Gorbachev visited Japan, where he met with a group of former internees. Gorbachev brought a list of 38,000 Japanese who had died during internment in the Soviet Union, promising to turn over a report on an additional 24,800 as soon as investigation was concluded. The list, which was released to the public in Japan, included inmates from Twenty-Fourth District Camp No. 2. The names were in an unreliable rendering of their Russian pronunciations in katakana, but even so Kenji was able to find those of men he knew.

At the time there were still many restrictions on travel to the Soviet Union, particularly in the case of a regional military outpost like Chita. But Kenji learned that youth and merchants' associations in the city of Chita in Aichi Prefecture—whose name coincidentally corresponded to that of the Soviet city—were planning to pay a goodwill visit to their counterpart in the Soviet Union. He contacted these organizations and arranged for himself and two other members of the Chita-kai camp veterans' association to accompany them on their trip.

The group took a charter flight from Akita Airport to Irkutsk, where they transferred to a Soviet domestic flight to Chita. It was July 1991, five months before the collapse of the Soviet Union and forty-three years since Kenji had last set foot in Chita. "The railway station was almost exactly the same, and most of the rest of the city hadn't changed much either."

Kenji and his companions headed to the outskirts of town to the site of the prison camp. "Traveling by bus to the camp site from the train station, where we POWs had disembarked long ago, I was surprised at how short a distance it was. It had seemed much longer back when we had been forced to walk it. The Zabaykal Military District Headquarters, the military hospital, and the wooden fences along the route that we had marched to our worksites were all as they had been. The monument to the fallen soldiers of the Japanese Fifth Army Division that had been erected during the Siberian Intervention was still there, too. But the prison camp had been demolished, and nothing remained but empty fields."

Next Kenji and his friends visited the Chita municipal cemetery. They were shown to an area where they were told the Japanese were buried; they placed flowers on the graves and installed a plaque that Kenji had brought from Japan.

"Through Tachikawa Sports I happened to know a metalworking shop that made sports trophies and such. I talked to the owner and got him to make this plaque. I didn't discuss the idea with anyone else, and of course I paid for it myself. Even though it was made of duralumin, I imagine with exposure to the elements it has probably corroded by now. But I only did it for myself, so that's OK."

The inscription on the plaque read, "In memory of the spirits of our comrades-in-arms (senyū) who arrived here with us in 1945 but who never returned home. 10 July 1991." This text, which had been written by Kenji, was accompanied by his name and those of the two other Chita-kai members, along with a Russian translation; "It seemed like adding that would maybe help prevent it from being vandalized.

"I chose the word senyū although we had just been prisoners of war and hadn't actually fought together. There wasn't really any better word. In Japanese senyū has a bit of a militaristic ring, but the closest European equivalents, camerade or kamerad, simply mean companion or friend. Besides, senyū was not actually used much in the Japanese army. Back in the day, in fact, the song 'Sen'yū,' about a soldier mourning a fallen comrade after a charge, was banned for being unmanly."

Among the members of the group representing the Japanese city of Chita was a woman whose husband had died in a prison camp in nearby Novaya. She and Kenji went there by bus to try to visit the grave, but could not locate it.

"It wasn't as though he had been laid to rest in a proper cemetery or anything. He'd just been buried somewhere near the camp. I figured we wouldn't be able to find the grave, and that was how it turned out. There wasn't much we could do, so we offered incense out on the edge of town. That seemed to help put her mind at ease."

When they returned to the hotel in Chita, a Mongolian plasterer working inside began to talk to them in Japanese. He would speak up when no Russians were around, but whenever one appeared he would fall silent.

"When we asked him why he was able to speak Japanese, he said that he had picked it up before the war as a child in Inner Mongolia through playing with the children of Japanese settlers. Since when we met it was still under the Soviet system, it must have been difficult for him to speak with foreigners."

The Mongolian man invited Kenji to his home. The other two members of the Chita-kai were also invited, but declined; at the time, the secret police was still active, and they were worried about what might happen should they accept. That evening, the man's son came in a car to pick Kenji up at the hotel. The man lived in an apartment with his Russian wife and their two children. They seemed middle class and owned some electric appliances.

"He said he missed Japanese things, so I spent a couple of hours talking to him about Japan. I also heard a little bit from him about how in the 1960s during the Cultural Revolution and the era of Sino-Soviet tensions he fled across the border to the Soviet Union because the Chinese government had become so oppressive."

As we shall see later, during the Cultural Revolution in China anyone who had connections with Japan was liable to be a target for criticism. And while Outer Mongolia had gained independence from Qing China in 1911 and in 1924 had become a socialist people's republic under the influence of the Soviet Union, Inner Mongolia had remained Chinese territory. With the founding of the Chinese Communist regime, Inner Mongolia became an autonomous region, but colonization by Han Chinese proceeded apace. In the time of Sino-Soviet tensions, several hundred thousand people are said to have been purged on suspicion of connections to the Soviet Union or the Mongolian People's Republic.

"The man said that after fleeing to the Soviet Union, he had served as an intelligence source on China. I've read that refugees in those days were carefully watched by the secret police, and if they did not collaborate their lives would become very difficult. I think the reason he took a chance on talking to a complete stranger like myself was that he was nostalgic for a Japan that was connected with memories of his childhood before a lot of unpleasant things happened to him. He must have been about fifteen or so when the war ended, the same age as the generation of little imperial patriots of Japan. During the Cultural Revolution he must have been at risk of being treated as a Japanese sympathizer.

"When I asked him what books he'd read back when he was a child, he mentioned Sakurai Tadayoshi's *Nikudan* [Human Bullets], a patriotic tale for younger readers depicting the Imperial Japanese Army's siege of Port Arthur during the Russo-Japanese War. I think

he'd had such a hard time later on in life that he'd come to some ideal-
istic fantasy of prewar Japan."

The man told Kenji he wanted to know more about the history
of the war. After returning to Japan, Kenji sent him a copy of Robert
Sherrod's *Taiheiyō sensō shi* (A Concise History of the Pacific War).
"But it seemed that rather than an objective account like that, he was
more interested in heroic tales. He was not too good at writing letters
in Japanese, and after a while I stopped hearing from him."

Kenji visited Ulan-Ude and Irkutsk on the way home to Japan
from Chita. With this trip, he felt as though he had reached some sort
of accommodation with his memories of Siberian internment. But
there would soon be unforeseen developments.

4

In 1988, the Japanese government established a program to provide
a solatium to former Siberian internees, in a move would eventually
lead to Kenji's involvement in a lawsuit against the government concerning postwar compensation.

To apply for the program, one had to have served for fewer than
three years in the Imperial Japanese Army and be ineligible for a military pension or an annuity under the *kyōsai nenkin* pension plan for
public service employees. The solatium took the form of government
bonds worth ¥100,000 (about $1,200), a silver cup commemorating
the recipient's service, and a certificate signed by the prime minister.
Applications, available at local government offices, were to be sent to
the body set up to administer this program, the Public Foundation for
Peace and Consolation (Heiwa Kinen Jigyō Tokubetsu Kikin).

Here we must discuss a bit of background information on how
the postwar Japanese government dealt with the issue of compensation for wartime damages. Briefly stated, it refused to pay any such
compensation, under the rationale that the burdens of war were something to be endured equally by all Japanese nationals (*kokumin*) and
thus it was unfair to compensate any specific victims. However, in
truth the main concern seemed to be that if compensation were to
be offered to any one group, this would unleash an endless torrent of
similar claims, both domestic and international.

The government consistently denied compensation even to the surviving family of military personnel or auxiliaries killed in action, or to victims of the air raids or atomic bombings of Japan. What it did instead was to expand the system of military pensions predating the war.

This pension system had been temporarily suspended at Japan's defeat, to be revived in 1953 after the termination of the Allied Occupation. Eligibility for benefits required a minimum of twelve years of service for noncommissioned officers and enlisted men and thirteen years for officers. The amount of pension was determined by rank and length of service; under the revived system, then, career military men of higher rank received higher amounts. A former general might receive ¥8 million (about $80,000) or more per annum, and other senior officers, ¥5 million or more. Although by 2014 government expenditure on military pensions had fallen to ¥421.7 billion due to a decline in the number of recipients, in 1988 it stood at ¥1.7166 trillion, about 3 percent of the national budget.

For the most part, soldiers like Kenji who were conscripted late in the war were ineligible for pensions. Men who had been sent to zones of heavy combat might be allowed to add to their official years of service, but for those who were not career military men to begin with this did not make much difference. Thus the solatium through the Public Foundation for Peace and Consolation was designed to cover such internees. The disbursements taking the form of a "solatium" or "relief" was no doubt because of the government's aforementioned principle of not offering "compensation."

In addition to military veterans and the families of public servants who died in the line of duty, other Japanese groups were demanding wartime compensation, including the victims of the air raids and, most prominently, of atomic bombs. Though such efforts led to the Atomic Bomb Survivors Relief Law in 1994, this was merely a systematization at the national level of various medical insurance and health maintenance plans that had previously been carried out at the local level—its aim was medical assistance, not compensation. Likewise at the international level, the "atonement project" aimed at former "military comfort women" begun in 1995 took the form of a private-sector foundation, the Asian Women's Fund, to disburse "atonement money," while the government limited its official involvement to programs providing medical treatment and welfare support.

The position adopted by the Japanese government may thus be summarized as follows: The suffering caused by the war was something to be borne equally by all Japanese nationals, so no official compensation would be made. When particularly strong claims were voiced, "solatia," "relief," or "medical assistance" might be offered; in addition, somewhat greater measures might be exercised through foundations or funds established not by the government directly, but by private-sector or quasi-governmental organizations. One journalist has described this as "No compensation. No apologies. But 'consolation'—that is the government's stance."*

It should be noted here that the government has consistently refused compensation to all victims, not only (as is sometimes believed) those of foreign nationality. The principle is the same across the board, regardless of whether one is Japanese or not. The only difference is that individuals without Japanese nationality tend more often to fall outside the range of applicability of "solatia" and health care benefits.

It has been argued that Japan has never really faced up to the damage it caused during the war to the people of Asia. But that is by no means to say that it has been lavish in its compensation to Japanese nationals. If there are those who think that Japan's policy denies only foreign nationals, then it is because they are uninformed about wartime victims within Japan itself.

In one sense, the 1988 "solatia" to Siberian internees can be seen as a template for subsequent dealings with foreign victims of the war. The creation of the Public Foundation for Peace and Consolation, separate from the government, closely resembles the format followed by the later Asian Women's Fund.

Efforts to seek compensation for former internees began soon after the war ended. But with the Joint Declaration signed between Japan and the Soviet Union in 1956, the Japanese government formally renounced all rights to compensation from the USSR—essentially as the South Korean government also did with its claims toward Japan in the 1965 Treaty on Basic Relations between Japan and the Republic of Korea, or other Asian countries in various bilateral negotiations restoring diplomatic relations with Japan.

---

* Kurihara Toshio, *Shiberia yokuryū* (Iwanami Shoten, 2009), p. 154.

Consequently, in the 1980s a movement arose among former internees to demand payment of wages for their forced labor from the Japanese government. They argued that the state had an obligation to provide living expenses and wages to military personnel, and that in the case of prisoners of war, it was international custom for such payments to be borne by their country of origin. The Third Geneva Convention (1949, ratified by Japan in 1953) requires that POWs be paid for any labor required of them by the detaining authorities, that detailed accounts be kept by the detaining power, and that the home country bear responsibility for payment of any credit balance due to prisoners upon termination of their captivity (as contained in a statement of accounts issued by the detaining power). In fact the Japanese government did pay the entirety of the wages owed to Japanese in the Pacific theater who had labored as POWs of the United States, Britain, the Netherlands, and Australia. But the Soviet Union had not issued any statements of accounts of internee labor, and the Japanese government had not paid any wages.

In 1981, sixty-two plaintiffs from the National Council for the Compensation of Siberian Internees (Zenkoku Yokuryūsha Hoshō Kyōgikai, or Zen'yokukyō) filed suit in Tokyo District Court against the Japanese government, seeking compensation for unpaid wages during their period of detention. In 1989 the court decided against them, ruling that the majority of the plaintiffs had been repatriated prior to Japan's ratification of the Geneva Conventions and were thus not covered by them; moreover, the losses suffered by the plaintiffs were damages of war to be borne equally by all nationals of the country.

Zen'yokukyō responded by appealing to Gorbachev during his 1991 visit to Japan to issue statements of accounts to the internees, a request that was later fulfilled. Russian president Boris Yeltsin, visiting Japan in 1993, further stated that "on behalf of the Russian people and the government, I would like to express my apology for these inhumane acts [of the internment]."*

After the collapse of the Soviet Union, official Soviet documents were discovered showing that in negotiations immediately before

---

* Ibid., p. 147.

Japan's surrender, the Japanese government and the Kwantung Army had offered the labor services of Japanese POWs to the Soviets. Many former internees felt angry and betrayed at this news.

Zen'yokukyō appealed the 1989 decision of the Tokyo District Court. The Tokyo Higher Court ruled against them in 1993, a decision upheld by the Supreme Court in 1997. However, in its ruling the Supreme Court wrote that "the discontent embraced by the plaintiffs is understandable" and that compensation might be given "at the discretion of the legislative branch."*

Meanwhile, separate from this movement and the court cases it inspired, efforts were also made to bring about compensation through the ruling Liberal Democratic Party. In 1982, the government and LDP agreed to create a private advisory council to the director-general of the prime minister's office called the Discussion Group for Issues of the Postwar Settlement. Its brief was to consider measures to provide some form of compensation to three groups: Siberian internees, persons ineligible for military pensions, and persons who had lost their overseas assets as a result of evacuation from Manchuria and other former Japanese-occupied areas.

The council issued its report in 1984. With regard to the Siberian internment, it proposed that some form of solatium should be made, noting that hardly any recompense had been given for the brutal labor endured by the internees and citing the example of West Germany, which had compensated POWS from its own army who had been held by the Soviets. But the council also pointed to the principle of the suffering of war being borne equally by all nationals and argued that new policy measures directed toward a particular group would not be equitable.

In 1986, the LDP drew up a bill providing a special allowance to former Siberian internees; however, it was never submitted to the Diet. In 1988, the aforementioned legislation establishing the Public Foundation for Peace and Consolation was enacted, and the foundation began its activities that year. Initially, however, Kenji did not apply for the program.

"They didn't express any responsibility for having involved us in that ridiculous war; despite the defeat, their only concern seemed to be with inventing some scheme that would be in line with bureaucratic

---

* Ibid., pp. 142–43.

niceties. They paid out full pensions to high-ranking military personnel, but guys like me were supposed to be content with ¥100,000 in government bonds and a silver cup from a foundation whose executives were a bunch of former bureaucrats parachuting into a cushy retirement. This is bullshit, I thought. If it had been right after the war, I would have appreciated any amount, no matter how little, and been grateful to the country for giving it to us in such difficult times. But at that point, I thought, 'I don't need their money and I won't have anything to do with this.'"

However, in April 1990 Kenji changed his mind and applied after learning that a fellow internee, a Chinese man of Korean descent who had been a soldier in the Imperial Japanese Army, was ineligible for the solatium. He wanted to share it with him.

5

Kenji first learned of O Unggeun (Ch. Wu Xionggun) in 1989, soon after joining Veterans Against War, through O's memoir, "Marugoshi no heishi" (Unarmed Soldier), which was serialized in the organization's *Fusen* newsletter. This memoir related how O had been drafted into the Kwantung Army on 10 August 1945, less than a week before Japan's surrender, and sent unarmed into combat, where he was severely wounded. Captured by Soviet forces, he was treated at the military hospital in Chita and, after several different camps, was sent to the Twenty-Fourth District Camp No. 2 in November 1947. Reading this, Kenji recalled a prisoner named Kurehashi Shūgō who had been transferred in alone to his camp.

"He had a space on the sleeping platform near me, though at the time we barely spoke to one another. But since a lone transfer was quite unusual, I thought there must have been some special reason for it. I also remembered that he spoke Russian pretty well, and that he was said to be a Korean. So I figured it might be him."

A number of items in the memoir matched Kenji's own recollections. O was from the area that had been called Jiandao Province under the Manchukuo regime (now the Yanbian Korean Autonomous Prefecture in Jilin Province of the People's Republic of China). While in the field hospital, O happened to get his hands on a Japanese textbook for learning Russian and managed to master the language while working in the camps. Later he was selected as an interpreter at a maintenance facility for locomotives in Chita, where he was asked by the political commissars to help identify individuals with a "prior record" (meaning a history of working for the Japanese military police or special services). When he refused, he was dismissed from his post and sent to Camp No. 2.

Kenji guessed that "Kurehashi" had been the Japanese-style name that O, like all Koreans, had been forced to take during the war by the Japanese government. He obtained O's address from the editors of *Fusen* and wrote a letter to him in China, giving a number of details about the camp during the period both men had been there and inquiring as to whether O was in fact the "Kurehashi" Kenji remembered.

After a while, a reply came. "He didn't seem to remember me, but said that he was certainly the person I remembered." This began an exchange of letters between the two.

According to statistics from the Japanese Ministry of Health, Labour and Welfare, individuals from the Korean peninsula serving in the armed forces of the Japanese Empire numbered 116,294 regular military personnel and 126,047 military auxiliaries. From Taiwan came 80,433 regular personnel and 126,750 auxiliaries. Of the Koreans, 22,182 are listed as having been killed in combat or gone missing in action.

While estimates vary, around 10,000 Imperial Japanese Army personnel of Korean descent are thought to have become prisoners of the Soviet army. Those who returned to South Korea after their internment were regarded with suspicion as former soldiers of the Japanese Empire and possible Communist spies. In February 1949, when a group of some 500 internees attempted to cross the thirty-eighth parallel to repatriate to South Korea, South Korean troops mistakenly opened fire on them, killing thirty-seven.[*]

In South Korea, former internees were subjected to interrogation by state security police, police surveillance, and discrimination in jobs and other aspects of daily life—worse treatment than that experienced by internees returning to Japan. The rehabilitation of their reputations

---

[*] Shirai Hisaya, *Kenshō Shiberia yokuryū* (Heibonsha, 2010), p. 240.

would not come until 2005, when the government of the Republic of Korea established the Truth and Reconciliation Commission to investigate and redress abuses committed under Japanese colonization and the autocratic regimes that followed.*

Taiwanese soldiers of the Imperial Japanese Army were also held in Siberia. One such veteran recounts that he was unable to return to Taiwan because of Kuomintang repression and so chose to remain in Japan.† The Kuomintang party, defeated in the Chinese civil war by the Communists, relocated the government of the Republic of China to Taiwan and until 1987 ruled the island as a single-party dictatorship under martial law; had this man returned, he probably would have faced treatment similar to that of his Korean fellows.

In November 1948, O Unggeun returned to his home in Jiandao Province, soon to become part of the People's Republic of China, where he suffered a series of hardships. He graduated from Yanbian University and became a doctor but, as noted earlier, many like him were attacked during the Cultural Revolution for presumed connections to Japan or the Japanese military. O was forced to wear a large placard around his neck that read "soldier of the Japanese Kwantung Army and ideological reactionary element" as he was beaten by Red Guards.‡

O knew nothing of the Public Foundation for Peace and Consolation or other Japanese government programs—and in any case, non-Japanese nationals were ineligible. But Kenji felt money of this kind should go to precisely people like him. In Kenji's view, it made no sense that Koreans who had been drafted as Japanese were being refused payments because they were now foreigners. He applied for his ¥100,000 in government bonds and sent half of it to O. "At first I was going to send the entire amount, but then I decided to split it equally with him, out of consideration for his feelings and to communicate a sense of solidarity."

Prior to the war Koreans and Taiwanese had possessed Japanese nationality, until in 1947 the Japanese government issued an Alien Registration Ordinance declaring that Japanese nationals registered in Korea, Taiwan, and other areas outside the home islands would

---

* NHK, *Shōgen kiroku heishitachi no sensō: Chōsenjin kōgun heishi, harukanaru sokoku*, television documentary, broadcast 27 March 2010.
† Sakai Atsuko (director), *Taiwan aidentitii*, film (Uzumasa, 2013).
‡ Hayashi Eidai, *Wasurerareta Chōsenjin kōgun heishi* (Azusa Shoin, 1995), p. 293.

"be regarded as foreigners . . . for the time being." Then, once the Occupation ended in April 1952, these individuals were summarily stripped of their Japanese nationality. From that time on acquisition of Japanese nationality had to follow the established procedures for naturalization, which included examination of the applicant's financial status and tax records; the decision was left to the discretion of the Ministry of Justice.

When Korea had been annexed by Japan in 1910, its inhabitants had not been given a choice regarding nationality—Japanese nationality had been forced upon them. Nor was there any legal means for renouncing it, apparently because the Japanese government was afraid that Koreans in the anti-Japanese movement who had fled to Manchuria might, by renouncing Japanese nationality, place themselves beyond the jurisdiction of Japanese law enforcement.* In the Twenty-One Demands and the Treaty Concerning Southern Manchuria and Eastern Mongolia in 1915, the Japanese government claimed that the Korean residents of Jiandao Province were Japanese nationals and that the jurisdiction of the Japanese government should therefore extend to the area in which they lived.

Later, in 1944, as the Pacific War intensified, Japan began conscripting Koreans into its armed forces, and eventually the Koreans of Jiandao Province were also called up. Thus it was that Korean and Taiwanese personnel like O were commandeered into the Imperial Japanese Army as "Japanese" without having been given any choice about their nationality, and then—also without any choice on their part—lost that nationality and their eligibility for pensions and other benefits.

In May 1990, Kenji sent the ¥50,000 to O, along with the following letter: "Several years ago the government made a law to pay ¥100,000 to veterans who had been Soviet prisoners of war. But this law does not apply to foreigners. As an expression of my feeling of apology as a Japanese, I am sending you half of the ¥100,000 that I received."†

A letter of heartfelt thanks soon arrived from O, who was, however, dissatisfied that he was ineligible for the program because he was

---

* Eiji Oguma, *The Boundaries of "the Japanese,"* vol. 2, *Korea, Taiwan, and the Ainu, 1868–1945* (Melbourne: Trans Pacific Press, 2017), pp. 142–51.
† Oguma Kenji, "Shiberia yokuryū no moto Kantō-gun heishi Go Yūkon [O Unggeun] no koto," *Aurora*, 30 December 1997.

not a Japanese national. He insisted that he, too, should have the right to apply for the money, and asked Kenji for an opinion on what he should do.

"To be honest, I didn't know how to respond," says Kenji. "Rationally, it was unfair for him not to be paid the solatium. But I also knew the Japanese government would have its guard up."

Kenji did some research before replying to O, explaining that when Japan had restored diplomatic relations with China and South Korea, the three governments had renounced the right to any claims for compensation arising out of the war, and that for O to be paid the solatium, the legislation establishing the Public Foundation for Peace and Consolation and its program would have to be revised.

This still did not satisfy O. Kenji wrote him again, saying that the Japanese government had refused wage payments even to former POWs of Japanese nationality. Kenji had applied for and received an official statement from Russia detailing his unpaid wages, but even with this certification, Kenji explained in his letter, the Japanese government and the courts would not change their position.

For a while, letters stopped coming from O. Then, at the beginning of 1996, there was an unexpected turn of events: O decided to come to Japan to initiate a lawsuit, and his lawyer invited Kenji to join in as a plaintiff.

6

Over the years O and other Koreans who had been interned in Siberia had begun action of their own. Former internees now living in South Korea formed the Siberia Sakpung (North Wind) Society after diplomatic relations between Russia and the Republic of Korea were restored in 1991; they visited the Russian embassy in Seoul and demanded labor certificates for their period of internment. Factors in the timing of this activity were the democratization of South Korea earlier in 1987 and the end of the Cold War, making diplomatic relations possible.

Prior to democratization, any demands for postwar compensation from Japan were suppressed by the South Korean government, which had renounced all rights to compensation in the 1965 Treaty on Basic

Relations between Japan and Korea and which therefore viewed any demands for Japanese compensation as a criticism of its own policies. In an interview in the 1990s, the chairman of the Korean Association of Pacific War Victims and Bereaved Families commented, "When at a 1974 rally for victims in Busan we called for a march to the Japanese consulate to question Japan's wartime responsibility, we were immediately arrested by the police. We continued to face such obstruction until the democratization brought about by President Roh Tae-woo."*

Similar conditions existed in much of Asia prior to democratization, as in the testimony of a member of a Taiwanese association of veterans and auxiliaries of the Japanese military and their survivors: "If we engaged in political activity we were jailed. The Kuomintang government wanted nothing to do with people educated under the Japanese colonial system and completely obstructed our efforts to demand compensation from Japan." The Kuomintang government gave priority politically and economically to its own members and other refugees from the mainland, and expelled native Taiwanese—including the intelligentsia, who had been educated in Japanese style—from the center of social life. Koreans remaining in Sakhalin, which had been Japanese territory before the war, were likewise unable to engage in political activity under Soviet rule, making impossible any movement for repatriation to Korea or compensation from Japan.†

With the end of the Cold War and the success of democratization movements in a number of Asian countries, however, this sort of repression was lifted, and demands for postwar compensation from Japan began to be voiced across the region. In December 1991—the same year the Korean internees began their movement—thirty-five Korean former soldiers and auxiliaries of the Imperial Japanese Army filed a suit for damages and compensation in Tokyo District Court. Three of the plaintiffs were former "comfort women," so this suit also marked the beginning of demands by that group for redress.

This is sometimes misunderstood, but at that point compensation of former comfort women was seen as only a small part of the larger issue. The movement for pensions and other compensation of Korean and Taiwanese veterans and auxiliaries of the Japanese military had

---

* Asahi Shimbun Sengo Hoshō Mondai Shuzaihan, *Sengo hoshō to wa nani ka* (Asahi Shimbunsha, 1999), p. 56.
† Ibid., p. 57.

existed for much longer; in fact director Ōshima Nagisa's documentary on their efforts, *Wasurerareta kōgun* (The Forgotten Imperial Army), dates back almost three decades earlier, to 1963.

The next year, in 1992, a former Siberian internee of Korean descent residing in Japan named Lee Chang Sok filed suit for a military pension, but the Kyoto District Court ruled against him in 1998, finding the provisions regarding nationality in the Military Pension Law constitutional and stating that compensation for wartime damages should be left to the discretion of the legislative branch. Lee protested, "During the war I risked my life fighting for Japan . . . If I were Japanese they would give me a medal. It's not about the money. All I want is equal treatment."* Yet in 2002, the decision against him was upheld in the Supreme Court. Undeterred, in 2003 members of the Siberia Sakpung Society in Korea filed suit in Tokyo District Court demanding an official apology and compensation for their internment in Siberia.

As related earlier, Kenji had sent O Unggeun ¥50,000—half of his solatium payout—in May 1990. According to journalist Hayashi Eidai, who has reported extensively on wartime compensation movements by non-Japanese nationals, "News of this soon reached others in Yangbian with a Siberian connection, who questioned why the Japanese government paid the solatium only to Japanese nationals and began to speak of their right to demand the same."†

According to Hayashi, in China at the time there were 315 other Korean residents of the former Manchuria who, like O, had served in the Imperial Japanese Army and been interned in Siberia. In order to facilitate negotiations with the Japanese government, O began to compile a roster of the Siberian returnees scattered around the country. Eventually a China Council of Internees of the Former Soviet Union was established around five former POWs, with O as its chairman. The group was able to locate 250 former POWs or their surviving family members; it also arranged with Zen'yokukyō in Japan to be recognized as a branch of that organization, which forwarded the necessary forms for requesting labor certificates from the Russian government.

---

* Kurihara, *Shiberia yokuryū*, p. 145.
† Hayashi, *Wasurerareta Chōsenjin kōgun heishi*, p. 311.

However, the China Council suddenly suspended its activities in 1992, right around the time of the visit of the Japanese emperor to China in October to commemorate the twentieth anniversary of the restoration of diplomatic relations between the two countries. Hayashi notes that there was probably pressure from the Chinese government; he speculates that the organization was possibly seen as an anti-government movement and that international considerations might also have played a part, with China not wanting to antagonize Japan and thus endanger the receipt of foreign aid.* In this period, China was isolated internationally, having drawn severe criticism for its brutal crackdown on the protests in Tiananmen Square in 1989. But among the Western bloc, Japan was the least enthusiastic about sanctions against China and was also its biggest source of foreign aid— thus the favor shown to it by China.

In recent years, documentary corroboration for Hayashi's conjectures has emerged: in 2013 it was reported that although materials confirming the wartime existence of "military comfort women" of Chinese nationality had surfaced in the archives of Japan's Defense Agency shortly before the emperor's 1992 China visit, diplomatic officials in both China and Japan made a confidential agreement not to allow the issue to escalate in view of the event.† It would not be until the mid-1990s that the Chinese government would begin to take a more harshly critical attitude toward historical issues involving Japan.

Whatever the reason, O and his associates halted their activities for a time. O told Hayashi in 1995 that even if he had to act alone, he wanted a labor certificate from the Russian government, since through it he would be able to prove that at least one Korean had definitely been interned in the labor camps in Siberia.‡ The following year, O came to Japan.

The trip was at the invitation of an activist group led by a Korean resident of Japan named Jong Dugoe (Jp. Sō Tokai). Jong was born in 1915 and came to Japan in 1920, where he was raised as an acolyte in a Nichiren Buddhist monastery in Kyoto. He developed relationships

---

* Ibid., p. 312.
† "Nittchū tōkyoku, ianfu toriagenu gōi: '92-nen no tennō hōchū mae," *Asahi shimbun* digital edition, 10 December 2013.
‡ Hayashi, *Wasurerareta Chōsenjin kōgun heishi*, p. 312.

with anarchists and pan-Asianists such as Ōkawa Shūmei, and in 1934 went to Manchuria.

After the war, Jong was arrested in Manchuria by the Kuomintang and in 1947 "repatriated" to Japan. But because of the Japanese government's policy of denying nationality to former colonial subjects, he found he was no longer legally Japanese. In 1969 he filed a lawsuit seeking recognition of his Japanese nationality. In 1973 he burned his alien registration certificate in front of the Ministry of Justice, insisting that he was a citizen of Japan.*

For a while afterward Jong wandered about the country before taking up residence in the Kumano-ryō, a dormitory run by the student government association of Kyoto University. Working with sympathetic Japanese, he organized an association to support a lawsuit by survivors and surviving family members of victims in the *Ukishima Maru* incident of 24 August 1945, in which a ship carrying Korean wartime laborers returning from Japan to their homeland exploded and sank in the waters off the port of Maizuru, killing over 500. The suit, which sought compensation and recognition of the authorities' dereliction of duty with regard to safety precautions, was submitted in 1992 and decided in 2003, in a ruling that acknowledged partial responsibility on the part of the Japanese government.

During O's trip to Japan in March 1996, Jong's group arranged rallies and speaking engagements in Kyushu, Kyoto, and Tokyo and also took O to submit petitions to Diet members, political parties, and the office of the prime minister. Kenji was asked to participate in these efforts. "I invited my friends who had been in the camp with us, and we went along to give moral support."

Kenji did not actually see much hope in such activism. O had written to Kenji that he wanted to come to Japan to file a lawsuit because his efforts in China were not getting him anywhere. But while Kenji could sympathize with his frustration, "in terms of what might actually be accomplished, I felt it would be dishonest to tell him anything that might prove overly optimistic." So his reply to O had been that he should not expect any results.

Even so, Kenji accompanied O and his associates on their visits to Diet members and the prime minister's office. "We were treated with

---

* For biographical details on Jong see Jong Dugoe, *Manshūkoku imin* (Fūbaisha, 2003).

polite condescension and failed to have much of an impact, but I still wanted to give O an opportunity to voice his grievances."

Meanwhile Kenji was asked to join O's lawsuit by the lawyer who had agreed to represent O and the other plaintiffs pro bono. The suit would be against the Japanese state, seeking compensation for damages and a formal apology. The lawyer, who knew the prewar pan-Asianist Jong quite well, liked to call himself "a dyed-in-the-wool conservative." His fundamental stance was that since large numbers of young people from Korea, China, and Taiwan had risked their lives fighting for Japan, the country "must restore its integrity as a nation by answering their sacrifice and suffering with profound thanks, compensation, and assistance." In his words, "Nations do not fall because of economics. They do not even fall as a result of defeat in war. They fall when they have lost their sense of justice and integrity."*

In the suit, the lawyer quoted exclusively from conservative intellectuals such as Nakano Seigō, Komuro Naoki, and Satō Seizaburō. Satō, a well-known member of the LDP's brain trust, had said in a magazine article at the time, "We should treat all former subjects of the Japanese Empire with complete equality. Japan is wrong in not taking a more compassionate stance toward Japanese war orphans in China and in not paying military pensions to Taiwanese and Koreans who served as military personnel or auxiliaries in the Imperial Japanese Army and Navy."†

This conservatism set the lawyer and his cohorts apart from the Japanese supporters of other suits brought during the same period by former "comfort women" and similar plaintiffs. Kenji, however, was not especially concerned about the ideological underpinnings of the suit, which he agreed to join. He describes his reasoning as follows:

"Jong struck me as a bit fishy, and I didn't see any hope for actually winning the lawsuit. To be honest, when they asked me to join it, I was taken aback. But I decided to go along with it because I believed that what they were saying was right. I felt that as a Japanese I had to do something for O. I didn't worry at all about the trouble I might have getting mixed up in something like this, or about the harm it might do to my reputation with the people around me. Why should I? I'd lived

* Text of lawsuit complaint, 25 September 1996, p. 53.
† Itō Takashi and Satō Seizaburō, "Ano sensō to wa nan datta no ka," *Chūō kōron*, January 1995, p. 40.

my life as the lowest of the low. I've never cared about my reputation or what other people might say about me."

There are virtually no other wartime compensation lawsuits filed by non-Japanese Asians in which Japanese have participated as co-plaintiffs. Japanese advocacy groups for Siberian internees cooperated with Korean and Chinese internees, given the actual varied backgrounds of the "Japanese" veterans who were affected, but they never joined as co-plaintiffs.

The lawsuit was filed in Tokyo District Court in September 1996. It was certainly an unprecedented case, involving a Japanese former POW and an ethnic Korean former POW of Chinese nationality bringing suit against the Japanese government with the support of a group of conservative pan-Asianists.

7

At the first public hearing for the lawsuit in January 1997, the court adjourned after the presiding judge expressed the opinion that the case should be tried as an administrative suit rather than a damage claim. After a change in judges, the second public hearing convened on 13 May, and the plaintiffs were given an opportunity to state their case.

That day, Kenji made his way from the subway to the court along with two veterans he had gotten to know through Veterans Against War, all three of them wearing white sashes marked with their former ranks and unit designations. This bit of political theater was Jong's idea, though there was no media coverage. The three veterans were accompanied by Jong, other supporters, and Kenji's family.

In court, O Unggeun gave testimony on the circumstances leading up to his internment in Siberia. At one point his attorney asked him to sing the song marking his departure for the front. O sang a military march with the following lyrics:

Our brave and loyal soldiers, beyond compare,
Will serve in Heaven's place to strike injustice;
Accompanied by our cheers,
They now set forth
To defend their homeland.

Later, O recounted, "I did not want to do it, but at the request [of my lawyer], I stood before the Japanese judges and sang the song from fifty-five years ago when I boarded the train at Shiyan, seen off by my mother and little sister, with the Rising Sun flag fluttering in the breeze."*

Next, Kenji took the witness stand to describe the circumstances of his internment and his acquaintance with O. For the most part he stuck to reading the statement he had prepared for the occasion:

> I did not become a plaintiff in this case for monetary reasons. I did it to speak on behalf of O Unggeun in the hope that by doing so I could urge Japan to become a country that truly respects human rights.
>
> I spent about three years after the war in a prison camp in the Soviet Union, where O was also confined. He was born in 1925 in the Yangbian district of what was then Manchuria.
>
> Conscripted as a Japanese subject of Korean ethnicity, he was admitted [into the Imperial Japanese Army] in Haila'er in northwestern Manchuria on 10 August 1945—the very day that the Soviet army attacked, following the declaration of war against Japan on 9 August. Badly wounded in the fighting, he was sent to a hospital in the Soviet Union. After his release from the hospital, he returned through North Korea to his former home at the end of 1948, where he became a Chinese national. As a veteran of the Imperial Japanese Army, however, he experienced discrimination in many aspects of his life, and in particular suffered nearly fatal persecution during the Cultural Revolution.
>
> Some years ago, I received a solatium and a letter acknowledging the hardships I experienced as a result of my Siberian internment. But Japan does not recognize O's eligibility for the same benefits because of his foreign nationality. This I cannot accept.
>
> Please think for a moment of why O was forced to endure internment in Siberia. The former Japanese Empire annexed Korea and declared all persons of Korean ethnicity to be Japanese subjects. Thus he, like me, was conscripted in accordance with his duty as a Japanese, inducted into the Kwantung Army, and made a prisoner

---

* Case appeal statement, 11 July 2000, p. 60.

of war. Insofar as the solatium is awarded in recognition of Siberian internment, he has a right to receive it.

The Japanese state conscripted O as a Japanese subject and caused his internment in Siberia. That same Japanese state cannot irresponsibly and illogically claim that he is ineligible because he is now a foreigner.

This is blatant discrimination, and a disregard of human rights that cannot stand up to international scrutiny.

We must think of issues of this kind not in ways that find acceptance only in Japan, but with a reasoning that is also deemed sound internationally.

During World War II, the countries of the West also possessed colonies and had people of other races and nationalities fighting in their armed forces. None of these countries discriminate in their wartime compensation on the basis of factors such as nationality. This holds true not only for the victors—the United States, Britain, France, etc.—but also for the vanquished such as Germany and Italy. Italy has compensated individuals from Ethiopia, Somaliland, Eritrea, and Libya who served in its colonial armies. And while Germany did not possess colonies, I want to cite the example of a certain Latvian lieutenant that I read in the book *Baruto-kai no hotori nite* [On the Shores of the Baltic Sea], written by the wife of a military attaché at the Japanese legation in Latvia before the war.

When Germany invaded the Soviet Union in 1941, this lieutenant joined a Latvian unit of the German army in order to win the independence of his homeland, which had been annexed by the Soviet Union in 1940. Though on Germany's defeat he fled to Sweden, he continued to receive a military pension from Germany until his death in 1980. I have also read of a Ukrainian soldier in the German army who emigrated to the US after the war but who also received such compensation.

Please take note. Neither of these men were ever German nationals. As far as Germany was concerned, they were never anything other than foreigners.

How different is the attitude of the Japanese state toward O Unggeun, who did his duty as a Japanese subject by serving in the Japanes military.

Fighting for one's country is an act that could very well mean giving up one's life. Whether one is ordered into or volunteers for this act, it establishes a kind of tacit contractual relationship of employment between the state and the individual.

In this relationship, nationality is irrelevant.

This is the common understanding of the modern nation-states. Japan's thinking on human rights does not hold up internationally and cannot be called that of a civilized modern nation.

Here is my request to our country: Postwar compensation of this kind has no statute of limitations. Stop trying forever to evade responsibility. Cease burdening future generations with this negative legacy.

In closing I have a request to make of all the judges. When O Unggeun visited Japan last March, I accompanied him, along with other like-minded individuals, to appeal this matter to the Diet, Diet members, political parties, and the prime minister's office.

We certainly met with sympathy, but still nothing changed.

Since neither the legislative nor the executive branch of government will do anything for us, we have no option other than to appeal to the judiciary. I may be naive, but I believe that the spirit of the law resides in protecting the innate rights endowed upon all human beings. We do not need any more sympathy. We hope that you will squarely regard the facts and the essence of this case and deliver a judgment consonant with reason.*

Kenji comments about reading this testimony before the judges: "I really didn't think we would win the case, but I had twenty minutes of oral argument to use, so I used them to say what I wanted to say. A great many of my comrades were killed due to being drafted into a senseless war and then put to senseless labor. My father and my grandparents lost everything they'd saved up for old age in that war, and they suffered immensely. Maybe it was useless to say such things to the judges, but I decided I would speak my mind in any case."

After the oral arguments were completed, Kenji took O on a holiday tour. "I put him up at a hot springs in the Izu Peninsula. He'd brought me a gift from China. He had a good heart."

---

* Statement by Oguma Kenji, 13 May 1997.

As mentioned earlier, there was no media coverage on the day of the trial. A newspaper sent reporters before the trial, and there was a small feature article, but that was all. At the time there were a number of compensation cases in progress, and this one did not draw the broad public attention that, for instance, the "comfort women" issue did. Kenji says,

"I didn't really follow the other compensation cases that were going on at the time. Even when our own case was covered in the press, we didn't seem to get much reaction or support. I figured that was as much as could be expected, and so it didn't bother me. But my old friends from the Veterans Against War days stuck by me to the end."

The remainder of the trial proceeded almost entirely through exchanges of documents between the lawyers and the judges, without any further testimony by the plaintiffs. Finally, in February 2000, Tokyo District Court delivered its verdict dismissing the plaintiffs' claims. Compensation for damages was rejected on the grounds that such were hazards of war that must be borne equally by all nationals. The question of a public apology was left to the discretion of the legislative branch.

By this time O had returned to China. As he later wrote in his appeal, when informed of the court's decision, he was beside himself with disappointment and rage, and took to his bed. "As a Korean, why should I have to bear the burden imposed on Japanese nationals by the Japanese state? I would like the Japanese judges to explain this to me in a way that I can understand." In O's words, "Neither the law nor justice nor the human heart seems to get through to Japanese judges."[*]

In 2001 the Tokyo Higher Court dismissed O's appeal, and in 2002 the Supreme Court upheld this decision, closing the matter. Kenji recalls,

"Once the final dismissal of the case was read in the Supreme Court, we were more or less pushed right out the door, I suppose because people sometimes make a fuss at that point. I guess you could call me eccentric for having done what I did. After the final decision I recall one of Jong's supporters telling me on the telephone that she saw at least some meaning in having left behind a record of such a trial. I realized then that you could look at it that way, and

---

* Case appeal statement, pp. 61, 63.

that thre might be some value to our case becoming part of the mountain of documents in the court archives."

It is up to historians to sort through that mountain of paper and determine its significance. The attorney in the case wrote of Kenji in his brief, "Even if the state did not have a conscience, by his actions he demonstrated, in place of the state's injustice, that this nation and its people do indeed have one." Whether this assessment is accurate or not awaits, as the expression goes, the judgment of history.

8

When the lawsuit was initiated in 1997, Kenji was already seventy-two. That year he finally retired completely from Tachikawa Sports, where he had still been working one or two days a week.

"Ōki-san took over all of Tachikawa Sports, but closed it in 1998 when he turned sixty and became eligible to collect his pension. We'd just been working to make a living, so I didn't feel a great sense of loss on seeing it go."

Then in 2002, after the Supreme Court rejected Kenji and O's final appeal, Kenji suffered a stroke. He had been at the community center attending a conversational English class on the invitation of a younger housewife from the Tama Hills Nature Conservancy when he suddenly became dizzy and unable to stand up.

"They called an ambulance for me, and I was taken to the hospital. For folks of my generation, calling an ambulance seems like making too big a fuss. But some of the younger women in that class had called ambulances before for their kids, so they had less resistance to the idea. If they hadn't done so, it would have been too late and I probably would have ended up half-paralyzed."

Despite some slight paralysis on his left side that lingered for a while, with physical rehabilitation Kenji was able to recover almost completely by the spring of the following year. One could say that his efforts to deepen his ties to the local community had proved a blessing in this case. However, Kenji was seventy-seven at the time of his stroke, and he took the occasion to withdraw from both the Katakuri meals-on-wheels program and the Tama Hills Nature Conservancy.

"About two years before that, I'd begun to get really out of breath on the steeper trails when patrolling Naganuma Park. So I thought it was time for somebody like me, without any special skills or knowledge, to leave."

The next year, in 2003, his wife, Hiroko, had a fall in the garden and broke her wrist. After that, she became depressed and was frequently at the doctor for various physical and emotional ailments. She was so dispirited that she became unable to handle the housework, and Kenji took over the cooking duties.

"Actually, since the 1990s I had already been taking care of meal prep on Tuesday and Friday nights so Hiroko could have time to learn to play go and take English and painting lessons. Because I had jotted down the basics of the kitchen she had taught me back then, I was able to manage when I took over all the cooking at the age of seventy-eight. The newsletter that Katakuri distributed along with the meals-on-wheels did a feature on me, saying it was great that there were men my age learning how to cook.

"In Siberia I did whatever I had to do in order to survive, and after the war I did anything and everything as well. Whether it's cooking or anything else, being self-sufficient is fundamental. Besides, if you can cook, then you can eat the things you like."

In 2005, O came to Japan once again to attend a conference of Zen'yokukyō, which had invited him from China along with the head of the Sakpung Society of former internees from Korea. O paid a visit to Kenji's home in Hachiōji, accompanied by a newspaper reporter and a Zen'yokukyō activist.

At the time, Zen'yokukyō was winding up its activities. In 2005, a coalition of the Democratic Party, the Communist Party, and the Social Democratic Party proposed legislation in both Houses for the government to pay former internees between ¥300,000 and ¥2,000,000 (about $3,000 to $20,000) each, according to the duration of their internment. But this bill was voted down in 2006 by the ruling coalition of the LDP and Komeito. The ruling coalition proposed an alternative bill, which would, as of 2010, dissolve the Public Foundation for Peace and Consolation, often criticized as a cozy sinecure for politicians and bureaucrats, and use its remaining assets to fund a "special solatium" to Siberian internees, evacuees from former Japanese-occupied territories, and individuals ineligible for military pensions. This bill was passed, and benefits were distributed once again.

The program offered a choice of ¥100,000 worth of vacation vouchers, a clock, a fountain pen, a stationery box, or a plaque. This time, too, non-Japanese nationals were ineligible. Kenji chose the vouchers, converting them to cash and contributing half to Zen'yokukyō.

Kenji continued to vote against the LDP. In the 2009 election he voted for the Democratic Party, whose win and takeover of the regime from the LDP, he says, "gave me hope."

In June 2010, the Democratic Party government enacted the Siberia Special Measures Law, which represented a compromise between previous bills by the Democratic Party and the LDP: former internees would be awarded money on a sliding scale from ¥250,000 to ¥1,500,000, depending on the duration of their internment, out of the capital that would be returned to the national treasury by the Public Foundation for Peace and Consolation when it was dissolved that year. The money could be interpreted in two ways—as a de facto direct payment of compensation by the Japanese state, or as simply a redirection of the remaining funds of the foundation, as in the LDP-Komeito bill. The text of the law did not use the word "compensation" (hoshō), but it did call for documenting the facts of the internment, and in his speech presenting the bill to the Diet, Democratic Party member Satō Taisuke described it as being for apology and compensation. There were some 70,000 surviving eligible internees, though once again, non-Japanese were excluded. With this success, Zen'yokukyō disbanded in May 2011.

"I'd been aware of Zen'yokukyō's activities since the 1980s, but had not participated. We didn't talk about movements like that in the Chita-kai, either. As with military pensions, the state gives money where the power is; people without a voice don't get any. Zen'yokukyō was on the right track, but after its loss in the Supreme Court [in 1997], I'd given up on it. I respect it for rebuilding the movement after that and managing to achieve what it did.

"Still, it all left a bad taste in my mouth, and at first I didn't apply for the new program, since they were basically doling out money left over from the dissolution of that cushy job for retired bureaucrats. I still held a lot of resentment toward the state. The state, unlike the human heart, is a soulless thing."

Yet once again, Kenji ended up applying for the solatium. He had lost contact with O, but found a new worthy recipient.

"The application deadline was March 2012. A year before that, in March 2011, I read an article in the Zen'yokukyō newsletter, *Aurora*, about how the daughter of a man who had died after being sent from Sakhalin to a camp in Norilsk in the far north was collecting funds to place a memorial tablet for him there. So I applied for ¥250,000. I gave half of it to help fund this memorial, and I gave the other half to Zen'yokukyō. That was the end of it for me.

"Whether it was a one-shot payment or an apology or whatever, the time to do it was right after the war—not like they did, finally doling it out after having been badgered about it for years. I felt no gratitude for anything that was given out that way by an institution like the state. I will say, however, that it was because it was a Democratic Party government that they did anything for us at all."

March 2011 was also the time of the Tōhoku earthquake and the Fukushima nuclear accident. "I learned from later news reports that the nuclear disaster had been an accident waiting to happen. The government showed its true colors by trying to minimize the reality of what had happened. We should give up on nuclear power plants." In 2012, Kenji had solar panels installed on the roof of his house.

From around 2012, Kenji began to have trouble walking. He was classified at "support level 1," the mildest category of nursing-care certification in Japan's national health system. In January 2015, Hiroko passed away.

Since about the turn of the new century, the aging of Japanese society had become a significant concern. In some depopulated rural areas, more than half of the remaining residents were over sixty-five years of age, and Kenji's neighborhood in Nan'yōdai, like many other once-new housing developments in Tokyo's outer suburbs, was rapidly graying as well. In Nan'yōdai District 1, the proportion of the population aged sixty-five or older was 44 percent in 2014; in nearby Kitanodai it was 43 percent, and in Mitsuidai, 40 percent. Though nominally part of metropolitan Tokyo, these developments were fast losing their ability to be self-sustaining.

Near Kenji's home the number of vacant houses was beginning to be noticeable. Many of the established shops in Nan'yōdai went out of business, and purchasing daily necessities in the neighborhood became impossible. Fortunately Kenji is still able to drive, and even at the age of eighty-nine is thus able to do his own shopping.

Kenji finds himself irritated by many current social developments.

"I am more or less resigned to the idea of politicians continuing to visit Yasukuni Shrine* and of pundits claiming that the Nanjing Massacre is a fabrication. But I always feel a quiet rage burning within me. The headlines in the weekly magazines are full of xenophobic lies, slander, and attempts to play down the truth of history.

"In the past many people spent their whole lives at the bottom of the heap, but it also used to be said that 'Poverty is a stranger to industry.' The way things are set up these days, though, if you aren't a regular full-time employee of some company there's no way to get ahead, no matter how hard you try. I don't think this is true only in Japan, but it feels hopeless. Employers have lost their sense of ethics. I feel sorry for young people.

"The way I was brought up, when I was twenty I knew nothing about the realities of the world or how it worked. I wasn't given any information, and I couldn't choose the government. There was no freedom to criticize. Nowadays, if you want to know the truth, you can. But far too many people refuse to look at things they don't want to see, and they don't even try to learn. Give it twenty more years and things will be even worse. I think there might even be a major economic collapse if interest rates on Japanese government bonds go up."

At eighty-nine Kenji is still living day by day, taking care of himself, keeping his own house. He reads scholarly books on post–Cold War Yugoslavia and World War II diplomacy. He is a member of or donor to a number of nonprofit organizations, including Amnesty International, Moyai (for the poor and homeless), Peshawar-kai (for aid to Pakistan and Afghanistan), Katakuri, and Doctors Without Borders, and regularly sends postcards protesting the incarceration of "prisoners of conscience."

---

* At Yasukuni Shrine in Tokyo, Class A war criminals are enshrined along with soldiers and sailors fallen in Japan's modern wars.

"Amnesty's newsletter comes with postcards preaddressed to the governments and chief officials of various countries with English text protesting the incarceration of specific individuals. So I say I am sending letters, but what I am really doing is just signing them and dropping them in the post. I doubt they will even be read, but something within me keeps me at it."

As long as he can manage it physically, he wants to keep cooking for himself and living independently. Looking back over his life, he says,

"For a while after I was released from the tuberculosis sanatorium, I figured I might live to the age of fifty at best. I lived the first half of my life at the bottom, then I was lucky enough to be able to lead a regular life. But many people I met along the way were never able to do that. Compared with them, I have it pretty good at this point."

At the very end of my questions to him, I asked Kenji what had been the most important thing to him at the most difficult points of his life. In situations like Siberia or the sanatorium, when the future seemed completely shut off, what had been most precious to him?

Kenji's answer: "Hope. If you have that, you can survive."

Oguma Kenji and Oguma Eiji, sharing their impressions of a Chinese edition of this book.

Afterword

This book is based on a series of interviews with a Japanese man, born in 1925, who experienced internment in Siberia following the end of World War II. But it differs from previous war memoirs in two important respects.

First of all, it depicts not only his wartime experience, but his everyday life in prewar and postwar Japan. Since many war memoirs fail to include such information, we cannot learn about the circumstances from which their protagonists went off to war, or the sort of lives they led when they returned. This book, on the other hand, gives a continuous account of daily life before and after the war in addition to describing the experience of the war, and thus addresses questions about how the war affected people's lives and how the postwar consciousness of peace took shape.

Second, this book introduces a social-science perspective. It considers contemporary economics, politics, and law as it depicts, through the experience of a single individual, the conditions of social mobility, educational achievement, employment opportunities, and industrial structure during the periods in question. So it is at once a personal history and a living history of the twentieth century that incorporates aspects of both institutional and economic history.

In contrast to the majority of those who have left memoirs and other records of this period, who generally had an educated middle-class upbringing, the subject of this personal history is a small-business owner who grew up in a shopkeeper's family. His trajectory is therefore different from the typical "student-soldier to salaryman" narrative found in many of these accounts. With the addition of the sociological perspective just mentioned, I believe there are aspects of his story that may offer a unique contribution to the study of contemporary Japanese history.

In recent years there has been growing interest not only in the history of wartime Japan, but also in accounts of the immediate postwar period and the era of high economic growth that followed. This is not surprising, considering that the generation born after that era of high economic growth now occupies center stage in our society. As the boom times have ended and issues of inequality have reemerged, greater attention is being paid to how the economic development and transformation of industrial structure that took place during the Shōwa era (1925–1989) influenced the lives of ordinary people and altered the social order.

This book is an attempt to connect such contemporary concerns with a historical interest in the war experience. Furthermore, by placing an individual's trajectory at the center of the war experience, and linking it to both prewar and postwar history, I hoped to create an account that would offer greater interest and a broader appeal than previous works of this kind.

In academic terms, this is a work of oral history, popular history, and social history. And in sociological terms, it is an effort both to provide a war memoir and to respond to interest in the transformation that has taken place in Japan's social structure during the lifetime of its central character.

The subject of this book is my own father. I would like to write briefly here of how it came into being.

The interviews that formed the basis for this book were conducted between May and December of 2013. Joining me in conducting them was Hayashi Eiichi, an outstanding young historian who has used similar interviews as a basis for writing personal histories of Japanese soldiers who remained in Indonesia after the war.

Hayashi's first published work, *Zanryū Nippon hei no shinjitsu* (The True Story of a Japanese Soldier Who Stayed Behind; Sakuhinsha, 2007) was based on his undergraduate thesis, which I supervised. When I mentioned to him that my father had survived Siberian internment, he said, "Let's go talk to him sometime." That planted the seed of this book.

The first interview was a rambling affair, with my father's stories going off in a number of different directions. But I was astonished at what detailed memories he had, not only of his time in Siberia, but also of growing up on a shopping street in Tokyo before the war, and of the vicissitudes of life in the early postwar period.

Then it occurred to me: if the interviews were done in chronological order, and supplemented with background information regarding the politics and economics of the periods in question, a historical text of some value might result. With this in mind, I proposed to Hayashi that we conduct a series of in-depth interviews with my father. He readily agreed, and we began visiting my father at his home in Hachiōji every two weeks or so, interviewing him for about three hours each time.

I had previously conducted an interview project focused on Korean residents of Japan, which was published as *Zainichi issei no kioku* (Recollections of First-Generation Korean Residents of Japan; Shūeisha, 2008). And Hayashi had, as mentioned, interviewed a number of veterans of the Imperial Japanese Army. Since we shared this prior experience, interviewing my father was not particularly difficult.

The process we followed was this: I served as interviewer, while Hayashi took detailed notes of the conversation on a laptop computer. I would review and revise the notes the same day, and later would check them against an audio recording of the interview before producing a final draft. I would then take this manuscript to my father so that he could read it and make corrections.

Since my father essentially has only one lung, speaking at length was tiring for him. Aside from that, though, he was an ideal interview subject for a historian. Not only were his recollections vivid, but his narrative was coherent and followed a clear storyline. His memories were not distorted by excess of emotion; he recounted what he had felt and observed at the time quite honestly and without adornment. Hayashi remarked on several occasions that such interviewees were rare.

I was also frequently struck by how perceptive my father could be. For example, in the first chapter there is a passage in which my father was talking about his elder brother Teruichi beating the big drum at a neighborhood festival in Kōenji as the hit tune "Tokyo ondo" played over loudspeakers. He then commented, "I think the reason that tune was so popular was because so many people had recently moved into Tokyo from outlying regions."

The acuteness of sociological observation here—connecting the experience of the festival music with the broader hypothesis concerning demographic movement into the city—is not something that everyone naturally possesses. Moreover, this was a story about his older brother, which he might have inflated with excessive feeling;

instead, he used it as a source of valuable objective information—again, not a common thing. Since my father has had no academic training, such observational skills were either innate or developed entirely on his own. His perceptiveness and objectivity is evident in many aspects of the testimony presented in these pages.

In a sense, my father is a dispassionate man. He never attempts to add romantic coloring to tragic experience or events that seem dramatic. He speaks consistently of the facts—coolly, objectively, and with an occasional touch of humor.

He always says, "That's the way people with real life experience are." I can't judge whether that is true of everyone. He did choke up a bit when he spoke of parting from his grandparents to enter the army, but that was the only time in our interviews that he became emotional. He was always quite detached in everyday life as well. I have clear memories of how cool and calm he was during the commotion surrounding the postwar compensation lawsuit.

An individual with such a personality inspires trust as an interview subject. Ironically, such people rarely leave written records of their personal experience. People who write personal histories are generally blessed with a good education and writing ability, or else are motivated by some powerful obsession. The former provide a viewpoint limited to that of a particular social class; the latter tend to lack objectivity. My father belongs to neither category, and in fact he had written next to nothing about his personal experiences.

When I began our interviews, I did not have a clear intention of publishing the results. But as they went on, my thinking changed. With Hayashi-san's permission, I began to complete this manuscript, which was serialized in the monthly journal *Sekai* from October 2014 to June 2015. I did this because of my belief that it is a historian's duty to help transmit to future generations the memories of individuals like my father who would not otherwise have recorded their experiences.

Is the trajectory of my father's life typical of the Japanese of his era? This question has a direct bearing on the academic merit of this book, and it is a difficult one to answer. His experience of Siberian internment is certainly unusual, and his participation, with an ethnic Korean veteran of the Imperial Japanese Army, in a postwar compensation lawsuit against the Japanese state was, as far as I know, unique. Some might conclude from this that he is not at all typical.

But what makes a person typical? In Japan, being a "salaryman" is often assumed to be typical. Salarymen were never in the majority, statistically speaking, at any point in history. Yet the illusion of the salaryman as the typical Japanese was widespread for a certain period after the war.

An example of this is was the 1963 novel by Yamaguchi Hitomi— also made into a movie—entitled *Eburi Man-shi no yūgana seikatsu* (The Elegant Life of Mr. Everyman). The protagonist, like my father, was born in 1925, as the premise was that his individual age would coincide with the years of the Shōwa era (1926 being Shōwa 1), just as his name, Eburi Man, signaled that he was supposed to be Mr. Everyman.

"Mr. Everyman," however, was depicted as a full-time salaried employee of a major electrical appliance manufacturer, living in company housing, even though less than 10 percent of the working population at the time lived such a lifestyle. It came to be regarded as typical simply because the people who wrote books, and who purchased them, tended to be middle-class city dwellers, many of whom had themselves graduated from university and become salarymen.

By the same token, even though farmers are widely perceived as the genuine "common people" of Japan, they no longer made up a statistical majority of the population by the 1950s. Moreover, not everyone living in rural villages was actually a "farmer"—my father spent a certain period after the war in the countryside, and he never farmed.

The text of this book makes it clear that my father's trajectory through life—whether he was aware of it or not—paralleled developments in Japanese society as a whole. Despite this, he frequently behaved in ways that were not typical of the majority of Japanese at the time. Since this is the case, how does my father's life compare to that of the "majority" or the "typical" Japanese?

My answer is that there is no one, anywhere, whose life represents the majority in all aspects. Sociology defines deviant behavior as that which diverges from the norm. Yet even if there was an individual who never deviated from the norm, this would still not make him or her typical.

People usually lead fairly unassuming, "ordinary" lives, but every life has moments of crisis, moments of heroic action. At the same time, every life is determined, in large part, by the contemporary social context. Put another way, if only the moments of crisis or heroic action are depicted, the entirety of a subject—be it an individual or a group—will not be portrayed. Likewise, merely depicting everyday life will not accurately represent the total picture either. It seems necessary to me to grasp all of this comprehensively and position it within the contemporary social context in order to arrive at a fully three-dimensional historical narrative.

As I've said, the subject of this narrative was not part of the educated urban middle class. In that sense, this book is a life history of a member of the "silent majority." While it contains some dramatic elements—war experience, a major court case—these are just part of the more comprehensive narrative of an entire life, which I feel is a distinctive feature of the book.

While the course of a person's life embodies certain fluctuations and deviations, they are also determined by the overall structure of society. In this book I have attempted to portray the ups and downs of my father's personal experience in the context of the history of East Asia—not only Japan, but the Soviet Union, China, Korea, Taiwan, and so on—that determined his life. Within Japan itself, furthermore, a variety of regions, social classes, and government policies come into play. The intent of this book is to offer a glimpse of this totality by closely examining the details of my father's life as a single individual.

As a matter of fact, I had made one previous attempt at interviewing my father, in 2003, but all I asked him about was his experience of the Siberian internment. At that time, I wasn't interested in hearing about his life in prewar and postwar Japan. And even with regard to Siberia, I didn't ask him about the management of the camp or the nature of contemporary Soviet society. Despite my father's experience of such things, my perspective at that time prevented me from being able to elicit these memories from him.

Collective memory is created through an interaction between teller and listener. If the listener does not have the capacity to hear what is being said, he cannot elicit memories from the teller. Of course, this book was possible because of its exceptional narrator. I also believe, however, that the expansion of my own knowledge and interests as a listener that resulted from a further decade of life experience had a positive effect on the outcome.

I suppose it is only natural that I developed a closer relationship with my father in the course of these interviews. We had more things to talk about, and I came to a better understanding of his speech and behavior. It was also simply a joy to me to see the vitality and brightness that returned to his features as he talked about the events of the past. And I think it brought him joy to have someone show such intense interest in his personal experience.

But these kinds of interactions do not occur without prompting from a listener. Not only in Japan, but throughout the world, vast stores of experience and memory are vanishing for lack of someone to listen to them. There is value in listening to the memories of others—relatives, neighbors, colleagues. And the process is even more fruitful for the listener than the teller, because the foundation of our existence as human beings can only be established through such interaction with others, and with the past.

Human beings experience anxiety when they do not have a clear sense of their reason for living. The goods that flood the marketplace represent one way of assuaging this anxiety. But better, more productive, and more sustainable than passive and ephemeral consumption is to engage with those around us, speak with them, and build relationships with them.

I reiterate: memory is a creative interaction between teller and listener. History is one form of this mutual interaction. We might say, in fact, that history consists of the effort to listen to voices and assign them meaning. Listeners, by eliciting and giving significance to the facts and experiences of the past, give them future life. Without listeners, these facts and experiences fade away—and the people who failed to listen also lose their footing. All of us living today are confronted with this choice: to listen or not.

Eventually, and inevitably, my father will die. However, by listening carefully to the experiences of others and giving them meaning, we can ensure that they continue to live after they are gone. This is something any of us alive today can do—something, in fact, that only we can do. I hope the readers of this book will join in this endeavor.

Oguma Eiji
May 2015

The Interview Process

The series of interviews with Oguma Kenji were conducted according to the following schedule and process.

2013

29 May	Preliminary interview
27 June	From birth to induction into the army
4 October	From basic training to the surrender
12 October	Transport to Siberia and life in the internment camp
25 October	The "democratic movement" in the camp
2 November	From repatriation to the tuberculosis sanatorium
15 November	Life in the sanatorium and in Niigata after release
22 November	Life in Tokyo during the postwar boom of the late 1950s and 60s
29 November	Life in the 1970s and 1980s and remembrance of the war
6 December	Reading history and the postwar compensation lawsuit
20 December	Life in Nan'yōdai and the citizens' movement

2014

31 May, 5 June, 11 June, 20 June, 25 August (follow-up interviews)

All interviews were conducted by Oguma Eiji. Hayashi Eiichi transcribed the 2013 interviews, all of which were conducted at Oguma Kenji's home in the Nan'yōdai district of Hachiōji. Each interview took approximately three hours, and all were preserved as audio recordings.

In the 2013 interviews, the questions focused on the time periods listed above for each interview. The 2014 interviews consisted of follow-up questions supplementing the initial interviews for each period. In 2014 and 2015, various other aspects of the content were confirmed in a number of telephone conversations and informal conversations.

The first draft of the book was written in the summer of 2014. Kenji checked the content of the manuscript and made necessary corrections for accuracy without manipulating or embellishing the facts. After this, each chapter was serialized in the journal *Sekai* from issue number 861 (October 2014) to 870 (June 2015), then published in book form by Iwanami Shoten in June 2015. Interviews have continued from that time to the present.

As part of a cooperative Northeast Asian publishing program commemorating the seventieth anniversary of the end of World War II, a Korean edition was published in August 2015 by Dong Asia Publishing and a Chinese edition (traditional orthography) in September 1915 by Lienching Publishing in Taiwan. A second Chinese edition (simplified orthography) was published in January 2017 in the People's Republic of China by Imaginist.

Oguma Eiji and Oguma Kenji. (Photo by Lee Soon-Koo.)

Filming *Father and Me*

Dialogues with Former Siberian Internees in Korea by Oguma Eiji
(originally published in the monthly magazine *Sekai*, no. 887, October 2016, pp. 242–57)

On 15 August 2016, the Korean television network MBC broadcast an hour-long documentary entitled *Father and Me* on Japanese and Koreans interned by the Soviet Union in Siberia at the end of World War II.* This essay is a record of my experiences in visiting Korea and Siberia to take part in it.

1

My father, Oguma Kenji, is a ninety-year-old former internee of a POW camp in Siberia. From 2014 to 2015 I serialized his reminiscences in this magazine under the title *Ikite kaette kita otoko* (The Man Who Made It Back Alive). The work was released in book form by Iwanami Shoten under the same title in 2015 and was also translated and published in China, Taiwan, and Korea. In March 2016, I received an email from Kim Manjin, a producer at MBC in Korea, who had read the Korean edition of my book and wanted to make a documentary about it.

As related in that book, from the late 1990s my father supported an ethnic Korean veteran of the Imperial Japanese Army from China named O Unggeun (Ch. Wu Xionggun) in a lawsuit seeking postwar compensation from the Japanese government. The two had originally met at a labor camp in the city of Chita in Siberia. About 640,000 Japanese military personnel, auxiliaries, and others were interned in Siberia, of whom about 60,000 are believed to have died during that time from the bitter cold, malnutrition, overwork, or infectious diseases. How many of their number were of Korean ethnicity is unknown; one Korean researcher estimates 2,421, but it is difficult to say how accurate this figure is.†

---

* In Japan, 15 August is the date marking the end of World War II; in Korea, it is commemorated as the end of Japanese colonial rule as a result of Japan's defeat in that conflict.
† According to research by V. P. Galitskii cited in Lee Pyeong-rae, "Dainiji taisen go,

From various memoirs, it appears that Korean POWs were separated from their Japanese counterparts around the spring of 1946. Beginning about the middle of 1948, a number of the Koreans were sent along with returning Japanese prisoners to the Japanese port of Maizuru, eventually making their way back to the Korean peninsula. In December 1948, some 2,300 Korean POWs (excluding those suspected of war crimes) were sent via the Siberian port of Nakhodka to Hungnam in North Korea.* Of this group, about 500 returned to

Chūō Ajia to Shiberia ni renkō sareta Kanjin horyo no shōgen," *Chūō Ajia kenkyū 9* (2004), Soviet records count the total number of Siberian internees at 609,448 Japanese and 10,206 Koreans. Of these, 546,572 Japanese and 10,134 Koreans were repatriated to their respective countries by 1956; 61,855 Japanese and 71 Koreans died in internment. Another 40,369 Japanese and 7,785 Koreans were released locally for illness or other reasons. From these figures, Lee calculates the number of long-term Korean internees to be 2,421—the total interned (10,206), minus the 7,785 released locally. Meanwhile, a 2010 report by a commission established by the South Korean government finds that there were approximately 15,000 Koreans enlisted in the Kwantung Army at the time of the surrender in 1945, some 10,000 of whom were taken prisoner by the Soviets, including an estimated 3,000 who were interned over the long term. (Commission on Verification and Support for the Victims of Forced Mobilization under Japanese Colonialism in Korea, Fact-Finding Report Concerning the Issue of Korean Prisoners of War Interned in Siberia [Japanese edition, 2013], pp. 23, 36, 57.)

Lee says that 7,785 were released locally soon after being interned either because of ill health or because it was discovered that they were Koreans. The report of the Korean government commission follows this analysis, which however does not account for why the remaining 3,000 internees continued to be held after it had become clear that they too were Koreans.

It may rather be conjectured that many of those whose "release" is recorded by the Soviets actually deserted from the Imperial Japanese Army before being apprehended by Soviet forces. The Kwantung Army had conscripted large numbers of Japanese colonists and Korean residents in Manchuria in the weeks immediately before Japan's surrender. It is quite possible that such individuals, armed with local knowledge, were able to desert and return to their homes as Japanese military organization disintegrated after 15 August.

In any case the reliability of these figures remains in question, given, as detailed below, that the Soviets do not seem to have been fully aware of the existence of Koreans among their "Japanese" POWs until the spring of 1946. It is possible that the figure 2,421 based on Soviet records only represents the number of Korean prisoners repatriated en masse over several occasions including in December 1948, and that the number of dead—71—is only for those recorded after spring 1946, with many other Koreans subsumed into categories such as "released" or "Japanese dead."

* Lee Pyeong-rae, "Soren seifu no Kanjin horyo seisaku to kikan," *Dai 48-kai Zenkoku Rekishi Taikai ronbunshū* (2005), states that upon their arrival in Hungnam on 20 December the Korean repatriates numbered 2,161. Hayashi Eidai, who compiled the recollections of a number of Korean internees in *Wasurerareta Chōsenjin kōgun heishi* (Azusa Shoin, 1995), gives 2,300, which is the figure used by the Sakpung Society and others; in my interview with Park Jeongui, Park cites this figure as the one he heard announced at the transit camp. Prior to being transported to Hungnam, certain of the prisoners were detained by the Soviet Union for reasons including suspicion of war

South Korea, about 1,000 to China, and about 800 to North Korea.* The reason for Korean returnees going to China was that on the eve of surrender, the Kwantung Army had drafted a number of ethnic Korean residents of an area called Jiandao Province under the Manchukuo regime (now the Yanbian Korean Autonomous Prefecture in Jilin Province of the People's Republic of China). Among them was O Unggeun, who made his way home to Jiandao.

The Korean former POWs had a very hard time of it in the postwar period. Those who repatriated to South Korea were—like many of their Japanese counterparts—suspected of communist indoctrination, placed under police surveillance, and subjected to occupational and other forms of discrimination. Those who repatriated to China and North Korea, on the other hand, found themselves suspected of having collaborated with the Japanese forces. O, a Chinese national, was accused during the Cultural Revolution of such collaboration.

In 1988, the Japanese government paid former internees a solatium in the form of ¥100,000 (about $1,200) in government bonds. But because only Japanese nationals were eligible for this program, my father, who had been carrying on a correspondence with O, shared half of his payout with him. Though O was grateful, he felt that the discrimination on the basis of nationality was unfair, and so he brought suit against the Japanese government, asking my father to join him as a plaintiff. My father agreed. The suit was filed in Tokyo District Court in 1996 and concluded in 2002 when it was rejected on appeal by the Supreme Court. Of the many postwar compensation lawsuits by non-Japanese nationals, this was the only one, as far as I know, in which a veteran of Japanese nationality joined as a co-plaintiff. This was also what interested Kim Manjin of MBC.

I first met Kim in May 2016. His longish hair and hat gave him the appearance of an intellectual artist. He was not very fluent in

---

crimes, which would partially explain the discrepancies in the numbers. Hayashi's book (pp. 228–36, 252–55) includes testimony by two of those detained Korean internees, the first of whom was put into a group with about sixty others and returned to North Korea in October 1949, crossing the Tumen River (on the border of Russia, North Korea, and China) by road; the other was sent with a group of returning Japanese to Maizuru in November 1953.

* Commission on Verification and Support, Fact-Finding Report, p. 48. Hayashi, *Wasurerareta Chōsenjin kōgun heishi*, p. 238, gives different numbers. All of these figures are based on testimony by returnees, and accurate statistics are difficult to establish.

Japanese, and I do not know Korean, so our discussions had to be carried out in English. Kim told me that I was to be the main character in the documentary, and that he wanted me not only to speak with my father, but to meet and talk with former internees in Korea. I agreed to participate, adding that in that case, I would also like to take the opportunity to visit Siberia.

The program was scheduled to be aired on 15 August, so filming began the following day. The crew shot footage of me interviewing my

father, teaching class at Keio University, and participating in an anti-nuclear demonstration in front of the prime minister's office. Throughout, I followed Kim's direction—"Ask your father a question," "Walk over this way," and so on—as the camera rolled. The following week, I was to travel to Korea.

Producer of MBC Kim Manjin and Oguma Eiji. (Photo by Lee Soon-Koo.)

2

On 30 May 2016, I took the Shinkansen bullet train to the port of Shimonoseki at the western end of Honshu. The crew wanted to film the voyage by ship from Japan to the Korean port of Busan, retracing the path that led to my father's internment in Siberia. After the ship left port, the crew used a small drone to take aerial footage of me on deck, leaning on the rail and looking out to sea.

The next day, 31 May, we headed to the apartment of Park Jeongui, a former internee living in Busan. Park was a member of the Siberia Sakpung (North Wind) Society of former Korean internees, which, since its founding in 1991, had linked up with parallel Japanese associations to demand compensation from the Japanese government; at one time the society had had more than fifty members, but was now reduced to a handful of survivors. Park came out to meet us, speaking fluent Japanese. The crew set up for filming, and our interview began.

Park was born in Busan in 1924. His father was a man of means who built a Christian church in the city. An excellent student, Park graduated from a highly regarded secondary school in Seoul, by which time the war had intensified to the point that he was unable to go on to higher education. So he went to work in Manchuria in one of his father's business operations.

Park Jeongui.
(Photo by Lee Soon-Koo.)

In March 1945, Park was drafted into the Imperial Japanese Army and assigned to the 362nd Infantry Unit, based in Haila'er. In August, on the eve of the Japanese surrender, the Kwantung Army implemented its "all-out mobilization" of Japanese colonists and Korean residents in Manchuria, including O Unggeun and Yi Byeongchu (d. September 2011), the former chairman of the Sakpung Society, who were inducted on 8 August, the day before the Soviet attack. As Park observed, "The Koreans in my unit were mostly from Manchuria, not Korea itself."

The Soviet attack commenced on 9 August. Park's unit, which had been stationed in Xing'anling, retreated southward and received news of Japan's surrender when they were in the vicinity of Qiqihar. They were taken prisoner by Soviet troops and transported to the industrial city of Krasnoyarsk in eastern Siberia. Park was sent to Camp No. 5 in the central part of the city as part of a battalion-level organization of about a thousand men. "There were about five Koreans in my company, but in the battalion when we arrived at the camp there were probably fifty of us altogether. Almost all the Koreans had been conscripted the day before the Soviet attack."

The prisoners suffered under the impact of the bitter -55°C cold of the Siberian winter, overwork, and malnutrition. Soviet society had been terribly weakened by the war, and food supplies did not always make it to the POWs.

"We were starving, so we bartered with Soviet women on the other side of the fence at our workplace for scraps of food. Pretty soon we ran out of things to trade, and I ended up washing my red loincloth, cutting the thong and waistband off of it, and exchanging it for about one meal's worth of black bread. The next day I saw that the woman had made a headscarf of the red cloth when she showed up on the other side of the fence again."

The hunger and cold took many lives. According to the memoir of former Sakpung Society chairman Yi Byeongchu, who was in the same camp, "In winter the ground would freeze to the depth of a meter or more, so the frozen corpses were stacked in a storage shed like firewood until the ground had thawed enough [the following May] to dig a mass grave."*

Park and his fellow prisoners were first put to work on a major infrastructure project: demolishing about 33,000 square meters of older buildings in the city and laying the groundwork for new highrise housing blocks. They transported mortar in wheelbarrows and poured it into forms for the foundations of the new structures. In January 1946, Park, who was close to having beriberi from malnutrition, fell into one of the foundation pits, injuring his back and neck. He was given a month off from work, but has continued to suffer from back and neck pain to this day.

At first the Soviets did not realize that there were ethnic Koreans mixed in among the Imperial Japanese Army POWs. Recurrent conflict between the Korean and Japanese prisoners—often resulting from discrimination and violence on the Japanese side—and requests by the Koreans to be separated led the Korean prisoners to be moved to another barracks around the spring of 1946.†

The leader of the newly separated Korean contingent was a former secondary-school teacher from Manchuria who, Park recalled, "had been an officer candidate in the Japanese army, which is why I think he was chosen." The Koreans still worked together with the Japanese prisoners at the job site, but now that they lived separately upon their return to camp, there was little further trouble.

The work assignments and other instructions were given to the Korean prisoners by their leader in Japanese, and their Korean foremen on the job site also gave orders in Japanese, but in their daily life

---

* "Yi Byeongchu no chinjutsusho," Gungun website, http://www.gun-gun.jp/sub-/i-byonju.htm, accessed 3 August 2016.
† According to Shirai Hisaya, *Kenshō Shiberia yokuryū* (Heibonsha, 2010), p. 239, Yi Byeongchu, who had learned some basic Russian from the Russian overseer of his work site, was among the Koreans who went to negotiate with the camp commandant to be segregated from the Japanese internees. Hayashi, *Wasurerareta Chōsenjin kōgun heishi*, pp. 122–27, records similar developments in other camps.

they spoke Korean with one another. Though Park himself claimed not to know why directions should have been given in Japanese, the Korean youth of the period had grown up under a colonial linguistic order in which commands and education were given in Japanese and everyday matters were handled in Korean. They had no experience of any other system.

Park, who had gone through secondary school with excellent marks, was good in Japanese. A keen lover of history, he wrote a story at the camp about a prince of the royal house of the ancient Korean kingdom of Silla—in Japanese. By contrast, among the Korean prisoners with no more than an elementary education there were some who knew very little Japanese. "Maybe half of us couldn't speak Japanese very well. This was particularly true of the ones from Jiandao Province [in Manchuria]. Most of the other half were so-so, and only a very few were really fluent." This ratio would seem to reflect the rates of advancement to secondary school and beyond under the pre-war and wartime Japanese system.

The unnatural superiority accorded to Japanese, however, did not last long. Wall newspapers written in hangul, the Korean phonetic script, soon began to be posted in the camp. "The paper was about the size of a standard sheet of newsprint pasted directly on the wall. I think there were a number of issues. No one on the Soviet or the Japanese side ever said anything to us about the content." Park's story was translated into Korean by another prisoner for publication in this wall newspaper. In many other camps, such newspapers were mobilized, with prodding from the Soviets, to support the "democratic movement" of political indoctrination and its Marxist agenda; Park, however, had no experience of that movement until he was transferred to Khabarovsk on his way home to Korea.

Instead, conversations in the camp revolved around food and work. Returning home was always on everyone's mind, so that came up quite often, but no one had the time or energy for discussing political issues; no one had any idea that Korea was going to get divided into North and South. Park was an intellectual among the prisoners. He also loved music and wrote a march for his fellows with lyrics in Korean that went something like this: "We are young! The Korean youth of the twentieth century. Thinking of the future of our homeland, we stand at the vanguard of our thirty million compatriots!"

In the summer of 1947, Park was transferred alone to Camp No. 1 in Krasnoyarsk, apparently because the Soviets suspected him of a relationship with a young Russian woman. At the time, a terrible number of young Soviet men had been killed in the war, and women were experiencing serious difficulty in finding marriage partners. "I was at the job site washing my face in a basin before returning to camp. When I looked up a woman was standing there holding a towel. She entreated, 'Please marry me! Please marry me!' But as a POW there was no way I was going to be able to make her happy, and I couldn't abandon my homeland to marry her, either. We never even held hands."

In Camp No. 1, about fifty Korean POWs lived separately from the Japanese with a Korean leader. "He was the type who liked to lord it over other people, and he was really full of himself. I thought he was a real snake." The man was from the northern part of Korea, and Park later heard from a friend that he'd been seen leading troops as an officer in the North Korean army when it invaded the South in 1950.

In 1948, repatriation of Japanese POWs began, and the population of the camps declined. Eventually the Koreans in Camp No. 1 were transferred across the river to Camp No. 4, where, together with the Koreans who were already there, they made up about a hundred men. Around October that year they entered a transit camp in Khabarovsk where Koreans from all over the Soviet Union were being held pending repatriation.

It was here that Park first encountered the so-called democratic movement. "Korean activists held political assemblies after work details and dinner and tormented 'reactionary elements.' They also made everybody sing Russian songs translated into Korean." Here Park also first encountered the *Nihon shimbun*, the Japanese-language newspaper distributed in the camps as propaganda for the movement.

In December, after a little more than a month at Khabarovsk, the entire group of about 2,300 prisoners was transferred to Nakhodka and put on a Soviet merchant ship bound for the North Korean port of Hungnam. After they landed and were given accommodations, the prisoners originally from northern Korea and Manchuria were permitted to return home after a comparatively short time. But the men from the south were detained for another forty days or so. They were told this was because South Korea would not accept them out of a fear of communist indoctrination. The North Korean government did not acknowledge the legitimacy of the South Korean government led by Syngman Rhee, and would not negotiate with it.

However, Park and his fellow prisoners from the south were able to arrange a return to their homes and, divided into three groups according to their regions of origin, crossed the thirty-eighth parallel separating North and South Korea. The South Koreans had not been informed, and thirty-seven of the POWs were mistakenly shot by border guards as they attempted the crossing.[*] The five hundred or so who made it across successfully were held for some two months in a detention center in Incheon, where they were interrogated by US forces and the South Korean intelligence agency. Even after their release, some were placed under surveillance as suspected communists. While in detention, Park was finally reunited with his parents, who came to visit him.

On returning home, Park passed the qualifying exam for a job at the Railway Bureau (later renamed the Korea National Railroad Administration). In June 1950, a year and a half after his return, the Korean War began. He took it fatalistically. Returnees he knew fought and died on both sides, North and South. Park himself escaped the fighting, since he was a railway employee engaged in critical transportation services and also had a bad back.

After the war he quit the Railroad Administration and worked for an oil company. He had lost his chance at higher education, and continued to have problems with back pain from his injuries in Siberia, but he received no assistance from the South Korean government. Prejudice against former Siberian internees was deeply rooted, and it was best to remain silent about his past.

With the democratization of South Korea in 1987 and the restoration of diplomatic relations with Russia in 1991, this political oppression and prejudice softened somewhat, and the Sakpung Society was founded. Learning through the National Council for the Compensation of Siberian Internees (Zenkoku Yokuryūsha Hoshō Kyōgikai) of the solatium paid to Japanese internees, the society attempted first to negotiate with and then to bring suit against the Japanese government to be given the same compensation, with little result.

---

[*] Shirai, *Kenshō Shiberia yokuryū*, p. 240.

Park commented, "Japanese behavior shows no remorse for the past. I wish Japan would reflect on its past the way Germany has." I glanced at Park's bookshelves, which contained a significant number of books in Japanese—a reminder of his complicated history as a former Japanese colonial subject.

3

After interviewing Park, I traveled to Seoul and met Kim Giyong, originally from Iwon County, South Hamgyeong Province, in what is now North Korea. He had a very different experience from Park.

Born in 1925, Kim was an excellent student. Although he graduated from the prestigious Seoul Secondary School (present-day Seoul

High School), he, like Park, was unable to continue with higher education because of the war, and went to work at the local government office in his home village. Drafted into the Imperial Japanese Army on 30 July 1945, he was sent to Unit 12005 of the Kwantung Army, stationed just south of the city of Heihe on the Manchurian border

Kim Giyong. (Photo by Lee Soon-Koo.)

with the Soviet Union. Arriving there two days before the outbreak of hostilities between the Soviets and Japan, he was trained in carrying out a suicide attack against tanks with an improvised explosive device strapped to his belly. Most of the other soldiers were Japanese colonists in their thirties or older who had been drafted in the "all-out mobilization" in Manchuria; it was only the Koreans who were in their twenties.

The Soviet forces attacked on 9 August. Kim and his unit were fortunate to be stationed in the hills; the troops on the flatlands were annihilated by Soviet armored units. Kim's younger brother was among those killed in combat. Captured by Soviet forces, Kim and his fellows were taken to Blagoveshchensk Camp No. 7, across the Amur River from Heihe. The first winter, about a hundred of the five hundred men in the camp died. "Most of the older Japanese soldiers had led a pretty soft life in Manchuria. They didn't hold up too well to the cold and short rations and hard labor."

As was true in many other of the camps, there were inequities in food distribution and work assignments based on rank. The officers and NCOs gave themselves extra rations, and the young Koreans, at the very bottom of the chain of command, were forced to serve veteran soldiers in the lower ranks. Such unfairness led to much unrest, and following some negotiation with the Soviet administrators, the fifty or so Koreans were moved to a separate barracks in the early spring of 1946. The man assigned as their leader had learned Russian at a technical school in Harbin (probably Harbin Academy, founded in 1920).

About a year later, the Koreans were transferred northward to a camp in Svobodnyy after several of them managed to escape by swimming across the Amur to Heihe.* Blagoveshchensk was a border town, immediately across the river from China. If he could make it across the river, a Korean prisoner from Manchuria or even the Korean peninsula had a chance of returning home, relying on the network of Korean communities scattered about northeastern China. At Heihe the Amur was several hundred meters across, but swimming it was not impossible.

Their new location of Svobodnyy was a small town, and both the cold and the food situation were much worse than in Blagoveshchensk. What was more, Kim suffered a particularly harsh experience of the "democratic" movement, which had begun back in Blagoveshchensk sometime after the separation of the Koreans, using the Japanese-language *Nihon shimbun* and Marxist texts written in Japanese. "When I was taken prisoner and interrogated by the Soviets, I made the mistake of telling them I had worked in a local government office in Korea. This was branded as collaboration with Japanese imperialism, and the Korean activists gave me a very hard time."

Later Kim was transferred several more times, to camps in Belogorsk and Vladivostok. In the spring of 1948, he sent a letter via the International Red Cross to his father, which out of concern for

---

* Hayashi, *Wasurerareta Chōsenjin kōgun heishi*, pp. 128–58, contains testimony from a Korean internee who escaped from Blagoveshchensk Camp No. 7 by swimming the Amur River, only to be returned to the Soviets by the Chinese Communist forces then in control of Manchuria. In my interview with him, Kim told me that there were other Koreans from Jiandao Province who escaped from the camp.

censorship simply mentioned that he was alive and well. "I'm told that when that letter arrived in my village, there was quite a fuss." His father, Kim Hanung, was a founding member of the Korean Democratic Party, which had been formed after the Japanese surrender before losing out in the power struggle in northern Korea and suffering the house arrest of its leader in January 1946. The KDP would gradually devolve into a satellite party of the Workers' Party of Korea, but as of 1948, Kim Hanung still sat on the Provisional People's Committee for North Korea. Yet even someone as highly placed as he was had not been privy to the knowledge his own son was being interned in Siberia.

After about two months, Kim received a reply from his father. It was very brief, but he learned later that in the meantime his father had been negotiating with the North Korean government on his behalf. In December 1948, Kim was sent along with other Korean prisoners (including Park Jeongui) via Blagoveshchensk and Nakhodka to the port of Hungnam in North Korea. He was held in a detention camp upon arrival, but his father soon came to see him and after a few days he was released.

From then on Kim found work as a high-school Russian teacher. In Siberia he had gotten hold of a Russian dictionary compiled by the Japanese army and mastered Russian on his own to the point that he had been able to work as an interpreter. At the time almost no one in North Korea was able to speak Russian—according to Kim, "Soviet officers said my Russian was quite good."

There was no freedom of speech, and he was unable to say much about his experiences in Siberia. He was urged to join the Workers' Party of Korea, but avoided doing so on various excuses. "Many others who returned with me from Siberia joined for economic reasons. Some were killed in the Korean War, and others fled to South Korea, concealing their past and starting a new life there."

Then in June 1950 the Korean War began. The North Korean People's Army had the upper hand initially, but US and South Korean forces counterattacked, and by October had pushed across the border into the North. Amid the confusion, rumors flew that individuals critical of the regime or associated with the former Japanese army would be executed; Kim recalled that in his village about two hundred people were summarily executed by the People's Army. When United Nations forces drew near his home, Kim was drafted into the People's

Army, but ran away from the camp to which he was assigned—a crime punishable by death. In December 1950, Kim and his family boarded a fishing boat and fled to South Korea.

In the South, the entire family was arrested by the military police. The boat was confiscated, and they were subjected to some two months of interrogation. As a former member of the People's Committee, Kim's father was tried by a military tribunal but got off lightly with a two-year suspended sentence. Kim was also suspected of being a spy, but thanks to his Russian-language ability was hired as an intelligence specialist by the South Korean navy. Kim had never imagined that the Russian he had learned in Siberia would prove so useful in both North and South Korea. "I thought I might be able to return to my village after a couple of weeks, but it's been seventy years now."

Once the war was over Kim resigned from naval intelligence and entered the business world. Despite his lack of a higher education, he was capable and diligent, and rose to the position of CEO of a travel company. When the Sakpung Society was founded, he became one of its leaders.

Kim had served in the Imperial Japanese Army, the North Korean People's Army, and the South Korean navy. Yet he did not receive benefits from any of these countries. When I asked him if that meant he had been abandoned by all of them, he replied, "Yes, abandoned. I think so." Like Park Jeongui, the young and capable Kim had been popular with the ladies in Russia. "I thought if I married one of them I'd be released, but since I wanted to go home, I didn't. They taught me a bunch of Russian songs, though. I probably know how to sing more songs in Russian than anybody in South Korea." And then he sang us a Russian folk song.

4

Both Park Jeongui and Kim Giyong spoke fluent Japanese. But this was not true of all the former Siberian internees in South Korea. As Park recounted in my interview with him, many of the Korean internees had received only a primary education and could not speak Japanese very well. Kim Hakbeom, who now lives on the outskirts of Daejeon in South Korea, was one such prisoner. When we visited him at his apartment, he greeted me with a warm smile. He spoke Japanese haltingly, and called me "sensei." We conversed mainly through an interpreter, but wherever he could, Kim used Japanese.

Kim was born in 1924 in Jangyeon County, Hwanhae Province, in what is now North Korea. After graduating from primary school he was working on the family farm when he received his conscription notice, entering the Imperial Japanese Army in June 1945. At school he had been taught that Japan was top in the world, and he said that even though he was a Korean, his head was full of the Japanese spirit. Yet when I asked him how he felt about being drafted, he replied, "I had no choice."

Kim Hakbeom. (Photo by Lee Soon-Koo).

Kim was assigned to a unit stationed in Haila'er, where the privates first-class, the superior privates, and the Koreans who were serving voluntarily lorded it over conscripted Koreans like him. Without ever seeing combat, he was taken prisoner and sent to a camp in Krasnoyarsk. In this respect his experiences were similar to those of Park and Kim Giyong.

When asked what life in the camp was like, Kim said, "There was nothing to eat, we were cold, we were hungry, and tired out from work." He continued, "It was cold, so cold. Fifty below zero. My feet froze." He showed me toes still blackened by frostbite. In December 1948, after three years in the camp, Kim was repatriated along with the other Korean internees. "After I got back, I was a farmer. That was all I could do." Before long he married and had children.

When the Korean War began, Kim was drafted into the North Korean People's Army. Handed a rifle and told their objective was Busan, he followed orders and kept marching south. Again, without ever actually fighting, he was taken prisoner by the South Korean army and lived another three years in a prison camp—a total of six years of his life spent as a prisoner of war, first in Siberia and then in Korea. Kim said that unlike in Siberia, in the South Korean camp, "We didn't work, and I don't have anything to say about it." But when I offered that it must have been hard to spend six years of his twenties in prison, he fell silent, then nodded. "It was hard."

After his release, Kim stayed in South Korea. He never again saw his wife and children in the North. He applied to a South Korean program to reunite families separated by the war, but no news ever came. With no education or special skills, he made a living in the South by farming and making charcoal. He remarried, "but my South Korean wife is now dead." They had two sons, one of whom had already passed away. Kim now lived with his surviving son and daughter-in-law.

Our conversation turned to the Sakpung Society, of which he too was a member. Kim said that the group had hoped to receive compensation and an apology from the Japanese government. Then he asked me, "Sensei, do you think I could get 60 million won or so from the Japanese government?"

The sum of 60 million won is roughly ¥6 million, or $55,000. As mentioned earlier, in 1988 the Japanese government paid ¥100,000 (about $1,200) in government bonds to former Siberian internees of Japanese nationality. Later, in 2010, a special measures law was passed to provide further disbursements to former internees ranging from ¥250,000 to ¥1.5 million. The maximum figure was given to a very small number of individuals detained to or beyond 1955; my father, who returned in 1948, received ¥250,000.

I was at a bit of a loss as to how I should respond to Kim's question, but I didn't think there was any point in sugar-coating things. "Given the hardships you have suffered, I think you deserve some sort of compensation, but even the Japanese internees have not received anything like the amount you are talking about."

Kim's expression changed. He said, "I heard that the Japanese got 150 million won." When I told him that my father had been an internee but had never received that much money, he asked how much my father did receive. I answered, "About 2.5 million won." Kim reacted in Korean, which the interpreter translated: "Is that all? Japan is a rich country, isn't it? What would anybody do with that little? You must be joking. I wouldn't even want it!"

I told him, "My father said the same thing. But he applied for the money anyway, because he wanted to give half of it to a Korean internee." At that point, Kim was at a loss for words, and waved me off.

"Stop it, goodbye." He was telling me to leave. Tears welled up in his eyes, and he spoke in Korean, "Why did you come now? If you'd come ten years ago, everybody in the Sakpung Society would still have been alive and well." He added, "Japan is a great country, a rich country. I was taught it was the best in the world."

As Kim wept, the cameraman kept filming. TV crews cannot afford to be too delicate in their sensibilities.

Producer Kim Manjin, who was at the filming, had met Kim Hakbeom earlier when the interview was being set up, but even to him the old man's tears were totally unanticipated. In the end we paid our respects and left the apartment, but an uncomfortable feeling lingered.

Afterward, Kim Manjin invited me to have dinner with him, the two of us. We discussed the project as a whole, and then he began telling me his own story.

Kim had graduated from university right at the time of the Asian financial crisis of 1997. South Korea was forced to undertake restructuring measures under the guidance of the International Monetary Fund, and there was a wave of corporate bankruptcies. Kim was fortunate enough to be hired by MBC Television, where he produced a series of documentaries. While working full time, he also earned a master's degree with a thesis on the dispute over historical perception between Korea and Japan that was critical of nationalism.

However, with the advent of the conservative Lee Myung-bak government, executives loyal to Lee were installed at MBC, which had previously won a reputation for its hard-hitting programming. Conflict immediately ensued between these executives and the production staff, resulting in a major strike in 2012, which Kim joined as what he called "a middle-rank activist." But the strike ended in defeat for the union. A number of prominent producers were driven out, and for about a year Kim was hung out to dry within the company. Some of the producers forced out at that time have since tried independent production for the Internet, but have been unable to gain much of an audience.

Kim observed, "In today's Korea, there is no freedom of reporting." At the time that we spoke in 2016, coverage of ongoing protest demonstrations in Seoul was being suppressed by top television executives. In the annual World Press Freedom Index compiled by Reporters Sans Frontières, Korea slipped by ten places that year to seventieth—similarly to Japan, which slipped eleven to seventy-second amid concerns about greater controls on the media under the conservative Abe cabinet. (In 2017, roughly a year after our conversation, a protest movement led to the fall of the conservative government in Korea, and its ranking rose again to sixty-third.)

Kim declared, "I am a non-nationalist. The internees were abandoned by every nation—Japan, South Korea, North Korea, the Soviet Union. Reading your book inspired me to make this documentary, and I worked hard to convince my superiors to let me do it. I am determined to air it on 15 August."

I responded, "I'll do what I can to help, but I hope we don't have too many more days like today." Kim said, "No worries."

5

Our next stop was the third-largest city in South Korea, Daegu—home of Moon Ryongsik, a former internee's son who has been active in pressing both the South Korean and Japanese governments to thoroughly investigate the facts of the internment. Born in 1960, Moon is a factory worker who has pursued political activism in his spare time.

The small factory where Moon worked and boarded was located on the outskirts of the city. During the week, he could not make time for us until after his work day, so our interview began at 8 pm in a corner of the factory building.

Moon's father, Moon Sunnam, was born in 1924 in Gaeseong in what is now North Korea. He completed no more than a primary education before being drafted into the Imperial Japanese Army, and the details of what happened to him after that remain unclear. When Sunnam returned home three years after the end of the war, everyone was surprised. After the Korean War he spent roughly four years in the South Korean army for financial reasons. Then he drifted from one job to the next, dying of a sudden illness in 1974 at the age of fifty.

When his father died, Moon Ryongsik was a first-year middle-school student. He had a younger brother and sister, but the sister died not long after their father. Moon dropped out of middle school and began working, meanwhile studying on his own to pass the middle-school equivalency exam and enter a technical high school. He was now employed in his younger brother's factory, which made wooden boxes for export goods.

Interview with Moon Ryongsik. (Photo by Lee Soon-Koo.)

Moon did not learn of his father's internment in Siberia until 1995, when a newspaper published a roster with the names of 6,134 Korean internees that a Korean journalist had discovered in Russia.* At this time, Moon heard from relatives in his hometown that his father had been an internee.

However, Moon did not then have the time or energy to pursue his father's story. He worked as a repairman for a major electrical appliances firm, but after the Asian financial crisis he was let go, and afterward he bounced around a number of jobs at smaller companies. He and his wife even ran a twenty-four-hour convenience store for a while, which meant a steady succession of sleepless nights.

The turning point came in February 2005, when the truth commission created by the Roh Moo-hyun government into the forced mobilization of Koreans during Japanese rule—as soldiers, military auxiliaries, laborers, and comfort women—began accepting grievance claims. It was then that Moon thought of filing a claim on behalf of his father.

---

* According to the Commission on Verification and Support, Fact-Finding Report, p.36, this list was discovered in Russian archives by a Moscow correspondent for the *Taejon ilbo* newspaper, who despite repeated calls could not provide specific details concerning the source.

Yet he lacked documentary evidence to support such a claim. Sunnam's younger brother testified that Sunnam had served in the Japanese army, but the claim was still rejected on the grounds of insufficient material evidence. Moon contacted Japan's labor and justice ministries for information, but was told in both cases that there were no records. Next he contacted the Russian government through the South Korean Ministry of Foreign Affairs, to no avail. He then thought of tracking down the reporter who had written the 1995 newspaper article, only to learn that he had emigrated to Canada in the wake of the Asian financial crisis.

Moon was about to give up when something occurred to him. He had queried the Russian government using the romanized Korean reading of his father's name: Moon Sunnam. That had brought up nothing, but perhaps the Russians had kept their records under the Japanese reading. He contacted the Russian government again, this time receiving a reply that an individual named Minamihara Junnan (the Japanized name that his father had been required to use) had been interned in a camp in Kazakhstan. "I'd never imagined this would be so difficult. When I finally located him, I thought I would cry," recalled Moon.

Armed with this new evidence, Moon applied once more to the truth commission. His claim was once again rejected, however, on the grounds that the body was charged with handling cases relating to the period of Japanese rule: those occurring after 15 August 1945 were therefore outside its jurisdiction.* He made a number of further

---

* Under the measures established by the South Korean government based on the findings of the truth commission, survivors of Japanese forced mobilization were awarded a one-time solatium of 20 million won (about $18,500) and an annual sum of 800,000 won in medical assistance. Although, as told in Moon's story, Siberian internees were initially excluded from this program because their hardships technically occurred after the war, as a result of protests and negotiations the government expanded eligibility to include surviving returnees and those who had died during their internment on the grounds that their suffering had been a consequence of forced mobilization prior to 15 August 1945. According to the commission's 2016 report, 512 individuals registered as Korean prisoners of war who had been interned in Siberia; review of eligibility for disbursements concluded at the end of 2015. (Commission on Verification and Support for the Victims of Forced Mobilization under Japanese Colonialism in Korea, Report of the Activities of the Commission [Japanese edition, 2016], pp. 48, 67.) Even with the expansion, however, eligibility was limited to residents of South Korea, so individuals such as O Unggeun, living in China, did not qualify. Moon's father, who died after returning from Siberia, likewise did not qualify for either the solatium (as he did not die during internment) or medical assistance (as he was no longer living).

efforts, including applying to the Russian government for verification of his father's labor, but the result was the same.

Moon showed me the responses he had received from the Japanese, Russian, and South Korean governments. All of them were cursory and impersonal, not at all commensurate with the effort it had taken Moon to obtain them. "I felt like this was simply the sort of reply you get when you're dealing with government bureaucracies." What supported Moon in his activism while he continued to work full time was the encouragement of the former internees of the Sakpung Society. Initially, all Moon had wanted to do was to track down information concerning his father, but on learning of the society he had telephoned its chairman, Yi Byeongchu, and begun attending its meetings.

After 2010, as its members grew increasingly old and frail, the Sakpung Society stopped holding regular meetings. Moon wrote letters to members of the South Korean National Assembly and the Japan-Korea Parliamentarians' Union appealing for revisions to the special legislation governing the scope of the truth commission. "It should be the job of politicians to create a good framework for dealing with issues. But they won't do anything. Are they just waiting for everyone involved to die?"

Moon has only a single photograph of his father, whose life was too hard for the luxury of family snapshots. In this photo, taken when Sunnam was in the South Korean armed forces, he appears in uniform. Showing it to me, Moon said, "My father had no education, and even after the war he was never able to find a decent job. I think he suffered a lot." He continued, "When I read the book you wrote about your father, it gave me lots to think about. Your father joined O Unggeun in his lawsuit, even without backing or support. Is he still in good health?" I could only reply, "Yes, he is."

Moon remarked, "Japan and South Korea have both ignored this issue for more than seventy years. What is a nation, anyway?" I asked, "What do you think it is?" to which he returned the same question. I replied, "A nation is a collection of people. It's not just the politicians, but people like you and me who make a nation. You have worked hard to try to make things a bit better. It's the accumulation of efforts like yours that make the world, Korea and Japan included, and it's through individual effort that we can effect change."

I did not speak with particular confidence—the words just came out. But Moon said, "That's a good way of putting it. It makes me feel better."

As I was leaving, I told Moon, "I am going soon to the town in Siberia where my father was interned. Do you want to visit the place where your father was?" He answered that he would like to, but had to work. I responded, "When it comes down to it, it is people who make life meaningful. Through what you've done, you've given meaning to your father's life." We shook hands, and parted.

When the filming was over, Producer Kim said to me, "Since I am a non-nationalist, I disagree with you. I don't think we can make our nations better." I said to him, "If you really believe that, why are you making this documentary?" He just smiled, and remained silent.

6

About a month later, in July, I traveled with the camera crew to Russia. Our destination was Chita, where my father had spent three years of his life. That day, as we followed the route my father would have taken to the prison camp, I communicated with him in Tokyo on a smartphone. Since he was already too old to travel, I had promised him I would use Skype to show him images of Chita.

We started at the Trans-Siberian Railway yards where my father had first alighted in Chita. We stopped the car and got out to look at the place, which I showed my father on Skype. "That's it, that's what it looked like," he said. The camera crew filmed me walking through the yards. We got back into the car, and I showed my father the scenery as we headed onward through the city. We crossed a river and followed a main street to a central square where a gigantic statue of Lenin stood. Facing the square was an immense military headquarters, unchanged since it was built in Tsarist times.

The site of the prison camp was on the northern edge of the city. Seventy-five years ago, my father used to walk daily along the road connecting it with the central square, going to and from his work assignments. As we walked along a hospital fence, my father, who was watching my live stream, said, "When you turn that next corner, you'll be at the camp." When we turned the corner, there was a stand of pine trees next to a health club and a nursery school enclosed by an iron fence.

The pines were right where they used to be in my father's time. I showed the hospital and the pines several times over Skype to my father, who said, "From where you are standing now, seventy years ago you would have seen the camp. You would have been able to see us."

Once we had confirmed the location in this way, the crew filmed me standing there. Kim the producer asked me, "This is the goal of your journey. How do you feel?" I answered, "I'm glad this makes my father happy." Kim said, "I think we got some good footage." After that we spent two days filming me riding on the Trans-Siberian Railway, walking the streets of Chita, and visiting the gravesites of internees.

The site of the former prison camp on the northern outskirts of Chita. (Photo by author.)

The graveyard I visited was at the crest of a hill outside the city, surrounded wherever one looked by grassy plains. But it was now empty; the remains of the internees who had been buried here had been disinterred in the first decade of the twenty-first century and returned to Japan, where they were held by the Ministry of Health, Labour and Welfare pending reclamation by family members. Remains not claimed within a certain fixed period were eventually transferred to the Chidorigafuchi National Cemetery in Tokyo, where unidentified Japanese war dead have been laid to rest.

All that remained to indicate that this site in Chita had once been a cemetery were white signposts and a stone monument erected by the Japanese government, inscribed in Japanese with the words "In Memory of the Japanese Dead, July 2013."

The monument had been erected only three years ago, yet the granite facing had already cracked and fallen away in places, exposing the underlying cement core. This made-in-Japan monument was simply not built to withstand the Siberian climate, where temperatures range from above 30°C in midsummer to −50°C in the dead of winter. Apparently the Japanese government had not thought things through that far.

After filming me in front of the monument, Producer Kim asked me, "Aren't you going to pray?" I replied, "This is a monument erected by the Japanese government. It's not like you to ask such a question. There are no longer any remains here." I added, "If I am to pray, I'll go to the site of the camp once more before we leave and do it there. My father said dozens of men died there."

Kim nodded, and remarked, "It says 'Japanese Dead,' but I imagine there were some Koreans among them." I said, "You know, among the dead there's really no such thing as nationality." The camera crew sent up a drone to film me from above as I stood in the midst of the grassy plain, and then we left.

The day before we were to depart Russia, I got some time to myself in Chita and went once more to the site of the prison camp. It took more than half an hour to walk from the electrical power plant on the south side of the city, where my father had worked the first winter, to the camp on the northern outskirts. When my father had walked it, half-starved and in −40°C weather, he said it had felt very long indeed. Walking the same route, I found myself a bit out of breath on the slope leading to the camp.

Then I reached the northern outskirt and turned a corner, and there it was. For someone without a historical memory of the place, all there was to see were some pine trees and a health club surrounded by a metal fence. But I imagined I could hear my father's voice: "From where you are standing now, seventy years ago you would have seen the camp. You would have been able to see us."

*The author in front of the stone monument at the former cemetery for
Japanese internees in Chita.*

Photo courtesy of Munhwa Broadcasting Corporation (MBC)